Oxford Studies in European Law
General Editors: Paul Craig and Gráinne de Búrca

EU HUMAN RIGHTS POLICIES

EU Human Rights Policies

A Study in Irony

ANDREW WILLIAMS

OXFORD
UNIVERSITY PRESS

Great Clarendon Street, Oxford OX2 6DP
Oxford University Press is a department of the University of Oxford.
It furthers the University's objective of excellence in research, scholarship,
and education by publishing worldwide in

Oxford New York

Auckland Bangkok Buenos Aires Cape Town Chennai
Dar es Salaam Delhi Hong Kong Istanbul Karachi Kolkata
Kuala Lumpur Madrid Melbourne Mexico City Mumbai Nairobi
São Paulo Shanghai Singapore Taipei Tokyo Toronto

Oxford is a registered trade mark of Oxford University Press
in the UK and in certain other countries

Published in the United States
by Oxford University Press Inc., New York

© A. Williams, 2004

The moral rights of the author have been asserted
Database right Oxford University Press (maker)

First published 2004

All rights reserved. No part of this publication may be reproduced,
stored in a retrieval system, or transmitted, in any form or by any means,
without the prior permission in writing of Oxford University Press,
or as expressly permitted by law, or under terms agreed with the appropriate
reprographics rights organization. Enquiries concerning reproduction
outside the scope of the above should be sent to the Rights Department,
Oxford University Press, at the address above

Crown copyright material is reproduced under
Class Licence Number C01P0000148 with the permission of the
Controller of HMSO and Queen's Printer for Scotland.

You must not circulate this book in any other binding or cover
and you must impose this same condition on any acquirer

British Library Cataloguing in Publication Data
Data available

Library of Congress Cataloging in Publication Data
Data available

ISBN 0-19-926896-7

1 3 5 7 9 10 8 6 4 2

Typeset by Kolam Information Services Pvt. Ltd., Pondicherry, India.
Printed in Great Britain
on acid-free paper by
Biddles Ltd., King's Lynn.

GENERAL EDITORS' PREFACE

The academic literature on the human rights law and policy of the European Union has burgeoned over the past decade, and in particular in the last four or five years since the project of drafting a Charter of Rights for the EU was initiated. At the same time the attention paid by the EU institutions to the topic has increased, with the enactment of anti-discrimination legislation, the development of external human rights and democratization policies, the proliferation of annual reports on human rights within and outside the Union, and the agreement recently reached on the desirability of EU accession to the European Convention on Human Rights.

Andrew Williams' book, however, makes a contribution to this increasingly crowded landscape which is both distinctive and powerful. Rather than focusing primarily on the Charter of Fundamental Rights or the recent constitutional Convention, he takes as his starting point the alleged double standard in the EU's human rights policy which was identified by a number of commentators some years ago. And instead of simply joining others in their call for the resolution of this apparent hypocrisy by the application of the same standards to the internal and external spheres of EU action, he sets about systematically analyzing the nature and causes of what he terms the 'bifurcation' in the EU's approach to human rights. He does this first by examining in some detail the two key areas of external EU policy in which the double standard is most apparent—those of development policy and accession policy—and compares the application of human rights standards in these fields with those of internal EU policies. He then proceeds to examine the possible explanations for the apparent hypocrisy, and having dismissed many of the existing versions, proposes an account of his own. His argument locates the origins of the bifurcation in the EC's retrospective use of a narrative of human rights as its founding myth, in order to compensate for the actual absence of any human rights dimension in the treaties by which it was established, while simultaneously ignoring Europe's darker past and ensuring that the content and meaning of its 'human rights' commitments remained undefined and undetermined. At the same time, the EU's discourse of European identity, which incorporated human rights as one of its elements, was founded on the notion of distinction or difference, thus setting in motion the conditions for a bifurcation between the external and the internal. Ultimately his argument is that unless the origin of this fundamental discrimination at the heart of the EU's narrative of identity is acknowledged and confronted, the EU's alleged commitment to human rights will remain fundamentally undermined by its own irony.

This is a theoretically sophisticated book which is at the same time solidly grounded in the law and practice of the European Union, and which brings to the sometimes tired debate on the EU's human rights policy a passionate yet clear-sighted argument for change.

Paul Craig
Gráinne de Búrca

PREFACE

Some years ago, at the beginning of the 1990s, I witnessed a human rights abuse. Perhaps others might have called it something different but that was how it appeared to me. It happened whilst I was living in Lilongwe, the capital city of Malawi. The victim was a young teenage boy. He was sprinting from the central market as I sat at a roadside bar. He clutched a pile of clothes as he ran and was being chased by three young men dressed in red shirts and brown trousers. This was the uniform of the Young Pioneers, the enforcers and propagandists of Hastings Banda, Malawi's self-styled Life President. The boy could not escape. He dodged the pedestrians crowding the road, threw the clothes he carried over his shoulder but still they caught him. One of the Young Pioneers grabbed the collar of his shirt and swung him to the ground. The others laid in with their boots. They kicked at his head, at his legs, at his torso heedless of the screams and then the blood. After about a minute, maybe less, they stopped. They dragged him partially to his feet, still rolled into a ball, and back towards where the chase had begun. No one objected, no one seemed interested. The boy was a thief and that was what the Young Pioneers did to thieves.

The event was not an isolated one. It may have touched me personally but I was already aware that violence permeated the country's 'justice' system. The treatment of suspects, the conditions in police stations, the children left unnamed and forgotten in adult prisons were all common concerns for groups such as Human Rights Watch and Amnesty International. The political oppression and dictatorial habits of Dr Banda's notorious regime had attracted growing attention from these organizations. Then the so-called 'international community', the donors, took notice.

In particular, I became aware that the European Community, or the Community as I call it in this book,[1] was beginning to show an interest in Malawi and its internal affairs. In the aftermath of the Cold War and the ideological 'victory' of democracy and the free market, the Community had adopted a new dynamic global approach. It was starting to get involved.

---

[1] I have used the term 'Community' to signify the whole historically linked project that incorporates the European Economic Community, the European Community, and the European Union.

Member States acting in concert through its auspices talked in terms of the then recently drafted Maastricht Treaty. They sought to develop and consolidate 'democracy and the rule of law' and respect for human rights and fundamental freedoms.[2] Development aid began to be considered in tandem with notions of 'good governance'. The suggestion of conditions being attached to aid became an acceptable political response to human rights abuses. Something was being done.

The feeling I had at the time was that the Community had emerged as a potentially powerful agent for human rights enforcement. It had assumed a pivotal position of international influence. Not only was it now the largest aid donor but it also portrayed itself as a new ethically bound force for justice in the world. Respect for human rights was to govern everything it did, or so it claimed. It therefore possessed significant authority.

As if to confirm my impression, whilst I was still in Malawi, the Community issued a *démarche* to the Malawian government calling for improvements in prison conditions, in police behaviour, in the release of political detainees, and the introduction of multi-party democracy. When no satisfactory action was taken by Dr Banda's regime, aid was cut.

The removal of balance of payments support crippled the Malawian economy already disintegrating under the strains of the worst drought in decades. Within eighteen months Banda's regime imploded. Multi-party elections ousted him and his party from power. Democratic institutions were installed and aid was resumed. The Young Pioneers were disbanded. International assistance in improving human rights and the criminal justice system began to flow. The aura of oppression and brutality, a small part of which I imagined I had witnessed, appeared to have been lifted. Banda had gone and the era of human rights and good governance had come to Malawi. That was the story, a success for the Community that now placed human rights at the centre of its external affairs.

The message that the example of the Community and Malawi represented was striking. Neither was it a solitary one. The revolution that had visited Central and Eastern European states had similarly produced a seemingly human rights based approach to the Community's external

---

[2] See, in particular, the Preamble to the Treaty on European Union which confirms the Member States' 'attachment to the principles of liberty, democracy and respect for human rights and fundamental freedoms and of the rule of law'. See also Article 177(2) (ex Article 130u(2)) of the EC Treaty: 'Community policy in this area [development co-operation] shall contribute to the general objective of developing and consolidating democracy and the rule of law, and to that of respecting human rights and fundamental freedoms'.

relations. Greater desire to promote a common foreign policy also pushed human rights considerations into the foreground. This all appeared indicative of a dramatic, almost 'born again', character shift for the Community.

On deeper reflection, I wondered whether this story of human rights advancement was as impressive and untainted as it would at first appear. Was it really representative of a fundamental change in ethical politics? Had respect for human rights become a decisive influence in constructing policy? Did the principle infuse the whole of the activities of the Community? Did it produce an environment of human rights promotion inside as well as outside the Community? Did human rights really 'now inform on everything the Union does' as Jacques Santer, then President of the European Commission, had suggested?[3]

These questions inspired the studies that have led to this book. They caused me to look more deeply at the role human rights play in the Community's affairs, specifically to consider the whole history of the Community's portrayal of human rights. For it was only in placing the 'new condition' in some kind of perspective that I felt an understanding of the deeper nature of the subject would be possible.

It was during the investigative process that I then became imbued with a sense of ambivalence pervading the Community. I saw that through its institutions it had constructed a complex system of stories, sometimes in the shape of policies, sometimes in law, sometimes in practical action, sometimes in political rhetoric. And when analysing these narratives it became apparent that there had developed a fundamental division between them. From a relative silence on human rights issues early in the life of the Community, and later the establishment of a working principle that the Community was founded on respect for human rights, a 'bifurcation' of rights discourse and action had seemingly evolved. An external approach had developed over time that was distinct from the internal in all of the three crucial aspects of human rights: their definition and scope; the methods of scrutiny employed; and the enforcement measures the Community was able, or chose, to use.

The effect of the nature of the bifurcation was to call into question the coherence and ethical basis for human rights policy-making. It suggested that there were fundamental uncertainties about the very values the Community expressed in this field. Indeed, it seemed as though the

---

[3] Jacques Santer, 'Foreword' to the Commission's *Report on the External Dimension of the EU's Human Rights Policy* (1995) COM(95) 567 final.

Community's human rights practices and narratives were imbued with a sense of irony. Not only was the distinction between internal and external approaches indicative of a gap between a universalising rhetoric of human rights and the Community's practices but it also suggested that some form of discrimination, perhaps racially motivated, had been instituted. This book provides a study of this ironical condition.

Originally the subject of a PhD thesis, the book takes into account the impact of the constitutional negotiations that have preceded the scheduled enlargement in 2004. In particular, the Draft Constitutional Treaty that emerged in 2003 from the Convention on the Future of Europe has suggested that human rights in the Community might undergo some fundamental realignment. Whether or not this is a realistic prospect is considered at various relevant points in my text.

The material in Chapter 3 was first published as 'Enlargement of the Union and Human Rights Conditionality' in the *European Law Review* December (2000), and is reproduced here, in considerably revised form by kind permission of Sweet and Maxwell.

Finally, I would like to acknowledge the contribution of a number of people in the completion of this book. Ralf Rogowski, my original supervisor, has remained a constant support and guide. I am also grateful for the continuing encouragement of Gráinne de Búrca and those at Warwick Law School who have always engendered a sense of enquiry and critique in the research conducted there. In particular, I would like to thank Upendra Baxi, Jayan Nayar, and Ken Foster. Finally, I thank Kathy, without whose love and assistance the book would never have materialized, and Antonia who makes everything worthwhile.

Andrew Williams
2003

CONTENTS

Abbreviations xiii
Table of Cases xiv
Table of EC Material xv

1. Introduction — 1
1.1 Human rights and the Community: the stimuli for reform — 1
1.2 The critique of incoherence and the analytical void — 6
1.3 A structure for analysis — 11
1.4 Conclusion — 15

2. Development Policy and Human Rights — 16
2.1 A history of human rights in development policy — 17
2.2 Key aspects of human rights in development policy — 40
2.3 Conclusion — 51

3. Accession to the Community and Human Rights — 53
3.1 A history of human rights in accession policy — 53
3.2 The key aspects of human rights in accession policy — 66
3.3 Conclusion — 78

4. The Scope of Internal-External Incoherence — 79
4.1 Distinctions in definition — 79
4.2 Distinctions in scrutiny — 94
4.3 Distinctions in enforcement — 105
4.4 Conclusion — 110

5. Explaining Incoherence: the Orthodox Arguments — 111
5.1 Legal competence — 112
5.2 Legal relevance — 118
5.3 Distinct conditions — 121
5.4 Realpolitik — 124
5.5 Conclusion — 126

6. The Invention of Human Rights in the Community — 128

   6.1 Human rights as institutional authentication — 129
   6.2 The myth of human rights as a founding principle of the Community — 137
   6.3 Conclusion — 157

7. European Identity and Human Rights — 162

   7.1 The myth of European identity — 163
   7.2 Human rights and the construction of *the* 'European Identity' — 174
   7.3 Identity as unity; identity as distinction — 184
   7.4 Conclusion — 192

8. The Irony of the Community's Human Rights Policies — 193

   8.1 The arguments — 194
   8.2 The significance of bifurcation — 196

Bibliography — 205
Index — 213

ABBREVIATIONS

ACP	African Caribbean and Pacific States
AG	Advocate General
CEE	Central and Eastern European
CERD	UN Committee on the Elimination of Racial Discrimination
CFSP	Common Foreign and Security Policy
CSCE	Conference on Security and Co-operation in Europe
DCT	Draft Constitutional Treaty
ECHR	European Convention on Human Rights
ECtHR	European Court of Human Rights
ECJ	European Court of Justice
ECRI	European Commission Against Racism and Intolerance
EIDHR	European Initiative for Democracy and the Protection of Human Rights
EP	European Parliament
EPC	European Political Co-operation
ERRC	European Roma Rights Centre
EUMC	European Monitoring Centre for Racism and Xenophobia
IGC	Intergovernmental Conference
RAXEN	European Racism and Xenophobia Information Network
SEA	Single European Act
TEU	Treaty on European Union
UNCTAD	UN Conference on Trade and Development 1964

TABLE OF CASES

Costa v. ENEL (Case 6/64) [1964] ECR 585 .... 132, 169, 172
Commission v. Council (Case 22/70) [1971] ECR 263 172
ERT (Case C-260/89) [1991] ECR I-2925 107
Groener v. Minister for Education (Case 379/87) [1989] ECR 3967 90
Hoekstra v. Bestuur der Bedrijfsvereniging voor Detailhandel
 en Ambachten (Case 75/63) [1964] ECR 177 169
Internationale Handelsgesellschaft v. Einfuhr-und Vorratstelle
 fur Getreide und Futtermittel (Case 11/70) [1970]
 ECR II 1125–1155 .... 90, 145, 148, 150
Nold v. Commission (Case 4/73) [1974] ECR
 I 491–516 .... 67, 81–2, 145, 150
Opinion 1/91 (Re the EEA Agreement) [1991] ECR 6079 131
Opinion 2/94 on Accession by the Community to the ECHR [1996]
 ECR I-1759 .... 82, 95, 97, 136, 138
Portugal v. Council (Case C 268/94) [1996] ECR I-6184 35–6
Ruhrkolen-Verkaufsgesellschaft mbH v. High Authority
 (Case 40/59) [1960] ECR 423–462 146
Rutili v. Minister for Interior (Case 36/75) [1975] ECR 1219 150
Sgarlata v. Commission (Case 40/64) [1965] ECR 215 146
SPUC v. Grogan (Case 159/90) [1991] ECR I-4685 82
Stauder v. City of Ulm (Case 29/69) [1969]
 ECR 419–430 .... 145, 147–8, 150
Stork v. High Authority (Case 1/58) [1958–1959] ECR 17–40 146
United Kingdom v. Commission (Case C106/96) [1998]
 ECR I-2729 .... 46, 113
Van Eick v. Commission (Case 35/67) [1968] ECR 329 146
Van Gend en Loos v. Nederlandse Administratie der Belastingen
 (Case 26/62) [1963] ECR I 55 .... 95, 132, 168–169
Wachauf v. Germany (Case 5/88) [1989] ECR 2609 107

TABLE OF EC MATERIAL

Regulations
Council Regulation 1608/93 (Haiti Embargo) 49
Council Regulation 1035/97 (establishing Monitoring Centre on
    Racism and Xenophobia) 88, 102, 103
Council Regulation 975/1999 (Development Policy) 41, 46, 90, 113
Council Regulation 976/1999 (Co-operation Policy) 113

Directives
Council Directive 2000/43/EC (implementing the principle of
    equal treatment between persons irrespective of racial or
    ethnic origin) 86, 114, 123
Council Directive 2000/78/EC (establishing a general framework
    for equal treatment in employment and occupation) 86

Decisions
European Ombudsman Decision adopting implementing
    provisions (1997) 96
Council Decision establishing a Community action programme to
    combat discrimination (2001 to 2006) (2000/750/EC) 86
Council Decision on Haiti (2001/131/EC) 45, 109
Council Decision on Fiji (2001/334/EC) 45
Council Decision on Cote d'Ivoire (2001/510/EC) 45, 50, 109
Council Decision on Zimbabwe (2002/148/EC) 45, 50, 109

Declarations
Copenhagen European Council Declaration on the European
    Identity 1973 .... 25, 40, 177–9
Joint Declaration Parliament, the Council and the Commission on
    Human Rights 1977 .... 55, 151–3, 180
Copenhagen European Council Declaration on
    Democracy 1978 .... 55, 154
Parliament, Council, Commission, Declaration against Racism
    and Xenophobia 1986 .... 87, 155
Luxembourg European Council Declaration on Human
    Rights 1991 .... 32, 106

xvi *Table of EC Material*

Laeken European Council Declaration 2001 .... 3, 122, 180

Resolutions

Parliament, Resolution adopting a Declaration of Fundamental
  Rights and Freedoms, [1989] 154
Joint Resolution of the Council and of the Member States,
  1991 33–4
Parliament Resolution on Human Rights, Democracy and
  Development [1991] OJ C326/259.. 33
Parliament Resolution on Progress in Implementing the Common
  Foreign and Security Policy [1995] OJ C151/223........................ 156

Common Positions

Council Common Position on human rights, democratic
  principles, the rule of law and good governance in Africa (1998) 48

Reports

Council

Council, EU Annual Report on Human
  Rights (1999) 9, 43, 46–7, 74, 99
Council, EU Annual Report on Human Rights (2000)............. 9, 80, 98–9
Council, EU Annual Report on Human Rights (2001)........................ 101
Council, EU Annual Report on Human Rights (2002)................... 6, 116

Commission

Commission Report on European Union (1975)......................... 179, 181
Commission Report on the Protection of Fundamental
  Rights as Community Law (1976)............. 136, 138, 149, 151, 160, 180
Commission Report on the Implementation of Measures Intended
  to Promote Observance of Human Rights and Democratic
  Principles in External Relations (1994)...................................... 41, 46
Commission Report to the Council and the European Parliament,
  The European Union and the External Dimension of Human
  Rights Policy: from Rome to Maastricht and
  Beyond (1995)..42, 80, 106, 113, 157
Commission Regular Report on Turkey's Progress Towards
  Accession (1998)... 76

Commission Regular Report on the Progress Towards Accession
    by Slovakia (2000) 72
Commission Report on the Action Plan against
    Racism (2000) 67
Commission Regular Report on Turkey's Progress Towards
    Accession (2000)... 77
Commission Report on the Implementation of Measures Intended
    to Promote Observance of Human Rights and Democratic
    Principles in External Relations (2000)....................................... 46, 47
Commission Regular Report on Turkey's Progress Towards
    Accession (2001).. 77, 83
Commission Regular Report on Romania's Progress
    Towards Accession (2002).. 70
Commission Regular Report on Bulgaria's Progress Towards
    Accession (2002)... 71

Parliament
Parliament Committee on Civil Liberties and Internal Affairs Report
    on the situation of the Gypsies in the Community (1994) 88
Parliament Committee on Civil Liberties and Internal Affairs, Annual
    Report on respect for human rights in the European
    Union (1993) 98, 156
Parliament Committee on Civil Liberties and Internal Affairs,
    Annual Report on respect for human rights in the European
    Union (1994) 98
Parliament Committee on Civil Liberties and Internal Affairs,
    Annual Report on respect for human rights in the European
    Union (1995) 98
Parliament Committee on Civil Liberties and Internal Affairs,
    Annual Report on respect for human rights in the European
    Union (1997) 9
Parliament Committee on Citizens' Freedoms and Rights, Justice
    and Home Affairs, Report on the situation as regards fundamental
    rights in the European Union (2000)....................................... 9, 96–7
Parliament Committee on Civil Liberties and Internal Affairs,
    Report on countering racism and xenophobia in the European
    Union (2000) 88, 104

xviii   *Table of EC Material*

Court of Auditors
Court of Auditors Special Report on the Management by the
    Commission of European Union Support for the Development
    of Human Rights and Democracy in Third Countries (2000)............ 48

Opinions and Communications
Commission Communication to the Council on human rights,
    democracy and development co-operation, 1991 32–3
Commission communication 'Towards a Closer Association with
    the Countries of Central and Eastern Europe', 1993 64
Commission Opinion Re-inforcing Political Union and Preparing for
    Enlargement (1996) 156
Opinion of the Economic and Social Committee on 'The European
    Union and the External Dimension of Human Rights Policy'
    [1997] OJ C206/117 8
Commission Communication to the Council and the Parliament,
    'Democratisation, the rule of law, respect for human rights and
    good governance: the challenges of the partnership between
    the European Union and the ACP states' (1998) 41, 43, 92–3
Commission Communication on Countering Racism, Xenophobia
    and Anti-Semitism in the Candidate Countries (1999) 70
Commission Opinion on Estonia's Application for Membership
    of the European Union (1999) 69
Commission Communication to the Council and the Parliament
    on Development Policy (2000) 38
Commission Communication on the Legal Nature of the Charter
    of Fundamental Rights of the EU (2000) 80
Commission, Communication to the Council and the Parliament,
    'The EU's Role in Promoting Human Rights and
    Democratisation in Third Countries' (2001) 9, 51, 91, 107

Memoranda and Reviews
Commission Memorandum on a Community Policy for
    Development Co-operation (1971) 26
Commission Memorandum on the Accession of the European
    Communities to the Convention for the Protection of Human
    Rights and Fundamental Freedoms (1979) 136, 180
Commission Agenda 2000 'For a Stronger and Wider
    Union' 1997 .... 59, 73–5, 106

Council Review of the Common Position on human rights,
   democratic principles, the rule of law and good governance in
   Africa (2001) 44
Commission 'Towards the Enlarged Union: Strategy Paper and
   Report' (2002) 71

Green Papers
Commission, Green Paper on relations between the European Union
   and the ACP countries on the eve of the 21st Century – Challenges
   and options for a new partnership (1996) 36–7

Proposals
Commission proposal for a Council Regulation on the Development
   and consolidation of democracy and the rule of law and respect
   for human rights and fundamental freedoms [1997] OJC 282/16 42

Staff Working Papers
Commission, Priorities and Guidelines for the Implementation of
   the 2001 European Initiative for Democracy and Human
   Rights (2001) 42

1

Introduction

1.1 Human rights and the Community: the stimuli for reform

The intersection between human rights and the Community's law and practice has proved to be both a contentious and complex subject. It poses questions that span both the macro and micro levels of Community affairs. Indeed, few areas of Community law and policy have escaped scrutiny in this respect.[1] Even before the notion of 'mainstreaming' became institutionally fashionable, human rights issues would surface across the spectrum of Community activity. Unsurprisingly, therefore, the subject has attracted significant scholarly and political attention. In particular, over the past thirty years, one can observe an exponential growth in the production of Community institutional pronouncements and deliberations connected with human rights concerns. Critiques and commentaries upon specific human rights policies adopted by the Community have also proliferated, tracking developments and proposing reform. Throughout, the role human rights can and do play in the Community's practice remains an implicit question.

The interest has been fuelled and heightened by an increasing number of constitutional 'moments' that have materialized since the early 1990s. In 1991 the Treaty of Maastricht substantiated the principle developed by the European Court of Justice (ECJ) confirming in Article 6(2) (ex Article F(2)) TEU that the 'Union shall respect fundamental rights, as guaranteed by the European Convention on Human Rights and as they result from the constitutional traditions common to member states as general principles of

---

[1] For a recent example of a broad examination see Philip Alston *et al* (eds), *The EU and Human Rights* (Oxford: Oxford University Press, 1999).

Community law'. In 1997 the Treaty of Amsterdam proclaimed in an amended Article 6(1) TEU that the 'Union is founded on the principles of liberty, democracy, respect for human rights and fundamental freedoms'. It also added an Article 7 to the TEU, since amended by the Treaty of Nice 2000, to provide a process by which the Community could bring sanctions against any Member State that was guilty of a serious and persistent breach of those principles in Article 6(1) TEU.

Potentially of even greater significance than these Treaty amendments was the decision of the European Council in Cologne in 1999 to establish a 'European Charter of Fundamental Rights' that might be 'integrated into the treaties'.[2] Such a Charter was intended to bring together the disparate sets of rights otherwise scattered across the landscape of the Community's laws. It would make clear the nature and scope of recognized rights providing a degree of coherence where little existed before. The process that led to the composition of the Charter was in itself significant. Gráinne de Búrca and others have commented that the 'Convention' created to produce a final text for adoption by the Council responded in part to principles that echoed the very subject matter being debated.[3] Human rights related concepts of dialogue, participation, and transparent decision-making were at least addressed through the Convention's practice. 'Civil society' was granted the opportunity to voice its opinions publicly on the emerging document even though it did not have formal representation on the drafting body.[4] All discussions and interim drafts were published on the Community's website.

Nonetheless, the fact that the subsequent text was only adopted initially as a declaration of intent rather than a legally binding document clearly undermined its constitutional impact.[5] This, however, has not stilled the institutional debate as to the Charter's prospects. The establishment of a new 'Convention' in 2002, to consider the constitutional future of the Community, included within its terms of reference the question of the

---

[2] European Council Decision on the Drawing up of a Charter of Fundamental Rights of the European Union, Presidency Conclusions, Cologne, 3 and 4 June 1999, Annex IV.

[3] Gráinne de Búrca, 'Drafting the EU Charter on Fundamental Rights' *European Law Review* 26/2 (2001) 126–38. See also, Sionaidh Douglas-Scott, *Constitutional Law of the European Union* (Harlow: Longman, 2002) 471–8.

[4] The composition of the Convention was a mix of Community and Member State parliamentary and other representatives together with lawyers from the ECJ, the European Court of Human Rights (ECtHR) and the Council of Europe. See website (http://european-convention.eu.int/bienvenue.asp?lang=EN).

[5] EU Charter of Fundamental Rights [2000] OJ C364/01.

Charter's inclusion in the Treaties.⁶ The possibility of the Community signing the European Convention on Human Rights (ECHR) was also resurrected. The Draft Constitutional Treaty (DCT) that emerged in May/June 2003 suggested both strategies should be adopted.⁷ Article I-7(1) DCT proposed that the 'Union shall recognise the rights, freedoms and principles set out in the Charter'. Article I-7(2) stated that the 'Union shall seek accession to the [ECHR]'. It is hardly prophetic to claim, therefore, that the subject of human rights in the Community's constitution will remain negotiable and uncertain for some time to come. Even if the DCT is adopted wholesale, significant questions will remain. What competence will the Community possess to construct a human rights policy? How will it be implemented and by whom? What will be the legal framework that guides it?

Beyond these textual advancements that have provided a focus for debate, a confluence of social, political, and economic challenges has accentuated the relevance and importance of human rights for the Community at the beginning of the 21st century. These are both peculiar to the Community and of more general applicability. The prospect and process of enlargement, for instance, has forced the Community to confront the raw rudiments of human rights violation and practice in those countries seeking accession. Turkey in particular has been the focus for the Community's expressions and actions of intent. The continuing denial of admission until the Turkish authorities have instituted basic and detailed improvements seemingly represents a most effective sanction.⁸ However, even though there remains concern over the human rights situation in various applicant states, attention has begun to shift to the consequences for human rights post-admission. A.G. Toth for one has reflected upon the problem of maintaining the standards that have been set for entry once entry is completed. He suggests that there 'can be no doubt that the admission of Central and East European States must be accompanied with written,

---

⁶ See European Council Declaration at Laeken, December 2001, EU Bull 12-2001 Annex 1 to Presidency Conclusions.

⁷ See the Draft Constitutional Treaty
(available at http://european-convention.eu.int/bienvenue.asp?lang=EN&Content=).

⁸ Considerable change occurred from 2002. In August of that year the Turkish Parliament abolished the death penalty, lifted restrictions on the use of the Kurdish language and ended key restraints on free speech. See Jonny Dymond, 'Turkey turns liberal with eye on EU', *Observer*, 4 August 2002. Strong criticism of the Community's approach has, nonetheless, been raised. See Harun Arikan, 'A Lost Opportunity? A Critique of the European Union's Human Rights Policy Towards Turkey' *Mediterranean Politics* 7/1 (2002) 19–50.

legally binding and judicially enforceable guarantees that they will observe human rights and fundamental freedoms, including the protection of ethnic and other (religious, linguistic, etc.) minorities'.[9] Such states supposedly 'lack any experience and tradition in the human rights field',[10] making them potentially dangerous recipients of any Community confidence in their ability to adhere to and improve their human rights obligations under the accession process.

Whatever the truth of this statement, and some questions could well be raised as to the longevity and seriousness of the Member States' own historical human rights commitment, the fear of an unchecked abusive regime *within* the European fold is manifest. How that fear may be assuaged whilst avoiding the political quicksand that the subject of Community internal scrutiny and enforcement of human rights poses is a key constitutional question. And it was one left largely unanswered by the DCT of 2003.[11]

A further acute human rights concern for the Community is its approach to development and its relations with the 'South'. The growing desperation over the scale of global poverty, the nature of international action designed to confront the problem, and the placement of the Community at the hub of its Member States' response to the crisis have all possessed a particular human rights dimension. Specifically the meaning and practical consequences of a right to development have taxed the Community without being satisfactorily resolved. Determining the scope of the obligations with regard to developing states whilst identifying those rights that should be respected and promoted in the process have brought collective notions of rights into play. Development policy has thus become a fundamental point of confrontation for the Community with regard to the global evolution of human rights concepts and their relationship with other notions such as good governance, democracy, and the rule of law. If the Community continues to seek an enhanced presence on the international stage, its approach to development will be crucial in the consideration of human rights futures.

---

[9] A.G. Toth, 'The European Union and Human Rights: the Way Forward' *CML Rev* 34 (1997) 491–529 at 527.

[10] Ibid at 526.

[11] See Andrew Williams, 'EU Human Rights Policy and the Convention on the Future of Europe: A Failure of Design?' *European Law Review* 28 (2003) 794–813 for an analysis of the DCT in relation to its failure to provide the Community with authority to adopt an effective internal human rights policy.

On a more parochial level, the re-emergence of a political right in European affairs has already begun to question the extent of the Community's role in acting as a human rights guardian within its domain. The strange affair of Austria and the advancement to power of the Freedom Party in 2000 triggered a constitutional debate about the extent of the Community's competence in internal human rights matters. The amendments to Article 7 TEU proposed at Nice (and subsequently embraced by the DCT of 2003) reflected a desire to produce some kind of effective monitoring and enforcement package that could be deployed against a Member State. The application of this possible regime remains something of a mystery at present. How the Community is to organize the resources and structures to scrutinize and act on human rights matters within its borders has yet to be determined. A continuing failure to attend to these matters may ultimately undermine Article 7 TEU itself, suggesting that the question of competence in such matters must be resolved sooner rather than later.

The burgeoning influence of racially discriminatory politics in a number of key European states has also emerged as a connected yet independent theme in the progress of the Community's human rights policies. The institutions have adopted the issue as something of a *cause célèbre* that warrants political rhetoric, legislation, and action. Racism has appeared as a major theme for consideration in the Council's Annual Report on Human Rights since 1999 both in an internal and external context. Initiatives have progressed from mere declarations of distaste at the rise of racism to Treaty amendments designed to combat the problem.[12] Investigatory organizations supported by the Community designed to monitor the issue have also proliferated.[13] Nevertheless, the progression of asylum seekers and immigration as a burgeoning political concern (particularly following the electoral success of the far right in various Member States at the turn of the 21st century),[14] has maintained the pressure on the Community to do more to enhance the principle of non-discrimination.

---

[12] See the revised Article 13 EC Treaty.

[13] See, for instance, the EU Monitoring Centre for Racism and Xenophobia, MERCATOR (a research network and information service concerning regional and/or minority languages of the European Union) and the European Bureau of Lesser Used Languages.

[14] Belgium, France, Denmark, the Netherlands, and Austria have all recorded significant rises in the level of support for anti-immigration parties since 1999. Occasionally this has led to electoral success. Witness in particular the gains in the popular vote achieved by Jean-Marie Le Pen and his party *Front National* during the 2002 French General Election.

All of these 'environmental' conditions (to which one can add, amongst others, the response to the perceived threat of terrorism following the attack on the World Trade Centre in New York on 11 September 2001, as well as the repercussions from the second Gulf War and perhaps concern over the accountability of insufficiently regulated multi-national corporations),[15] have combined to focus minds on the Community's human rights policies and how they might be structured. There are even suggestions that the Community should centralize human rights as a core objective and perhaps metamorphose into a human rights organization of some description.[16] Whether or not this is a realistic proposition, the desire to place human rights at the heart of the Community remains a serious concern. The question is, however, whether the Community is inherently constrained from effecting meaningful change to react to the human rights challenges it faces. Does it have the capacity to construct a workable policy?

1.2 The critique of incoherence and the analytical void

A number of fundamentally debilitating characteristics of the Community's existing human rights practices have often been identified when constitutional and/or policy reform has been contemplated. Philip Alston and Joseph Weiler have argued strongly that the paramount obstacle to effective human rights action is the absence of a recognizable institutional programme built on coherent aims and objectives. They note that 'despite the frequency of statements underlining the importance of human rights and the existence of a variety of significant individual policy initiatives, the European Union lacks a fully-fledged human rights policy'.[17]

Individually, Weiler has also referred to the absence of several factors that tell against a sense of institutional focus or direction.[18] The failure to appoint a human rights commission or a Directorate-General with responsibility for the area, the failure to create a budget to finance human rights

---

[15] The relevance of 'multi-national enterprises' (MNE), as called by the Council, for human rights development was acknowledged in the Council, *EU Annual Report on Human Rights 2002*, 12747/1/02 at 29–33.

[16] Armin von Bogdandy, 'The European Union as a Human Rights Organisation? Human Rights and the Core of the European Union' *CML Rev* 37 (2000) 1307–38.

[17] Philip Alston and Joseph Weiler, 'An Ever Closer Union in Need of a Human Rights Policy: The European Union and Human Rights' in Alston *et al*, note 1 above, 3–97 at 7.

[18] Joseph Weiler, 'Does the EU Need a Human Rights Charter?' *European Law Journal* 6 (2000) 95–7.

initiatives, and the absence of 'a horizontal action plan' to ensure recognized rights were properly protected, he maintains, all indicate an institutional unwillingness for the Community to become possessed of an effective human rights structure. The fragmentation of responsibilities for human rights actions and policy-making further exacerbates the position, doubling the sense of confusion.

Central to these observations has been the related critiques of incoherence and inconsistency. Although the Community's failure to adhere to a concerted human rights approach afflicts all of its activities wherever located,[19] the pivotal incoherence has been identified as that which distinguishes its external and internal practices. Weiler and Alston noted that '[t]here is an unfortunate, although perhaps inevitable, element of schizophrenia that afflicts the Union between its internal and external policies'.[20] Officials are compartmentalized along this fundamental fault line so that any practical or administrative coherence is unlikely to evolve naturally. Andrew Clapham also notes the presence of a 'skewed' human rights policy that 'seems solely focused on the behaviour of non-European States'.[21] The Commission has not been given the requisite powers to address human rights issues beyond the fundamental freedoms of the Treaty in or across its Member States and thus, as it 'fails to consider human rights issues within', the policy 'lacks coherence in the eyes of the rest of the world'.[22]

Weiler and Alston have highlighted three important and worrying effects of this incoherence.[23] First, the adoption of a discourse of universality and indivisibility of rights renders an external human rights policy suspect if it is not mirrored by internal approaches. It will not be 'taken seriously' if in practice the Community either operates as though universal principles do not apply to its own institutions or Member States or it washes its hands of any breaches of human rights norms. Secondly, incoherence suggests 'unilateralism and double standards' thus undermining the credibility of the Community's actions. Human rights become contingent principles, available when politically convenient, tools to be operated rather than ethical

---

[19] Inconsistencies in the Community's approach to third states are, for instance, frequently cited. Decisions to take positive action externally for human rights violations rarely seem to adhere to any governing principle. This may be due to the case by case nature that is the invariable practice of foreign affairs for Member States. The Common Foreign and Security Policy may be interpreted as a natural extension of such a practice.

[20] Alston and Weiler, note 17 above, at 8–9.

[21] Andrew Clapham, 'Where is the EU's Human Rights Common Foreign Policy, and How is it Manifested in Multilateral Fora?' in Alston *et al*, note 1 above, 627–83 at 641.

[22] Ibid at 642.   [23] Alston and Weiler, note 17 above, at 8–9.

guidelines to govern Community performances. Thirdly, a Community that fails to adopt a 'strong human rights policy for itself is highly unlikely to develop a fully-fledged external policy and apply it with energy or consistency'.[24] Thus, any long-term ambitions for the Community to acquire an identity in the world become compromised. Uniting all these perceived problems is the underlying concern that the credibility of the Community is at stake both as an institution concerned with human rights and in its ability to fashion a workable policy that will attain its objectives.

This begs the question as to the authority of the Community to assume *any* kind of human rights role. Why indeed should it be concerned with the promotion of rights in any sphere? The answer is treated for the most part as axiomatic by both commentators and institutions alike, a position confirmed rather than created by the Treaties of Maastricht and Amsterdam. Prior to these constitutional moments it was well established that respect for human rights formed one of the fundamental principles governing the operation of Community law.[25] The amendments to Articles 6 and 7 TEU, as we have seen, have apparently settled the issue by establishing the *'right'* if not entirely the competence of the Community to engage in human rights practices. Putting aside the possible interpretations of this right and the correlated duty imposed on the Community to act, there is little argument against the Community being concerned with human rights issues as a matter of general principle. Having established the convention, it is then appropriate for the policies and practices adopted by the Community to be evaluated. The charge of incoherence as exemplified by Alston and Weiler's commentary is a consequence of questioning the effectiveness and efficacy of the Community's position.

Both the critique and its importance have not been lost on the Community institutions. The Economic and Social Committee made the point that it is 'important for the EU to establish a clear link between both arms [internal and external] of its human rights policy...even if this only involves being asked to take a stand on values on which it challenges other countries and calls upon them to respect'.[26]

The European Parliament has been more explicit. It has stressed the 'need for the Member States to adopt or strengthen the provisions to

---

[24] Alston and Weiler, note 17 above, at 8–9.

[25] The story is a familiar one and need not be revisited here. However, a re-evaluation of the development of this principle is considered in Chapter 6.

[26] Opinion of the Economic and Social Committee on 'The European Union and the External Dimension of Human Rights Policy' [1997] OJ C206/117.

guarantee the effective protection of the fundamental rights of individuals in the European Union', particularly with respect to acquiring 'the credibility and consistency of European Union external action in this sphere'.[27] It has adopted the EU Charter of Fundamental Rights as the template for monitoring the human rights record within Member States to achieve this aim.[28]

The Commission has followed the Parliament's lead. It has declared that in external relations it will be 'guided by compliance with the rights and principles contained in the EU Charter of Fundamental Rights...since this will promote coherence between the EU's internal and external approaches'.[29] It too then has acknowledged an internal/external distinction worthy of attention.

Perhaps more importantly though, the Council has conceded that 'the European Union is aware that it must begin by applying to itself the principles for which it stands'.[30] It has also accepted the need to 'enhance the transparency of the Union's human rights policies'.[31] Whether this is an ambiguous commitment, in that it still does not state categorically that the Community may subject the Member States to a human rights regime equivalent to that adopted externally, it nonetheless confirms, if only by implication, recognition of the charge.

There is little resistance, therefore, to the notion that Community human rights policy has been and remains afflicted by a central condition of internal/external incoherence. Equally there is a rhetorical commitment to resolving the perceived deficiency. And indeed the Council's Annual Reports on Human Rights, the identification by the Commission and Parliament of the EU Charter of Fundamental Rights as a standard for consistency, and the development of Article 7 TEU at the Treaty of Nice, could all be touted as helping to resolve the incoherence.

---

[27] EP Committee on Civil Liberties and Internal Affairs, *Annual Report on Respect for Human Rights in the European Union* (1997) A4-0468/98 para. 2 at 8.
[28] See EP Committee on Citizens' Freedoms and Rights, Justice and Home Affairs, Report on the *Situation as Regards Fundamental Rights in the European Union* (2000) A5-0223/2001, which adopts a robust, although self-consciously limited, approach to the scrutiny of Member States. The initiative is considered in greater detail in Chapter 4.
[29] Commission, Communication to the Council and the European Parliament, on 'The EU's Role in Promoting Human Rights and Democratisation in Third Countries' COM(2001) 252 final at 3.
[30] Council, *EU Annual Report on Human Rights 2000*, 11542/00 at 8.
[31] Council, *EU Annual Report on Human Rights* 1999, 11380/1/99 at 1.

Despite all these largely rhetorical developments there is a lack of critical analysis of the problem that subverts any movement towards effective change. Particularly, there is a surprising dearth of investigation by either commentator or institution alike into three key areas of the condition. First, there is no comprehensive account of the extent of the problem. How deeply and to what extent is this incoherence manifest? Secondly, the analyses of why the condition has arisen possess little rigour. Most enquiries are centred on the issue of legal and constitutional competence, which although an important aspect fails to reflect the wider context and mechanisms of decision-making that have led to the development of the internal/external dichotomy. Certainly, it takes no account of any possible sociological or other critical perspectives. Thirdly, the significance and implications of the condition have not been fully explored. Few studies have helped to assess the importance of a failure to rectify the current position. It is difficult therefore for any sense of urgency to be invested in the political voices for change. A cry for Community 'credibility' seems insufficient when unaccompanied by a deeper reflection upon the possible consequences of continuing the practice of distinction.

These three critical failures represent a void in analysis. They make meaningful reform of both the Community's constitution *and* practice a difficult if not impossible task. For how can changes be effected without understanding the scale and nature of the condition that needs to be addressed? How can institutional practices be re-directed when the current paths have not been adequately tracked and understood? How can a policy for human rights be constructed that will change the decision-making behaviour of institutions, governments, and bureaucrats without an appreciation of the reasons for the evolution of previous conduct? And how indeed can the political will for reform be engendered without an understanding of the significance of the condition, and thus the dangers to be incurred should the necessary changes in practices fail to be implemented?

These questions form the basis of this book. In essence, the purpose is to provide a critical analysis that will inform the debate about human rights reform in general and the present putative movement towards coherence in particular. It is also to contribute to the evident challenge that has emerged with regard to the means by which human rights should or could be incorporated into a constitutional framework, an issue that takes us far beyond the limited, though noble, ambitions to incorporate the EU Charter into the Treaties and to have the Community accede to the ECHR. In short, it is to provide an insight into the character and potential future ethical direction of what may be called the 'European Project' and the role(s) human rights have and may play within it.

Before outlining the structure of the book a brief word about the method of analysis is necessary. In essence it is a form of textual interpretation. It is based on an appreciation that socio-political institutions such as the Community engage in the construction of narratives that are 'autocentric' (histories of themselves and their decisions and actions)[32] and self-sustaining (determining the precepts for future institutional conduct). These narratives are concerned with both the institutions' origins and their policies, for want of a better term. But they are not purely representations. The narratives also serve as a structure of conditions for present and future practice. Although they are endlessly in formation, changing with each re-narration, they nonetheless set parameters. The 'institutional narratives', as I have called them elsewhere,[33] if excavated from the Community's text, provide vital evidence for the precepts and beliefs that help to define those parameters. Thus, an understanding of the motivation and direction, the 'political unconscious,' of the narratives and the resulting policies can be developed.

For this book the institutional narratives that have shaped the history of human rights policy, and the incoherence that afflicts it, provide the central concern. Through their unearthing and examination we can better understand how they have developed to influence decision-making in this field. And more importantly perhaps we can acquire a deeper appreciation of their likely effect on future policy formation.

1.3 A structure for analysis

The book is separated into three parts. First, it explores the extent of the internal/external distinction. To do so, two key areas of *external* projection of the Community's human rights activities, development co-operation and enlargement, are considered in detail. A history of human rights in each policy area is provided followed by an analysis of the current state of the

---

[32] I have taken the term from J.G.A. Pocock in his attempt to distinguish between histories that create autonomous political societies and those that narrate 'other' histories, of those excluded from the political order concerned. See J.G.A. Pocock, 'The Politics of History: The Subaltern and the Subversive' *Journal of Political Philosophy* 6/3 (1998) 219–34.

[33] Andrew Williams, 'Mapping Human Rights, Reading the European Union' *European Law Journal* 9/5 December (2003) 659–76.

three main components of the Community's practice, namely, definitions, measures of scrutiny, and processes of enforcement.

The reasons for focusing on the two specific external policy areas identified are twofold. By extracting the stories of human rights and comparing them with the interior condition, the full scope of the internal/external incoherence can be revealed. They also represent two of the significant areas of human rights challenge faced by the Community identified at the beginning of this chapter. Undoubtedly, further evidence might be gleaned from other external policy fields, notably foreign and trade policies, but the wide range of external activity within development and enlargement is sufficient to illustrate the depth and breadth of the internal/external distinction phenomenon.

Thus in Chapter 2, the history of human rights in the Community's Development Co-operation policy is considered. A policy area that has been present within the Community's institutional structure ever since the Treaty of Rome, it represents the location from which the Community confronts the external in a structured and institutional manner. Through law, rhetoric, and practice, the Community has defined its relationship with the 'South' distinguishing itself from the colonial relationship that previously subsisted under the regimes of its Member States. A wide definition of rights that encompasses both the traditional designation of civil, political, economic, social, and cultural rights as well as certain collective rights such as the right to development, has been applied. Furthermore, the Community has instituted an extensive scheme for scrutiny and enforcement of all these rights that now includes diplomatic 'consultations', financial assistance, and intrusive sanctions.

Chapter 3 then turns to the narrative of human rights in enlargement and the process of accession to the Community. Here, the distinction between the approaches to human rights internally and externally is lent added pertinence. Its importance lies in highlighting the distinction between the human rights conditions applied internally by the Community and those directed to states seeking to become members. The historical development of a textual human rights conditionality that has been projected as a requirement for those countries seeking full admission reveals the evolution of an intrusive and demanding policy. An individually prepared strategy has been imposed to improve the human rights situation in all states seeking admission. An extensive understanding of rights has been applied so as to include civil and political rights, economic, social, and cultural rights, and as a specific and separate category, minority rights.

The pressures that may be applied to bring about systemic change across the human rights spectrum have also developed into a sophisticated approach. This combines constant monitoring with potential enforcement of standards through the withdrawal of aid or the threat of a delay in, or denial of, admission to the Community.

After uncovering the history of human rights practices in the two external realms, Chapter 4 details the scope of incoherence evident from the contrast with the interior condition. In its definitions of rights the Community applies a narrow conception internally. Using a limited range of sources, particularly the ECHR, the emphasis is placed predominantly if not exclusively on individual rights. Collective concepts, including minority rights, find little practical expression within the Community. There is therefore a broad divergence in the meanings ascribed to the rights discourse. Similarly, in relation to scrutiny, the Community possesses few effective means to monitor either its own or its Member States' human rights records. Some internal scrutiny is apparent but it lacks the consistency, structures, resources, and political force to match the external approach. When it comes to enforcement, those measures applied to developing and acceding states also find no effective interior equivalent. Thus, across the spectrum of rights practice divergences appear that denote the significant scope of incoherence. Recent initiatives that might alleviate the extent of the distinction, including the EU Charter of Fundamental Rights, the Council's Annual Reports on Human Rights, and the Vienna Monitoring Centre for Racism and Xenophobia, have as yet failed to counter the issue to any meaningful extent. Instead, they can even be said to perpetuate its corrosive effects.

The second part of the book then analyses why such a policy differentiation has arisen. In Chapter 5 the legal, political, and constitutional arguments most frequently raised are critically examined. Issues of competence, legal reverence for the ECHR system, differing human rights conditions inside and outside the Community, and political realism are all explored. However, whether individually or collectively they fail to provide an adequate explanation for the evident depth and breadth of distinction. Although important for our understanding of the standard interpretation of current incoherence, they do not address satisfactorily how and why the phenomenon has evolved. A re-evaluation of the history of the condition is therefore imperative.

Chapter 6 commences the process by re-examining the evolution of the Community's human rights story. It advances the proposition that the circumstances for the central internal/external distinction were set early in the Community's existence. Despite the absence of human rights principles in the EEC Treaty, a mythic account of institutional origin that attempted to deflect the consequences of that deficiency was constructed. In order to authenticate the Community as an international entity and a rightful holder of sovereign powers assumed from its Member States, it relied in part on a notion that respect for human rights was a founding principle. However, by failing to provide a coherent framework for the definition and application of these rights, or a constitutional structure for their uniform development, the Community created an enabling environment within which a *bifurcation*, as it may be termed, in human rights policies and narratives could evolve. No institutional constraint was built to prevent human rights policies taking divergent paths. Rather, the internal and external narratives were open to influences more concerned with politics and perhaps prejudice than principle. The very rhetoric of human rights as an independent and untainted construct promulgated by the Community was thus compromised in the process.

Chapter 7 then proposes that the present form and scope of the bifurcation were inspired specifically by the Community's adoption of a discourse of 'European Identity'. By seeking a means to encourage unity, or rather adherence to the European Project, through a mythic identity that looked towards a commonality of values frequently expressed in human rights related terms, the Community's institutional narrative took a hegemonic and exclusionary path. In asserting its authenticity as a representative institution of 'Europe', and thus a legitimate site of power and re-designation of sovereignty within its domain, the Community relied upon assumptions of difference. It sought a definition of itself on the basis of not only what it was but also what it was not. It therefore set the basis for distinction and the limits of its own possibilities that continue to constrain the decisions made.

Finally in Chapter 8, in the book's concluding part, the consequences of the presence and nature of the bifurcation are described. The phenomenon has direct implications for the Community's constitutional structure and its future human rights activities. The possibility exists that the conditions for conflict rather than integration through human rights language have been instituted. In particular, the presence of double standards undermine the Community's claims for a credible human rights policy by infusing it with a sense of irony. Scepticism and cynicism may plague the Community's policies and activities. Human rights initiatives may be viewed with disdain. Far from drawing peoples together they may be viewed as fundamentally suspect, even duplicitous. The Community's human rights policy may also be conceived as concealing attitudes of superiority and exclusion behind a language of universality and inclusion. The irony of a bifurcation that sees the representation of values and standards *disguise* more persistent, differentiated, complex, and contradictory appreciations may then act to undermine the constitutional precepts that purportedly underpin the whole Community project. The need to address the bifurcation and the irony it may induce is therefore of paramount concern in the Community's constitutional development of its human rights policies.

1.4 Conclusion

The central theme of this book is to consider the evolution of human rights in the Community and determine the possibility for constitutional and practical reform. Underlying the enquiry is a realization that the Community has now reached a stage when its history and present practice needs to be re-assessed if future human rights developments are not to founder in a state of legal and political confusion. In particular, the possibility that the Community might mimic the practice of states in maintaining a stance that sees human rights as an external affair needs to be addressed. As Richard Falk has stated, '[a] strong human rights culture is the necessary underpinning of an effective regime of human rights. Such a culture cannot take hold unless the political culture is supportive of human rights.'[34] If the Community has any ambitions to develop such a regime then it must re-examine its legal and political culture to determine whether the support for human rights is both a real and serious institutional and constitutional enterprise. The sense of irony that currently pervades the Community's policy construction has to be confronted in this context. Its evolution needs to be mapped and a deliberate course adopted that will overcome existing contradictory structures. Whether then the Community can be treated seriously in its future human rights endeavours is a central question for this book.

[34] Richard Falk, *Human Rights Horizons: the Pursuit of Justice in a Globalizing World* (London: Routledge, 2000) 57.

2

Development Policy and Human Rights

There are two reasons for selecting development policy as central for examining the extent of incoherence in the EU's human rights approaches. First, development co-operation has been an important component of the Community's institutional structure ever since the Treaty of Rome. It has formed a focus for external relations and has been invariably affected by the Community's initiatives in foreign policy. European Political Co-operation, its successor the Common Foreign and Security Policy, and the external commercial policy frameworks have all played significant roles in relations with developing states. Tracking the progression of development policy therefore provides the opportunity to consider perhaps the most complete expression of human rights in an external context. Secondly, the field of development represents the location where the Community confronts its 'other', those not of Europe, the 'uncivilized', 'undeveloped', 'strangers', in a structured and institutional manner. Through law, rhetoric, and practice the Community has defined its relationship with the 'South'. The part played by human rights in this process has been a vital one. Consequently, an analysis of development policy will provide a detailed picture against which the internal condition of human rights practice can be compared.

To undertake this endeavour the history or genealogy of human rights within development policy is examined. First, the narrative *context* for considering how the external condition has intersected and/or deviated from that which has developed internally is considered. Secondly, the three main aspects of human rights in this policy field, the definition and scope of human rights applied, the method of scrutiny adopted, and the enforcement mechanisms, negative in the sense of sanction and positive in the sense of practical initiatives,[1] deployed, are reviewed.

[1] For a consideration of the term 'practical initiatives' in the context of development see Demetrios James Marantis, 'Human Rights, Democracy, and Development: the European Community Model' *Harv HRJ* 7 (1994) 1–32 at 12–16.

2.1 A history of human rights in development policy

For some commentators human rights only assumed a role of any significance in the Community's development policy after the fall of the Iron Curtain.[2] The story suggests that once the Cold War began to lose its determining influence on all elements of external relations, the Community, along with the West in general, uncovered a hitherto largely hidden moral position. No longer were its foreign policies constrained by the contingencies that were instrumental when it came to protecting Western interests against the threat of Soviet domination. In the 'brave new world' that was proclaimed after 1989, human rights could emerge from the shadows to be 'freed from ideological conflicts and become a common standard of achievement for humanity'.[3]

It is important, however, to consider the whole evolution of development policy. Only then will it be possible to consider how and from where human rights practices evolved in this field. Even though there has undoubtedly been a seismic shift since 1989 the antecedent discourse and practices operated by the Community must not be ignored. In particular, the colonial legacy that permeated the relationship between the Community and the South was and remains relevant.

2.1.1 *The formative period: development policy 1950s–1960s*

The story of development policy in the Community has its origins in the post-War world of the 1940s and 1950s. At a time when the old regimes of Europe no longer had the resources or will to operate as colonial rulers, and movements for independence had acquired considerable momentum, new relationships had to be formed between the North and the South. The notion of 'development' took shape in the political and economic uncertainties of the time. Promoted most effectively by the USA in an effort to break the colonial mould whilst maintaining Western influence and liberal-capitalist systems in preference to communist revolution, the concept quickly gained international currency.[4] It was President Truman who first

---

[2] See, for instance, B. Simma, J Beatrix Aschenbrenner, and C. Schulte, 'Human Rights and Development Co-operation' in Philip Alston *et al* (eds), *The EU and Human Rights* (Oxford: Oxford University Press, 1999) 571–626, where scant attention was paid to the story of human rights in matters relating to development prior to 1991.

[3] Katarina Tomaševski, *Development Aid and Human Rights Revisited* (London: Pinter, 1993) 7.

[4] For a history of this movement see Gilbert Rist, *The History of Development* (London: Zed Books, 1997).

gave it official form. During his Inaugural Address of 1949 he identified 'peace, plenty and freedom' as the triad of aims that underpinned the approach. More specifically, he claimed that 'democracy alone can supply the vitalising force to stir the peoples of the world into triumphant action, not only against their human oppressors but also against ... hunger, misery and despair'.[5]

The principles of self-determination and democracy were therefore redolent within the concept, howsoever the USA may then have applied the doctrine in practice. Arturo Escobar indeed interprets the emerging discourse as conditioned by 'the control of communism, the ambivalent acceptance of the independence of former European colonies as a concession to preventing their falling into the Soviet camp, and the continued access to crucial Third World raw materials'.[6] But whatever the motivation, the conjunction of a philosophy of the free market and liberal democracy provided the central themes for the development discourse of the moment.

When the European Economic Community emerged from its chrysalis in 1957 it did not unquestioningly adopt Truman's conceptualization. Rather, it was France and her interests that dictated how the new Community's relations with colonies and ex-colonies would be governed. The *milieu* was conditioned at a late stage of negotiations for the Treaty of Rome when the French government made known that provision had to be made for its dependencies.[7] It could not countenance a position whereby its overseas territories were left outside the customs union. The disadvantage to areas still considered to be part of France would be wholly unacceptable. Equally, France did not wish to see its ex-Empire discarded so prematurely. There was a keen political desire to retain the 'familial' relations with its colonies and ex-colonies despite the clear anti-colonial movements that were taking hold throughout the world.[8]

Even though Germany had no interest in allowing the new Community to be saddled with the vestiges of colonialism, having been stripped of such interests after the First World War, the French insistence that provision be made operated as a veto on the whole Community project. The other negotiating states had little choice but to satisfy France's concerns.

---

[5] Quoted in Rist, note 4 above, at 71.

[6] Arturo Escobar, *Encountering Development: The Making and Unmaking of the Third World* (Princeton: Princeton University Press, 1995) 34.

[7] See Martin Holland, *The European Union and the Third World* (Basingstoke: Palgrave, 2002) 25.

[8] See Marjorie Lister, *The European Community and the Developing World* (Aldershot: Avebury, 1988) 1–18.

It was determined that a system of 'association' should be instituted within the new Community's structure, one that drew on the language of 'development' but was fundamentally preconditioned by French colonialist thinking. The foundation of development policy was therefore beset by an early contradiction when positioned within the context of global discourse.

The conflict was immediately evident from the Preamble to the Treaty of Rome, one aim of which was 'to confirm the solidarity which binds Europe and the overseas countries and ... to ensure the development of their prosperity, in accordance with the Charter of the United Nations'.

The reference to the UN Charter should have indicated an acceptance of its promotion of higher standards of living and 'economic and social progress and development' *and* 'universal respect for, and observance of, human rights and fundamental freedoms'.[9] It did at least acknowledge the global discourse attributed to 'development' as recognized through the United Nations but the relevant provisions in Part IV of the Treaty failed to amplify the connection. Rather, the economic aspects of 'association' provided the focus, avoiding any direct suggestion of a wider ethical dimension that might have incorporated a human rights element.

So it can be seen from Article 3(k) of the original Treaty of Rome that the general purpose of association with the 'overseas countries and territories'[10] was 'to increase trade and to promote *jointly* economic and social development' (emphasis added). Part IV of the Treaty then provided the detail. Article 131 specified that association was 'to promote the economic and social development of the countries and territories and to establish close economic relations between them and the Community as a whole'. It was to 'further the interests and prosperity of the inhabitants ... in order to lead them to the economic, social and cultural development to which they aspire'. Together these provisions ensured that the original colonial thinking would not disappear. The mutual benefit available through 'economic relations' was accompanied by the refusal to embrace any radical sub-text of self-determination and independence. The absence of a political development as opposed to economic and social development ensured the decolonization discourse would remain outside the Community's immediate concern. The position was emphasised by the provisions that proceeded to govern the association practice.

---

[9] See Articles 55(a) and (c) Charter of the United Nations 1945.
[10] The countries and territories were listed in Annex IV EC Treaty.

Article 132 EEC Treaty provided that the Member States would 'apply to their trade with the countries and territories the same treatment as they accord each other' under the Treaty.[11] The relationship would be formed through law by means of a legally constituted association agreement. The only possible reference to human rights was extremely tenuous. Article 135 suggested the potential for concluding agreements enabling the free movement of workers from the countries and territories within the Community and *vice versa*. A right of establishment was also promoted.[12] But these provisions did not provide the basis upon which a human rights narrative in the association relationship could be founded. There was no political will to provide the people of the associated states with rights in the Community and there was no apparent intention to address rights issues in the colonies and ex-colonies themselves. There was only concern for the economic aspects of the 'special relations' that were now to be fostered between the Community and the associated states.

The absence of a human rights or political dimension was in keeping with the general rhetoric employed within the Community at this time. Human rights were not evident as subjects of concern within the Treaty of Rome or the early practices of the Community.[13] Member States were not intent on questioning each other's record and were unlikely to differ in their approach when it came to the overseas territories.

However, a primary distinction that separates the internal condition from development policy had an important bearing on the evolution of human rights in each domain. Internally there was a concern to resolve the relations of conflict that had previously subsisted between the Member States. The Community expressly recognized the past violence and specifically assumed the role of redressing the conflict.[14] Member States combined in a project designed to end 'bloody conflicts' and work together to achieve liberty and prosperity. Human rights may not have been specifically mentioned but the understanding that the peoples of Europe should be the recipients of benefits and respect was a key element. At least that is the inference from the language of the Treaty of Rome.

---

[11] Article 183 (ex Article 132) EC Treaty.

[12] Article 183(5) (ex Article 132(5)) EC Treaty.

[13] See Chapter 6 for a more detailed account of the history of human rights *within* the Community.

[14] See in particular the Schuman Declaration 1950 and the succeeding European Coal and Steel Community Treaty 1951.

Externally, in the realm of development policy, as it was to become known, the Community was faced with dealing with the historical relations between the individual Member States, particularly France, and their colonies. Those relations were also based on conflict, conflict with an external 'other' and a conflict wholly generated by Europe's determination to impose its will on the 'South' for Europe's benefit. Colonialism was structured on a violence that fundamentally abused human rights as advocated by the West. But in contrast to the internal condition, nothing in the Community's structure of association, in its rhetoric, or in its actions, suggested any attempt to resolve the nature of the colonial relationship. Instead, the approach was based on a central ambiguity. On the one hand there was no intention to construct the Community as a successor to its colonial Member States. Colonialism had no part in the post-War world and there was no political will for the Community to assume the problems of decolonization. On the other, there was no intention to present the Community as a 'champion' of the colonized. That would entail a direct confrontation with Member States still significantly engaged in the colonial enterprise. Nevertheless, it did make economic sense to maintain a relationship with the colonies and ex-colonies and to continue to benefit from the colonial connections that had been formed over the previous centuries.

Consequently, to deal with the ambiguity the idea of 'association' enacted an institutional culture of denial and deflection rather than one programmed to heal past external violence. Colonialism indeed would have no textual presence. No mention would be made of the term. There would instead be 'special relations'[15] and 'development', the emphasis being on the economic. Political dimensions would be ignored, at least rhetorically, and the historical link between the Community and the colonial activities of its Member States would be expressed carefully and in such a way as to avoid criticism of both the past and present behaviour of Member States.

A prime example of the deflection at work appeared in the Commission's 1964 review of the 'Background to Association with the African States and Madagascar'.[16] In referring to the period before the formation of the Community, it observed that, '[t]hrough a process of historical evolution these territories had become, *as it were*, overseas extensions of the Member States' economies' (emphasis added).[17] In the Commission's words 'there has been a gradual shift from the empirical pattern of association, a legacy

---

[15] Article 182 (ex Article 131) EC Treaty.   [16] EC Bull 3-1964 at 21.   [17] Ibid.

of the past, to a far more conscious policy of association linked to the concept of development aid'.[18]

The tone inferred that the Community was faced with a situation and a relationship with the South that had arisen almost by chance. By failing to recognize the purposive actions of the European states in their colonial endeavours and intimating that such endeavours no longer persisted, the Community had embarked on a process that denied the abusive nature of the exploitative relationship that still subsisted. It deflected criticism away from its Member States' records. Equally, by adopting a language of law and suggesting that the relationship with the South was consensual through the institution of a contractual scheme of association the Community could legitimize the relationship and resist criticisms of neo-colonialism. But in taking this course the Community ironically became implicated in the colonial methods of its Member States. Indeed, the very process by which the association policy was drawn up, with little if any reference to the states and territories concerned, indicated the lack of movement away from old colonial methods of dealing with the South.[19] The dependent territories were simply *incorporated* into the association structure. The Implementing Convention relating to the association *imposed* a relationship that would last for five years and gave no scope for the beneficiaries to question any of its provisions.[20] Even independence would not release any ex-colony. Such dictatorial approaches did little to suggest a shift away from colonialist thinking. They were also accompanied by a general discourse that denied colonialism's heritage.

It was not necessarily unwelcome in the South to ensure that human rights would have little if any role to play in the new policy. 'Development' was considered an internal affair, albeit one that warranted assistance from the North. The Asian-African Bandung Conference held in 1955, for instance, kept separate its conception of human rights from that of 'economic development'.[21]

The Community had no difficulty embracing this practice. As the original association agreement came to be renewed, at a time when most of the recipient states had achieved independence, the Community was happy to describe the continuing relationship with the 'developing countries' as one of 'equality and reciprocity'.[22] These principles were founded 'in the

[18] EC Bull 3-1964 at 21.
[19] See Lister, note 8 above, at 18.
[20] Annex A EEC Treaty.
[21] Rist, note 4 above, at 83.
[22] EC Bull 9/10-1963 at 13.

institutions and machinery which we have created because these are the expression of political equality among our states and of our mutual recognition of each other's sovereignty'.[23]

The legal formation of association was portrayed as the basis of the legitimacy of the Community's activities. Non-interference was key, echoing the current orthodoxy promoted by and within the United Nations[24] as well as by the newly independent developing states. But whilst this had the effect of the 'new Europe' distancing itself from past colonial structures, if not practices, it also served to confirm that the members of the Community only had a general moral obligation to assist the peoples of the developing world. Officially, the Community held that the 'chief responsibility for economic and social development continues to be with the populations concerned and with their governments'.[25]

The move away from colonialism ensured that emerging nations in the South were prepared to co-operate with the Community on a mutually beneficial basis provided always that the practice of non-interference continued. The growing discourse in the United Nations, which sought to provide the South with the power to 'challenge the Northern countries' control of international resources'[26] and led to the creation of the UN Conference on Trade and Development (UNCTAD) in 1964, added to the sense of authority now assumed by the South. When the association agreement was renewed the President of the Federal Republic of Cameroon, M. Ahidjo was sufficiently empowered to comment that the aid provided to date, 'had been all the more valuable and appreciated because it has never had any kind of political strings'.[27]

The Yaoundé Convention signed in 1963, again for a period of five years, between the Community and the eighteen Francophone African states, ensured that the human rights aspects to development, such as they were, remained unarticulated. Instead, the objectives for the Convention were the 'economic, social and cultural progress' of all the parties, the diversification of the economies and industrialization of the associated states, and the extension of inter-African co-operation and trade.[28] In short, aid and trade.

---

[23] Ibid.
[24] See, for instance, Article 2(7) Charter of the United Nations and UNGA Res 2625 (XXV).
[25] EC Bull 2-1960 at 10.
[26] Olufemi Babarinde, 'The European Union's Relations with the South: A Commitment to Development' in Carolyn Rhodes (ed), *The European Union in the World Community* (London: Lynne Rienner, 1998) 127–46 at 142.
[27] EC Bull 9/10-1963 at 8.   [28] Lister, note 8 above, at 39.

The initial construction and implementation of the policy of association set important conditions for the evolution of human rights concerns in the field of development. Through the confluence of the Community's wariness in encouraging independence movements or criticizing the past practices of its Member States, and the newly independent states' refusal to accept any scrutiny of its internal political and human rights affairs, human rights from a civil and political perspective were simply ignored. It was in all parties' interests to concentrate on the economics of the relationship, a relationship supposedly founded on law rather than colonialism.

This is not to say that a human rights presence in development policy during the 1960s cannot be inferred. Rather, the narrative of rights was constrained in a way that was distinct from the internal experience. The legal moves to ensure that the Community could deflect internal opposition to its institution of supremacy through adopting human rights principles essentially focused on civil and political rights,[29] were not relevant to the external position. A different role for rights emerged in development policy. As Simma *et al* observed, human rights issues materialized in relation to 'humanitarian relief'[30] during this early period. There were traces of rights of an economic, social, and cultural nature flowing from the attention paid to the 'social' aspects of development referred to in the Treaty. The operation of the European Development Fund, created by Article 132(3) EEC Treaty, which focused its attention on the giving of aid rather than stimulating trade, was said by the Commission in 1960 to be within an 'atmosphere of freedom and healthy competition'.[31] The funding of projects of a social character was a particular aim. Projects would be 'to improve the public health and educational equipment of the country concerned and the social services and housing conditions of the local inhabitants'.[32] Admittedly, such matters were not expressed in rights terms but they did reflect social elements of the Universal Declaration of Human Rights.[33] That the projects needed to 'correspond to some economic development'[34] in the Commission's view obscured the potential rights dimension. Walter Hallstein, the President of the Commission, in 1963 presaged the possible link when he advocated that development was concerned with establishing 'living conditions conducive to the unfolding of human dignity',[35] a term that was later to become centrally implicated in the realization of human rights

---

[29] For a review of the story of this development see Chapter 6.
[30] Simma *et al*, note 2 above, at 574. [31] EC Bull 2–1960 at 10. [32] Ibid at 12.
[33] See, *inter alia*, Articles 25 and 26 Universal Declaration of Human Rights 1948.
[34] EC Bull 2-1960 at 13. [35] EC Bull 9/10-1963 at 18.

in development. Nevertheless, one struggles to uncover a human rights dimension during the foundational period of the Community until the late 1960s. A 'dependency relationship' was imposed between the Community and the developing states that not only suggested 'the charge of neo-colonialism was hard to refute',[36] but also set any effective role for human rights in this context largely untenable. It has even been commented that a policy of 'temporarily sacrificing both civil and political rights and economic and social rights was the reigning orthodoxy' in the development discourse at this time.[37] Whether there was a palpable change in mood for the Community's practice in the 1970s must now be considered.

2.1.2 *Seeking an external identity: development policy 1970–1991*

(a) *Lomé I and II*

In the period leading up to the imminent accession of the United Kingdom there emerged a determination by the Community to project itself to the external as well as to its own constituents. The manufacture of a 'European Identity', which had its roots in a discourse developed in the early 1970s, was the concept promulgated as a means by which the joint projection could be effected. At the Paris Conference of the Heads of State and Government in 1972 the problem of 'underdevelopment' was highlighted as one field in which Europe's 'voice' should be 'heard in world affairs'.[38] The Community was determined to 'increase aid and technical assistance to the least favoured people'.[39]

The following year, in the seminal Copenhagen Declaration on 'the European Identity'[40] development policy was noted as one crucial area in which the Community's identity vis-à-vis its relations with the rest of the world could be defined. Those elements of the European Identity expressed as fundamental to its definition (namely, the defence of the 'principles of democracy, of the rule of law, of social justice ... and of respect for human rights')[41] should therefore have had specific application in the field of development policy. Yet initially no direct textual link was made to this effect.

---

[36] Holland, note 7 above, at 31.
[37] Jack Donnelly, *Universal Human Rights in Theory and Practice* (New York: Cornell University Press, 1989) 163.
[38] See the text of this declaration in Press and Information Office of the Government of the Federal Republic of Germany, *Texts Relating to the European Political Co-operation* (Bonn, 1974) 26–39.
[39] Ibid at 27.   [40] See EC Bull 12-1973 118–22.   [41] Ibid at 119.

The lack of explicit incorporation of human rights issues in the development context at this important juncture established a central ambiguity. Were human rights concerns relevant to development policy or not? The texts did little to resolve the issue. The Commission's Memorandum on Development Co-operation of 1971 made no direct mention of human rights.[42] It did, however, contain an oblique reference to 'the pursuit of better conditions of life and of fulfilment for mankind'.[43] It pronounced that development policy was not to be restricted to the economic field and should include social improvements 'in the standard of education and health'. In truth this did not deviate substantially from existing Community practice in development assistance projects. What human rights matters could be inferred remained confined to interpretations of social welfare initiatives.

The accession of the United Kingdom in 1973 and the consequent inclusion of the Commonwealth countries within the Community's development policy offered the opportunity for a radical re-shaping of the Yaoundé Convention system.[44] When the Convention came to be renewed for the second time in 1975, negotiations between the Community and what were now termed the African, Caribbean, and Pacific (ACP) states, were framed with a 'more balanced economic order' in mind.[45] But this did not precipitate a change in approach as regards human rights despite the concurrent rhetoric of European Identity. Political neutrality remained an aim for Community and ACP states alike and this precluded any rights discourse impinging on the arrangements. Rather, Lomé I, as the Convention became known, was concerned with preferential access to Community markets, technical and industrial co-operation, and economic assistance to foster balanced development.[46]

However, Lomé I did succeed in providing institutional structures and a new discourse that would have an important bearing on the eventual involvement of human rights practices. First, it reaffirmed that the basis for development policy was contractual. The relationship was legally bound, at least in theory, by the arrangements negotiated between the parties. A sense of 'partnership' accompanied the Convention that

---

[42] Commission Memorandum on a Community Policy for Development Co-operation Summary, EC Bull Suppl. 5-1971.
[43] Ibid at 18.
[44] Yaoundé I was renewed by Yaoundé II in 1969 with little amendment.
[45] Lomé Convention 1975, Preamble, *The Courier* No 31, Brussels, March 1975.
[46] See Babarinde, note 26 above.

suggested the original 'francophone style of colonial relationship', as Holland describes it,[47] no longer held sway. This meant that any formal inclusion of human rights factors would have to be *agreed* as a result of a consensual acknowledgement that they represented valid topics of concern for both the Community *and* the ACP states. Secondly, Lomé I established the Council of Ministers that was supposed to concentrate on fundamental political issues as well as a Consultative Assembly and a Committee of Ambassadors. This provided the institutional structure within which human rights could be raised informally. Lomé I therefore determined that the parameters for involvement of human rights in development policy would be tightly constrained. Community initiatives outside the system would lack legitimacy within the terms of the contractual relationship and the institutional framework. Of course, it did not mean that the Community was prevented from raising human rights issues through other avenues, but development practice was conditioned so as to keep human rights a distant concern.

The absence of human rights in development policy was nevertheless finally challenged in the mid-1970s after it became apparent that gross human rights abuses were taking place under the very nose of the Community's development activities. In particular, the events that occurred in Uganda under the Idi Amin regime and in Equatorial Guinea, made a mockery of the Community's discursive moves to be seen as 'guardian' and promoter of human rights.[48] Even so, the only response the Community could give was self-consciously 'reserved and pragmatic'.[49] Some aid was cut but 'discretely' as Lister notes and with 'relatively little commotion'.[50]

The sensitive approach to human rights abuse continued despite the Commission's attempt to introduce a human rights element into the Lomé II Convention of 1979. A Commission memorandum drew attention to the, 'importance of *human rights* in the eyes of the European public, whose support is vital for the continuance and enhancement of a real co-operation policy'[51] but the argument that the new Convention should introduce a human rights component attracted severe opposition. Unsurprisingly, the lack of interference that was so warmly appreciated in the early days remained a crucial point of principle for the ACP states. The President

---

[47] Holland, note 7 above, at 35. [48] Marantis, note 1 above, at 6.
[49] *The Courier*, No 56, July-August 1979, viii as quoted in Lister, note 8 above, at 197.
[50] Lister, note 8 above, at 197. [51] EC Bull 2-1978 at 19.

of the Council of ACP Ministers, speaking on behalf of the ACP group, stated that although 'human rights were a matter of concern for both the ACP states and the Community Member States' it was not felt that 'these questions had anything to do with an economic and trade co-operation agreement'.[52] The position was bolstered by the observation that the Treaty of Rome itself contained no reference to human rights.[53]

The logic of the opposition to the Commission's initiative (and the fact that the balance of power in negotiating positions remained fairly even at this time)[54] ensured that direct mention of human rights issues were prevented from acquiring any meaningful presence in the new Lomé II text. Michael Addo attempts to suggest that certain aspects of the Convention touched human rights 'in a broader context' but it is difficult to accept the argument that a prohibition of discrimination in investment, linked with the human right to 'property (of aliens)' suggests that Lomé II contained any meaningful advancement of human rights *per se*.[55] It is too tenuous to maintain that such provision within the Convention was evidence of a hidden human rights programme *despite* the blatant and vociferous objection to such a link by the ACP states.[56] In comparison to the Community's internal discourse, which had seen the establishment of respect for human rights as a founding principle, development policy remained largely unfettered by human rights considerations.

(b) Lomé III

It was not until the Lomé Convention arrangements came to be renewed in the early 1980s that any alteration to the human rights aspects of development policy were formally addressed. Even then Lomé III, renegotiated in 1982 and signed in 1984, continued to use language that suggested a distinct approach from the appreciation of human rights that was simultaneously gaining ground *within* the Community.

---

[52] Report of the Opening Session of negotiations for Lomé II held in Brussels on 24 July 1978, EC Bull 7/8-1978 at 17.

[53] The fact that the Community, through first the ECJ and then the other institutions in their Joint Declaration of 1977, had begun to develop an appreciation of the need to respect human rights within and by the Community was ignored.

[54] See Marantis, note 1 above.

[55] See M. Addo, 'Some Issues in European Community Aid Policy and Human Rights' *Legal Issues of European Integration* 1 (1988) 71–7.

[56] It is interesting to note, however, that attached to the Convention was a statement that looked towards the 'observance and protection of the civil rights of ACP citizens...resident in the Community'. See EC Bull 1-1979 at 60.

In the Convention's Preamble, for instance, the parties reaffirmed their 'adherence to the principles of the [UN Charter] and their faith in fundamental human rights, in the dignity and worth of the human person, in the equal rights of men and women and of nations large and small'.

This was vague enough to avoid opposition by the ACP states but indicative perhaps of the approach intended for human rights in the Community's relationship. Article 4 then provided the guiding clause generating an instructive but non-binding Joint Declaration that was annexed to the Convention and provided a statement of interpretation rather than a framework for action.

The declaration indicated the parties' understanding of the human rights element. Crucially it focused on 'human dignity as an inalienable right and as constituting an essential objective for the attainment of the legitimate aspirations of individuals *and of peoples*' (emphasis added).[57] It further proclaimed that ACP-EEC co-operation 'must help eliminate the obstacles preventing individuals and peoples from actually enjoying their economic, social and cultural rights'[58] and then chose to specify the obligation to 'fight for the elimination of all forms of discrimination' and to 'work for the eradication of apartheid'.[59]

The failure to consider civil and political rights directly in Lomé III continued to run counter to the clear preference established by the Community internally, specifically with regard to its attachment to the European Convention on Human Rights (ECHR).[60] Admittedly, the notion of 'human dignity' could have suggested the need to protect certain civil and political rights but it by no means necessarily encompassed them all. Indeed, the resolution on human rights adopted by the ACP-EEC Joint Committee in Bujumbura in 1985 following the signing of the Convention placed the concept in terms of development rather than merely rights. It concluded that 'mankind, male and female, must be the essential beneficiary of development policy, and must be able to find satisfaction and well-being in his [*sic!*] every-day life without fear of aggression, unwarranted arrest or detention or any other political menace or coercion and maintains that *man cannot live with dignity under the current world economic system*'.[61]

Despite the mention of certain forms of intolerable civil rights abuses, the concept of 'dignity' appeared to have more to do with the search for

---

[57] Ibid.   [58] Ibid.   [59] Ibid.
[60] Again see Chapter 6 for consideration of the parallel story within the Community.
[61] ACP-EEC Joint Committee Resolution on Human Rights at Bujumbura (1985) para C.

global economic justice than addressing any particular human rights concerns.

Equally, the reference to the aspirations of 'peoples' indicated an appreciation of 'third generation rights' that were beginning to find expression in a more radical human rights discourse. For instance, international moves to acknowledge and promote a 'right to development' were gaining recognition throughout the early to mid-1970s.[62] The UN Declaration on Social Progress and Development in 1969 had maintained that 'social progress and development shall be founded on respect for the dignity and value of the human person and shall ensure the promotion of rights and social justice'.[63] The 'recognition and effective implementation of civil and political rights as well as economic, social and cultural rights without any discrimination' was a priority consideration.[64] The formula was repeated in succeeding UN productions thereby entrenching the notion of the indivisibility of rights within development.[65]

The discourse on rights adopted in the Community's development policy in Lomé III demonstrated a willingness by the Community to consider a broad range of rights concepts, not just those limited to the European sphere. It certainly did not embrace an unqualified approach to such concepts, as illustrated by the failure to clarify the nature of the rights being promoted or protected. But it at least provided evidence of the Community's intention to consider new discourses externally. It also, according to Addo, recognized the importance of 'the ability and the need to use Community aid to promote human rights in the ACP states'.[66] This was one of its defining characteristics, he suggests, a 'noteworthy innovation'.[67]

Although, civil and political human rights continued to be ignored as a governing factor there was a willingness to address some notable human rights 'situations' through public condemnation (apartheid South Africa being the chief target)[68] *and* to embrace rhetorically international human

---

[62] See, generally, on the progress of the 'right to development', Roland Rich, 'Right to Development: A Right of Peoples?' in James Crawford (ed), *The Rights of Peoples* (Oxford: Clarendon Press, 1988) 39–67.

[63] Article 2 Declaration on Social Progress and Development, UNGA Res 2542 (XXIV) (1969).

[64] Ibid.

[65] This process culminated in the Declaration on the Right to Development, UNGA Res 41/128 (1986).

[66] Addo, note 55 above, at 84.   [67] Marantis, note 1 above, at 7.

[68] See, for instance, ACP-Joint Assembly Resolution on Human Rights adopted 26 September 1985, which called for the Member States of ACP-EEC to 'break off all economic, financial

rights norms.[69] Apart from this, action remained rooted in the economic and social dimensions (particularly the former). The resolution on human rights produced by the ACP-EEC Joint Committee in January 1985 in particular specified that greater economic resources should be 'devoted to resolving the problems which undermine the possibility for the peoples of Africa, the Caribbean and the Pacific to enjoy their fundamental human rights *as defined by Article 25 of the Universal Declaration of Human Rights*' (emphasis added).[70]

Article 25 focuses upon the right for everyone to a 'standard of living adequate for [their] health and well-being'. Similarly, in the ACP-EEC Joint Assembly's 1986 resolution on 'People-Centred Development' the emphasis was on welfare not a general improvement of human rights *tout court*. Thus the Community's practice under Lomé III continued to take a narrative path that remained closely linked with its previous actions.

(c) Lomé IV

With the alteration of the global political landscape in the late 1980s the Community's development policy entered a new phase. The fall of the Iron Curtain prompted the Community to re-define its priorities. Countries emerging from Soviet control needed to be encouraged in their evolution into fully democratic free-market regimes. Assistance was shifted from the South to the East. At the same time, the dramatic 'victory' for liberal capitalist systems convinced many that a new ethical order had emerged, one that should ensure that the South in particular could no longer expect to be exempt from human rights and democratic standards. Lomé IV, signed in 1989, emphasized a development that entailed 'respect for and promotion of *all* human rights' (emphasis added).[71] These were described as being 'indivisible and inter-related, each having its own legitimacy: non-discriminatory treatment; fundamental human rights; civil and political

---

and military relations with South Africa'. Similar condemnatory outputs from the ACP-EEC institutions regarding South Africa continued regularly until transition at the beginning of the 1990s.

[69] See note 61 above at para D, which refers to the Universal Declaration of Human Rights, the International Covenants on Civil and Political Rights, and on Economic, Social and Cultural Rights, the African Charter of Human and Peoples' Rights and the European Convention for the Protection of Human Rights and Fundamental Freedoms. Paragraph E also noted the obligation of the Lomé III signatories 'to ensure the preservation and improvement of human rights'.

[70] Ibid at Article 3(ii).   [71] Article 5 Lomé IV, *The Courier*, No 120, March-April 1990.

rights; economic, social and cultural rights'.[72] The language had finally embraced the civil and political dimension without equivocation.

As with Lomé III, however, Lomé IV's adoption of an extended rhetoric was still bounded, as Marantis notes, by the 'weak institutional network' of the ACP-EEC framework.[73] Effective action on human rights concerns remained a distant prospect within the contractual arrangements, chiefly because the long-standing methods of doing business had no history of addressing such issues. By the same token, development policy remained focused upon the economic and social elements of a 'basic needs' perspective, one that was given added relevance by the increasingly hopeless position in which the South found itself despite decades of development.

The new international political setting nevertheless encouraged the Community to look beyond its ACP agreements, even to ignore them. Pivotal demonstrations of intent appeared in rapid succession in response to the dramatic events around the world that saw the overthrow of many human rights abusive regimes.[74] The European Council at Luxembourg in 1991 recognized the 'considerable progress' made in the world and began to build upon the Commission's linkage of human rights, democracy, and development.[75] It reiterated the principle of indivisibility of rights and affirmed that the 'promotion of economic, social and cultural rights, as of civil and political rights ... is of fundamental importance for the full realisation of human dignity'.[76] The Council then linked 'democracy, pluralism, respect for human rights, institutions working within a constitutional framework, and responsible governments appointed following periodic, fair elections, as well as the recognition of the legitimate importance of the individual in society ... [as] ... prerequisites of sustained social and economic development'.[77]

The Commission also issued a communication at this time that made explicit the connection between respect for and promotion of human rights

---

[72] Article 5 Lomé IV, *The Courier*, No 120, March-April 1990.

[73] Marantis, note 1 above, at 9.

[74] Such events were by no means restricted to those that occurred in Central and Eastern Europe. The Peoples' Revolution in the Philippines during 1986, for instance, and the transition that took place in South Africa in 1989–90 served as examples of social movements that removed seemingly intractable regimes and replaced them with putative human rights respecting governments.

[75] See the Luxembourg European Council Declaration on Human Rights, EC Bull 6-1991 at 17, which made reference to the Commission's Communication to the Council on 'Human Rights, Democracy and Development Co-operation', EC Bull 3-1991 point 1.3.41.

[76] Ibid.   [77] Ibid.

and democratic processes in developing countries.[78] In essence, this was the rhetoric of 'good governance'. Already formulated by the World Bank in 1989 and given credence on the European stage by the French and British governments, it was now incorporated wholesale into the language of development. The door was opened for the Community to adopt specific strategies to accompany the rhetoric.

(d) Resolution of 28 November 1991

The Council and Member States' Joint Resolution of 28 November 1991 ('the 1991 Resolution') provided definition for the Community's revised approach.[79] It set in train institutional responses to the question of human rights in development policy that suggested a more consistent and forceful strategy.[80] In particular, it gave a 'high priority to a positive approach' to stimulate respect for human rights. Increased assistance for those states that demonstrated 'substantive positive changes' in the condition of human rights and democracy was advocated. Nonetheless, this would not prevent the Community from taking appropriate action against those states guilty of 'grave and persistent human violations' or 'serious interruption of democratic processes'. In that event the Community was provided with the authority to adopt a number of graded responses.

First, confidential *démarches* to apply pressure on the offending state could be employed. Secondly, alterations in the 'content or channels' potentially re-directing development funds to non-governmental organizations could be made, thus ensuring the maintenance of aid even in the face of violations. And thirdly, suspension of co-operation (and aid) could be used as a last resort.

The Resolution did *not*, however, privilege respect for human rights. Rather, they were expressed as elements of a greater whole, a package of principles that was not necessarily undermined merely by a regime's failure to adhere to one component. Human rights were 'part of a larger set of

---

[78] Communication from the Commission to the Council on 'Human Rights, Democracy and Development Co-operation', EC Bull 3-1991 at 64.

[79] Resolution of the Council and of the Member States, EC Bull 11-1991 122–3.

[80] It would be true to say, however, that the Council did not go as far as the European Parliament would have liked. That institution made various recommendations in its Resolution on Human Rights, Democracy and Development [1991] OJ C326/259. It suggested that 'development aid is necessarily dependent upon human rights being respected' (para 2) that 'respect for democracy and human rights is a matter of concern to all countries...and to the European Community in particular where the situation with regard to third country nationals is constantly worsening' an admission that finds little support from the Council in *its* Resolution.

requirements in order to achieve balanced and sustainable development'. These included 'sensible economic and social policies, democratic decision-making, adequate governmental transparency and financial accountability, creation of market-friendly environment for development, measures to combat corruption, as well as respect for the rule of law, human rights, and freedom of the press and expression'.[81]

None of the stated requirements, a non-exhaustive list it should be emphasized, were accorded any priority. Human rights may have attracted considerable attention as already indicated but other issues loomed just as large in the Council's vision. In particular, military spending was a target. The Council noted that '[e]xcessive military spending not only reduces the funds available for other purposes, but [are] violations of international law, as well as often being meant and used for purposes of internal repression and denial of universally recognized human rights'.[82]

The Resolution suggested that the Community and the Member States would consider concrete measures to 'encourage developing countries to reduce their military expenditure' including increasing or decreasing 'support' where appropriate and re-directing funds towards economic and social development projects 'with particular emphasis on the education and health sectors'.

The implication of these pronouncements was that human rights matters were not seen as separable from other interests. They were linked demonstrably to issues of political concern to the Community.

2.1.3 *The post-Cold War period*

The 1991 Resolution undoubtedly represented a radical departure from existing human rights practice in development policy. But this was only the first institutional response to the new era heralded by the fall of the Berlin Wall. Further and more systemic changes were introduced both in legal terms and in the clear political will displayed to ensure the contractual relations with the ACP states in particular reflected the new environment.

(a) The legal dimension

The Maastricht Treaty completed in 1992 ensured that the new global era was accompanied by constitutional recognition that human rights should possess a significant presence in development policy. Article 177(2) (ex

---

[81] See note 79 above.   [82] Ibid.

Article 130(u)(2)) EC Treaty determined that the respect for human rights and fundamental freedoms (amongst other requirements) now became an official policy objective.

In *Portugal v. Council*[83] the European Court of Justice (ECJ) was asked to consider the whole legitimacy of Community activity that tried to give effect to this constitutional amendment. The Portuguese government had objected to the inclusion of a human rights clause in the co-operation agreement entered into with India. In response Advocate General La Pergola first suggested that it was 'clear that [the objectives laid down in Article 177 (ex Article 130(u)) reflect a complex vision of development, the product of interaction between its economic, social and political aspects, which are taken into account by the most recent cooperation agreements'.[84]

Within that vision, human rights and democracy occupied a central role, although treated separately through Article 177(2) (ex Article 130u(2)) rather than (1). Nonetheless, here was a Treaty provision that explicitly incorporated a human rights dimension into a policy field.

The ECJ followed the advice of AG La Pergola and confirmed the Community's authority to enact human rights initiatives under the Treaty provisions. It found that the Community was entitled to introduce such requirements and thus gave legal sanction to the fundamental nature of human rights in development policy practice.[85]

In explaining its decision the Court noted that it was common ground that fundamental rights formed an integral part of the Community's legal order. Portugal had argued that the Community was still not competent to adopt human rights measures 'either internally or externally'[86] but the ECJ disagreed as far as the latter was concerned. It concluded that Article 177(2) (ex Article 130u(2)) 'demonstrates the importance to be attached to respect for human rights and democratic principles, so that, amongst other things, development cooperation policy must be adapted to the requirement of respect for those rights and principles'.[87]

It then accepted the Advocate General's submission that the discursive practices of the Community, through its 'various declarations and documents', had already confirmed the importance of human rights in all its dealings. The ECJ thus determined that the Community was indeed authorized to include human rights provisions, which entitled suspension

---

[83] *Portugal v. Council* Case C268/94 [1996] ECR I-6184.   [84] Ibid.
[85] Paul Craig and Gráinne de Búrca, *EU Law: Text, Cases and Materials*, 2nd edn (Oxford: Oxford University Press, 1998) 336.
[86] See note 83 at 6189, para 23.   [87] Ibid at 6217, para 24.

or termination in the event of violation of human rights, within any development co-operation agreement. Competence for Community action in this regard was firmly settled in law.

(b) The political dimension and the re-negotiation of Lomé

At the same time as the ECJ was considering the legal position of human rights in the Community's development policy, the other institutions were taxed with the issue of renewing the Lomé Convention. It was extended on an interim basis in 1995 during its mid-term review. This provided the opportunity to revise Article 5 of the Convention to turn it into an essential element clause. Thus, should any state contravene 'respect for human rights, democratic principles and the rule of law' the Community would be entitled to suspend the Convention in relation to the state concerned. In other words, aid could be cut, although only as a last resort. This was very much in line with the growing trend for the Community to include essential element clauses in its association agreements with the newly emerging democracies in Central and Eastern Europe.[88] It reflected the desire, expressed by the Parliament, which exercised the right of veto over the adoption of any association and trade agreement, that human rights concerns should always appear within the Community's formal external agreements.[89] The political will to establish a framework for enforcement action in the event of a breach of human rights was thus firmly entrenched.

In addition to this amendment, and as something of a concession to the ACP states, the mid-term review also introduced a new system of political dialogue that would be instituted in the event of a suspected breach of Article 5 and that should precede any precipitous action by the Community.[90] As Holland comments, 'political dialogue—or perhaps more accurately political conditionality—was no longer taboo but became an essential element of a new approach to development issues'.[91]

The new political environment prompted a complete review of the relationship with the ACP states almost as soon as the ink was dry on signing the revised Lomé IV. The Commission's Green Paper of 1996 was the first major document to address the matter.[92] Here, economics continued to dominate

---

[88] See amongst others, E. Riedel and M. Will, 'Human Rights Clauses in External Agreements' in Alston *et al* (eds), note 2 above, at 723–54.
[89] Ibid.   [90] Article 366a Lomé IV.   [91] Holland, note 7 above, at 197.
[92] European Commission, *Green Paper on Relations Between the European Union and the ACP Countries on the Eve of the 21st Century: Challenges and Options for a New Partnership* (1996) COM(96)570.

the rhetoric with even the notion of an external identity described as being achieved through *inter alia* 'an effective and differentiated development policy, and a multilateral trade policy designed to open up markets in accordance with negotiated common rules'.[93]

But the Commission was nevertheless intent on strengthening the 'political dimension' of the agreement as well. It was quick to identify the 'promotion of a kind of world development that is more compatible with European political and social values'[94] as a guiding principle for the Community's policy. The adoption of a form of development that failed to guarantee 'social progress, respect for human rights and above all fundamental social rights' was described as 'incompatible with European political and social values'.[95] It did not shy away, therefore, from treating the principle of external non-interference as well and truly buried notwithstanding continued opposition to such a stance taken in the South.

The Commission was also intent on ensuring that development policy, and human rights within it, were not treated in isolation. The aims of the policy 'ultimately complement the Union's political and economic objectives', the Commission stated.[96] Respect for human rights and 'fundamental liberties' (as elements of the political aspects of development) together with the intended 'social benefits (better living conditions, preventing the disintegration of the social fabric) and its environmental concerns' that development should bring, were not to be ends in themselves. As the Commission admitted, '[i]t comes down to ensuring consistency between the objectives pursued within the European Union and the influence that it can bring to bear on the form of development in certain regions of the world'.[97] Such development would therefore have to meet 'some of the security concerns of the EU (risk of armed conflict, spread of nuclear weapons, terrorism, migration)' as well as any objective development criteria.[98] The Community's security in particular would be enhanced by the stability of developing nations, a stability that was assessed in terms of 'sustainable economic and social development, democracy and human rights, establishment of viable political structures and a capacity to manage change without resorting to violence'.[99]

The attempt by the Commission to draw together the internal interests of the Community with the rationale behind development policy suggests

---

[93] Ibid, 'Foreword' at 1. [94] Ibid, 'Main Topics for Discussion' at iii.
[95] Ibid, 'Chapter IV' at 37. [96] Ibid at 4. [97] Ibid.
[98] Ibid. [99] Ibid at 40.

that there was a conscious determination to eradicate the effects of distinction or incoherence between the external and internal spheres. However, the Commission's practice demonstrated the opposite. Human rights were treated as only one of several concerns when dealing with the South. Other economic and political interests continued to dictate Community policy, suggesting that the promotion of human rights was often contingent. For instance, the Commission later recognized that 'geopolitics, trade and global environmental problems' affected the Community's development policy choices[100] and that the Community pursued 'objectives and interests ... dictated by political, economic and trade interests that are shared by all or by a majority of Member States'.[101] This resulted in a self-confessed prioritization for 'stability and development of neighbouring countries and to aid for countries in crisis in the regions nearest to the EU'.[102] Consequently, any suggestion that human rights either held a position of preeminence in development relations or could even be considered as a fundamental guiding principle in the field was suspect. Instead the long-standing critique of the Community's neo-colonialist practice, through the relationship with the ACP states, was confirmed rather than radically altered. Marjorie Lister pointed out in 1988 that the Lomé Conventions were neo-colonial in character because, *inter alia*, they sought to 'further European political and economic goals' not to establish a new justice in relations with the South.[103] The institutional approach in 1996 showed no change in these dynamics despite the rhetorical flourishes that accompanied the post-Soviet new world order.

These political matters were reflected in the renewed ACP Convention that was completed in 2000. The Cotonou Agreement, replacing Lomé IV, was supposed to respond to demands for a strengthening of political dialogue between the Community and the ACP states. However, little in truth was changed from established practice. The requirement for a regular assessment of developments relating to 'the respect for human rights, democratic principles, the rule of law and good governance'[104] may well have instituted the possibility for additional scrutiny but placed within the format of the Community-ACP structures it is difficult to consider that this was an innovation worthy of the name. Holland indeed refers to

---

[100] Communication from the Commission to the Council and the European Parliament (2000) COM(2000)212 final.
[101] Ibid.   [102] Ibid.   [103] Lister, note 8 above, at 215.
[104] Partnership Agreement between ACP States and the EC and Member States, Cotonou [2000] OJ L-317/3 Preamble.

Article 8 of the Cotonou Agreement's incorporation of political dialogue as 'anodyne'.[105]

Still, Article 9 Cotonou reiterated that human rights *were* an essential element of the Agreement although seemingly inseparable from 'democracy based on the rule of law and transparent and accountable governance'. 3 Article 9 paragraph made the link explicit by stating that in the context 'of a political and institutional environment that upholds human rights, democratic principles and the rule of law, good governance is the transparent and accountable management of human, natural, economic and financial resources for the purposes of equitable and sustainable development'.

Throughout, the economic preferences of the Community, namely 'the principles of the market economy, supported by transparent competition rules',[106] were necessary components for the attainment of the Agreement's objectives.[107] The principle of respect for human rights continued to be addressed as a part of a whole. The drafting ensured that there were no boundaries within the contractual setting of the agreement. It follows that the Community authorized itself to address human rights concerns in all aspects of its development relations.

Could it be said, then, that the Community attained a new plane with the Cotonou Agreement? Admittedly, the requirements of the Community were expressed in more accessible language and clearer provision was made outlining possible action in the event of breaches of the essential elements as regards human rights, democratic principles, and the rule of law.[108] But the ethos of complicity that saw human rights as one element of a complex picture in development still owed more to the projection of a European ideal rather than a commitment to human rights as an independent and absolute moral necessity. By treating human rights in this fashion, the potential for decisions made *without* reference to human rights arises. Indeed, the text is a rendition of contingency as far as human rights is concerned that fully recognizes the exigencies of the Community's external policies. Indeed, the comments of the Hon Ms Billie Miller, President-in-office of the ACP Council of Ministers, at the opening of negotiations for a renewal of Lomé in September 1998 suggest a certain degree of impatience

---

[105] Holland, note 7 above, at 201. We shall examine the application of these provisions in detail in the next section of this chapter.

[106] Agreement, note 104 above, at Article 10(2).

[107] The objectives are 'poverty reduction and ultimately its eradication; sustainable development; and progressive integration of the ACP states into the world economy': ibid Article 19(1).

[108] Ibid Article 96.

with the Community's assumption that human rights should be of central concern in what was essentially a matter of economics. She stated that '[d]emocracy, the rule of law and respect for human rights' were part of 'our national civic ethic' and that if they were 'prerequisites of development ... we should be among the richest and in need of no assistance'. Human rights might 'constitute attributes of development, and as such they are vital to sustained development' but 'they will never be a substitute for it—or for our attention to the economic essentials'.[109]

Such a critique emphasizes the continuing conflict of interests and discourses that afflict the Community and its human rights policy in development relations. It remains to be seen whether the new political environment established by Cotonou will see any fundamental realignment of the Community's position in this respect.

2.2 Key aspects of human rights in development policy

The historical review of human rights in the Community's development policy provides the legal and political hinterland for the current state of the Community's human rights practice. Three key aspects of rights concern me here: first, the definition of rights employed, secondly, the methods of scrutiny adopted, and thirdly, the enforcement measures applied.

2.2.1 Definition

The genealogy of human rights in development policy suggests that their definition has always been fluid. Even though the term 'human rights' appeared in this context as early as 1973 with the Declaration of European Identity[110] their meaning and scope was not subject to further clarification. Rather any definition was left vague. International human rights discourse may have given some indication of definition but this was hardly an area of universal agreement at the time. As we have seen the Community's early development practice suggested an emphasis on economic and social aspects, particularly in the 'basic needs' doctrine, but that did not necessarily preclude concern for civil and political rights, which certainly became more prominent after the mid-1970s.[111]

---

[109] See Press Release 2169/98(presse 329), Brussels, 30 September 1998.
[110] See note 40 above.
[111] The reaction to the atrocities undertaken in the Idi Amin regime in Uganda was a key factor.

The sources of law relied upon in development relations since then have been vast. The Universal Declaration of Human Rights and the UN Charter provided the base conditions for original activity and the Commission has built on this grounding. In 1994 it stated that 'Community action to defend and promote human rights is taken in accordance with the United Nations Charter and the universal principles and priorities adopted by the international community at various world conferences'.[112] In Council Regulation 975/1999, authorizing the Community's human rights activities in development, a more complete picture was provided by suggesting Community action to promote human rights and democratic principles was 'rooted in the general principles established by the Universal Declaration of Human Rights, the International Covenant on Civil and Political Rights and the International Covenant on Economic, Social and Cultural Rights'.[113]

The Regulation went on to be specific about other applicable instruments. It stated '[h]uman rights within the meaning of this Regulation should be considered to encompass respect for international humanitarian law, also taking into account the 1949 Geneva Conventions and the 1977 Additional Protocol thereto, the 1951 Geneva Convention relating to the Status of Refugees, the 1948 Convention on the Prevention and Punishment of the Crime of Genocide and other acts of international treaty or customary law'.[114]

The last phrase opens the door for other sources to be drawn into the precedential net. In this spirit the ACP-EEC Joint Assembly has also referred to the African Charter of Human and Peoples' Rights[115] as has more recently the Commission.[116]

The broad spectrum of rights instruments used to underscore the Community's practice has been criticized as creating a sense of uncertainty and vagueness about the standards purportedly being promoted.[117] Whether

---

[112] Commission, *Report on the Implementation of Measures Intended to Promote Observance of Human Rights and Democratic Principles* (1994) COM(95) 191 final, at 2.

[113] Council Regulation 975/1999, Preamble para (6) [1999] OJ L120/1.

[114] Ibid, Preamble para (8).

[115] See note 63 and ACP-EEC Joint Committee Resolution on Human Rights, 31 January 1985.

[116] See Commission Communication to the Council and the Parliament on 'Democratisation, the Rule of Law, Respect for Human Rights and Good Governance: the Challenges of the Partnership Between the European Union and the ACP States' COM(98)146 at 4.

[117] Diego Nogueras and Luis Martinez, 'Human Rights Conditionality in the External Trade of the European Union: Legal and Legitimacy Problems' *Columbia Journal of European Law* (2001) 307–36 at 333.

this may or may not be an issue when it comes to determining those rights to be enforced through sanctions or supported through positive measures, it does indicate that the Community has been willing to consider other conceptions and expressions of rights beyond those normally associated with the internal rights discourse. In particular, it embraces notions of collective rights. The protection of minority rights, and of 'indigenous peoples, their rights and cultures' have been specifically identified as objectives of the Community's action.[118] The 2001 Commission staff working paper examining the programming for human rights and democracy in third countries, for instance, specifically points to the need 'to protect minorities and indigenous peoples'.[119] Furthermore it highlights how East Africa and South America have both benefited from projects designed to intervene in such matters.[120]

The breadth of definition applied to rights has more recently been placed within a formulaic framework that purports to govern the Community's approach. Three guiding principles of definition have been identified: first, that of *universality*, which implies that no provision of a national, cultural, or religious nature can override the Universal Declaration of Human Rights, in other words, all rights expressed in that document are applicable in all contexts; secondly, that of *indivisibility*, which maintains that civil and political rights shall be treated as of no greater importance than economic, social, and cultural rights—priority should not be given to one or the other; and thirdly, that of *interdependence* between human rights, democracy, and development, in which structure 'man' is identified 'as a holder of human rights and the beneficiary of the development process'.[121]

This tripartite definition partially mimicked the Vienna Declaration that emerged from the World Conference on Human Rights in 1993. Paragraph 5 of that Declaration stated that, 'all human rights are universal, indivisible and interdependent and interrelated'.[122] The fact that the Community has also brought within the notion of interdependence concepts that extend

---

[118] Commission Proposal for a Council Regulation on the Development and Consolidation of Democracy and the Rule of Law and Respect for Human Rights and Fundamental Freedoms [1997] OJ C282/16.

[119] Commission, *Priorities and Guidelines for the Implementation of the 2001 European Initiative for Democracy and Human Rights* SEC(2001) 891 at 2.

[120] Ibid at 9.

[121] See Communication from the Commission to the Council and the European Parliament on 'The European Union and the External Dimension of Human Rights Policy: from Rome to Maastricht and Beyond' COM(95)567 final.

[122] Vienna Declaration and Programme of Action UN Doc A/CONF.157/23.

beyond the normal corpus of international human rights norms does not undermine the basic principle established at Vienna. Indeed, even though the principles of universality and indivisibility have been re-iterated almost as a matter of course, the Community has felt empowered to address not only the full spectrum of civil, political, economic, social, and cultural rights but also wider conceptions of rights. In particular the collective notion of the right to development has been given some credence by the Community.

The right to development has been an officially recognized concept since the UN Declaration on the Right to Development in 1986.[123] Article 1 denotes that the right is 'an inalienable human right by virtue of which every human person and all peoples are entitled to participate in, contribute to and enjoy economic, social, cultural and political development, in which all human rights and fundamental freedoms can be fully realised'.

The Community has tentatively yet positively embraced this concept.[124] It has even recognized that its purpose is to meet 'equitably the developmental and environmental needs of the present and future generations'.[125] Whilst the Community may still like to stress the individual human being as the beneficiary of the process, there is an implicit acceptance that collective rights are to be promoted through this discourse. Whether this will ever translate into an acceptance of a *duty* to provide development assistance must remain doubtful.

The theme of interdependence has not, however, been restricted to human rights. The Community has also used the concept as a reason for linking other notions such as 'good governance' to human rights practices. Defined by the Commission as 'the transparent and accountable management of all a country's resources for its equitable and sustainable economic and social development'[126] it is a concept that 'remains implicit in a political and institutional environment respecting human rights, democratic principles and the rule of law'.[127] Integration of these issues is essential to provoke an acceptable programme of development in the Community's eyes. Similarly, rights are inextricably linked with 'equitable growth, social services, environment, gender issues, capacity and institutional building, [and] private sector development'.[128]

---

[123] UNGA Res 41/128 (1986) Annexing the Declaration on the Right to Development.
[124] See European Political Co-operation Bulletin, 29 March 1990, 155–60.
[125] Council, *EU Annual Report on Human Rights (1999)* 11380/99.
[126] See note 116 above, at 8.   [127] Ibid.   [128] See note 100 above, at 7.

On one level the inter-relationship between human rights and these other concepts has encouraged the Community to involve human rights matters throughout its aid programme. As the Council has recently stated, 'human rights and democratic principles are regarded as horizontal aspects, which must be integrated into all development programmes'.[129] Another perspective might conclude that the association with essentially free-market principles has diluted human rights. Either way, the result has been a policy influenced by a wide interpretation of human rights meanings. The Community has recognized these general rights claims and provided itself with the authority to intervene accordingly. The definition of rights in development is therefore extremely flexible. It provides the opportunity for future evolution of specific rights constructs particularly those associated with collective rights.

2.2.2 Scrutiny and enforcement

As the history related in this chapter reveals, the means by which the Community scrutinizes and enforces human rights standards in its development policy have undergone an extraordinary change over the last ten years. From a position whereby rights abuses were barely the subject of condemnation let alone enforcement in the 1970s, a sophisticated policy has evolved that draws together diplomatic pressure, positive measures, and sanctions to promote and protect human rights. Since 1991, this range of action has been utilized with varying degrees of success and enthusiasm. A sketch of these initiatives will provide a flavour of the Community's practice.

(a) Diplomatic pressure

The system of *démarches* available first through the European Political Cooperation and latterly through the Common Foreign and Security Policy (CFSP) has always encroached on the area of development relations.[130] This has been inevitable given the number of developing states accused of human rights abuses over the years. However, under develop-

---

[129] Council Review of the Common Position on Human Rights, Democratic Principles, the Rule of Law and Good Governance in Africa, 25 June 2001.

[130] For a review of this area of human rights activity see Andrew Clapham, 'Where is the EU's Human Rights Common Foreign Policy, and How is it Manifested in Multilateral Fora?' in Philip Alston *et al* (eds), note 2 above, at 636–41.

ment policy alone diplomatic initiatives are restricted to fairly formal structures of political dialogue.[131]

The means by which discussions on human rights would be held were first formalized by Article 366a Lomé IV as amended in Mauritius in 1995. 'Consultations' could occur in the event of any party having failed to 'fulfil an obligation in respect of one of the essential elements referred to in Article 5' as a first step towards suspension. The fact that this procedure was not employed until 1998 may have delayed the introduction of this form of political pressure but it did not detract from the establishment of the principle.[132] Since then various instances when the Community has demanded consultations have arisen.[133]

The Cotonou Agreement attempted to clarify the procedure. Article 8 stated the basis upon which dialogue should take place. The focus was described as 'political issues of mutual concern', specifically 'the arms trade, excessive military expenditure, drugs and organised crime, or ethnic, religious or racial discrimination'. Respect for human rights was left as an element of 'regular assessment'. Article 8(6) stated that the dialogue should be flexible and 'formal or informal according to need, and conducted within and outside the institutional framework, in the appropriate format, and at the appropriate level including regional, sub-regional or national level'. Hardly the institution of a transparent and comprehensive structure but it did recognize the importance of maintaining contact on human rights issues within a political context.

The Article 8 procedure seems to have been applied with some vigour by the Community. Actions against Haiti, Cote d'Ivoire, Zimbabwe, and Fiji are all evidence of political dialogue being assiduously instituted.[134] It is also developing into a recognized precursor to further issues of scrutiny or enforcement. Article 96, which deals with the procedures in the event of a breach of respect for human rights that amounts to a contravention of the essential element clause of the agreement, will only come into play if the dialogue fails to resolve the position. A situation of 'special urgency'

---

[131] The place of *démarches* and political pressure applied within the CFSP is not considered directly in this book. However, see Clapham, note 130 above, for a review of measures applied externally under this policy area.

[132] Togo was the first state to be called for consultations in June 1998. For an account of the event see Karin Arts, *Integrating Human Rights into Development Cooperation: the Case of the Lomé Convention* (The Hague: Kluwer International, 2000) 234–5.

[133] See ibid at 239–40 for details of the occasions.

[134] Council Decisions 2001/131/EC, 2001/510/EC, 2002/148/EC and 2001/334/EC respectively.

is the sole exception. The scope for a graded response to a human rights situation has therefore been well set.

(b) Positive measures and scrutiny

Ever since the 1991 Resolution, positive measures have been considered an essential element of human rights policies in the Community's development relations. Marantis sees them as complementary to negative measures and the means by which the 'structural obstacles to sustained and equitable development' can be overcome.[135] Arguments have been rehearsed regularly as to their advantages when compared to negative measures.[136] Unsurprisingly perhaps, they have been seen as an important method by which the human rights aspects of development policy can be better pursued.

A wide range of initiatives has been instituted as a result. Initially, the process of offering support to such measures was confused and confusing particularly in relation to the financing and choice of projects. But in 1994 resources were grouped together under one budgetary heading entitled the 'European Initiative for Democracy and the Protection of Human Rights' (EIDHR) (budget chapter B7-70). Developing countries occupied a specific budgetary sub-section[137] and during 1998 the Council reported that a total of 45 projects were supported with the application of 19.7 million euro.[138] Other headings also covered states in the developing world, such as those relating to human rights and democracy in Southern Africa (B7-7021), the Special Programme for democracy and good governance in Nigeria (B7-7022) and human rights and democracy in Asian countries (B7-707) amongst others.[139]

Even this reorganization proved unsatisfactory. Criticisms were levelled at continuing problems of transparency, and doubt over the legal authority for the Community to take positive action.[140] This led to Council Regulation 975/1999, which determined that in development policy action could include 'the implementation of measures in support of democratisation, the

[135] Marantis, note 1 above, at 14.
[136] See Marantis, note 1 above, and Simma, note 2 above, respectively.
[137] Heading no B7-702: see Commission, *Report on the Implementation of Measures Intended to Promote Observance of Human Rights and Democratic Principles* (for 1994) COM(95) 191 final, Annex 3.
[138] See note 125 above, para 4.3.1.
[139] Interestingly, only the heading for 'subsidies for certain activities of organizations pursuing objectives in support of human rights' under the EIDHR could be interpreted as enabling funds to be provided for human rights projects taking place *within* the Community.
[140] See *United Kingdom v. Commission* Case C106/96 [1998] ECR I-2729.

strengthening of the rule of law and the development of a pluralist and democratic civil society and in confidence-building measures aimed at preventing conflicts, supporting peace initiatives and addressing the issue of impunity'.[141]

Article 2 of the Regulation specifically authorized the promotion and protection of the rights referred to in the Universal Declaration of Human Rights. It then proceeded to set out the areas and means that could be undertaken legitimately by the Commission.

At the same time, the Commission also responded to criticism from the European Parliament concerning its positive measures by undertaking to adopt a more transparent reporting mechanism.[142] The result was a comprehensive survey of action under the EIDHR for the years 1996–1999.[143] For the first time considerable effort was taken to ensure 'transparency and accountability in the deployment of Community funds'.[144] Individual projects illustrating general policy directions were described and many procedural as well as policy aspects addressed. The analysis was indeed broad and even encompassed some engagement with academic debate.[145] The review was therefore significant in monitoring the Community's own practices.

Equally, it is clear that the procedure now adopted for assessing human rights conditions and instituting programmes are rigorous. Three stages are involved. First a country's record of ratification of 'international instruments with a view to establishing a standard profile' is considered. Secondly, the 'current human rights situation, ... encompassing any bilateral or regional dialogue' is assessed. Thirdly, a 'multi-annual programme for each country' is outlined, identifying 'the priority measures to be taken into account'.[146]

The measures available to the Community and particularly the Commission are also broad. Regulation 975/1999 sets out the matters that can be

---

[141] See note 113 above, Preamble para (11).

[142] See in particular European Parliament Resolution A4-0381/97 and attached Report by Parliament Vice-President Imbeni on the Report from the Commission on the implementation of measures intended to promote observance of human rights and democratic principles (for 1995).

[143] See Commission, *Report on the Implementation of Measures Intended to Promote Observance of Human Rights and Democratic Principles in External Relations for 1996–1999* COM/2000/0726 final.

[144] Ibid.

[145] Specifically, the Commission was concerned with A. Cassese *et al*, *Leading by Example: a Human Rights Agenda for the Year 2000* (European University Institute, 1998) and Philip Alston's edited collection of reports, see Alston *et al* (eds), note 2 above.

[146] See note 143 above, para 3(g).

embraced in its Preamble. These include the promotion and protection of the human rights of those 'suffering from poverty or disadvantage, which will contribute to reduction of poverty and social exclusion'; support for 'minorities, ethnic groups and indigenous peoples'; support for 'local, national, regional or international institutions, including NGOs' involved in human rights protection; support for 'education, training and consciousness raising'; and support for 'action to monitor human rights'.

The Commission's review further identifies as 'key areas' for action:

Institutional and administrative reforms connected with democratisation and the rule of law including ... support for regional systems to protect and monitor human rights ... Human rights education ... Strengthening civil society ... including an emphasis on free and independent media, action against the exploitation and abuse of women, and the rights of ethnic, religious and cultural minorities.[147]

The Council has separately set out the basis for encouraging the 'on-going democratisation process in Africa' by concentrating on the protection of civil, political, and social, economic, and cultural rights and 'guarantees of freedom of expression, information, association and political organisation'.[148]

The projects instituted under the above guidelines range from supporting the rights of the handicapped in Madagascar (Project no 99/0350) to assisting the monitoring of prison conditions in Egypt (Project no 98/Mas24).[149] The Commission has thus confirmed its willingness to become involved in the day-to-day detail of human rights promotion work. The sheer scale of such enterprises leaves the internal human rights activities (beyond concerns over citizenship rights and social rights associated with the economic aspects of the Treaties) far behind in their ambition.

The Community has therefore instituted a process of positive action that has attained a sophisticated structure. The fact that the development initiatives have been heavily criticized by the Court of Auditors in relation to a failure in definition of country strategies, a lack of a clear set of project selection criteria, and shortcomings in programme management does not detract from that fact.[150] Indeed, the criticism reflects an institutional

[147] See note 143 above, para 2.1.
[148] Council, Common Position on Human Rights, Democratic Principles, the Rule of Law and Good Governance in Africa [1998] OJ L-158/1.
[149] See note 143 above, paras 1.2.3 and 1.4.1 respectively.
[150] For a criticism of the Community's practices see Special Report no 12/2000 on the management by the Commission of European Union support for the development of human rights and democracy in third countries, together with the Commission's replies [2000] OJ C-230.

willingness to create programmes of action *and* to review their operation and effectiveness. This makes for a policy that has substance. But in the world of human rights, positive measures have rarely been viewed as sufficient. Action to prevent abuse has always focused upon negative measures if only to reflect public condemnation of a state's practice.

(c) Negative measures or sanctions

Sanctions, or negative measures, have not been limited to development policy.[151] They may be applied in all the Community's foreign affairs by reason of Article 300(2) (ex Article 228) EC Treaty. Where the Member States decide upon a common position or joint action under the CFSP to 'interrupt, in part or completely, economic relations with one or more third countries', the Council is entitled to institute 'the necessary urgent measures'. These include all 'negative' operations.[152] Nevertheless, it is within development policy that the full range of action available to the Community is most apparent.

The scope of measures that may be taken against a developing state arises in part because of the condition of dependence that suffuses the relationship with the Community. The provision of aid as well as trade benefits ensures that such states are inevitably in a position of vulnerability in respect of any sanctions. The suspension or interruption of aid or trade can have immediate and significant effects on any economy let alone an under-developed one.

The Community has appreciated this vulnerability and has introduced a wide range of measures by which it might be exploited. In addition to those measures available under Article 300(2) (ex Article 228) EC Treaty 'essential elements' clauses may be used to suspend or terminate benefits provided under third country agreements.[153] Equally, trade preferences, under the General System of Preferences, have introduced a scheme of conditionality with particular reference to international labour standards.[154]

---

[151] See I. Macleod, I.D. Hendry, and Stephen Hyett, *The External Relations of the European Communities* (Oxford: Oxford University Press, 1996) 352–66.

[152] The sanctions issued against Haiti in 1993 and 1994 provide an indication of the type of measures that might be contemplated. There, Council Regulation 1608/93 placed an embargo on petroleum products and under the ECSC trade in goods relevant to that particular Treaty was restricted ([1993] OJ L139/8).

[153] For a comprehensive consideration of such clauses see, for instance, Riedel and Will, note 88 above.

[154] See Barbara Brandtner and Allan Rosas, 'Trade Preferences and Human Rights' in Alston *et al*, note 2 above, 699–722.

The resultant possibility for action has thus been devised on a wide scale.[155]

In the specific area of relations with the ACP states, the authority for any action now occurs under the Cotonou Agreement. This has built upon a steadily increasing body of precedent that has emerged from the Community since the 1991 Resolution. Sanctions were then made available for the Community to react to serious interruptions in democratic processes or to 'grave and persistent' human rights violations.[156] Although clearly envisaged as a last resort, it was nevertheless determined that such a course of action should continue to be available despite the preference for positive measures. This was recognized within Article 366a Lomé IV as revised in 1995 and subsequently followed at Cotonou.

Under Article 96 Cotonou, enforcement measures assume a key position within the agreement's structure. Article 96(2) states that if political dialogue fails to deal with a situation of human rights all relevant information can be placed before the Council of Ministers for a 'thorough examination ... with a view to seeking a solution acceptable to the Parties'. If no solution is forthcoming *or* the situation is a 'case of special urgency' 'appropriate measures may be taken' by the complainant party. Such measures must be 'taken in accordance with international law' and must be 'proportional to the violation'. Suspension of the agreement may be considered but only as a last resort. Thus for instance, in 2002, Zimbabwe had budgetary support and development projects suspended.[157] Cote d'Ivoire also suffered the suspension of direct budget aid in 2001.[158]

The availability of sanctions as a method of enforcement, variably applied since the mid-1970s, is now framed by these structures. The power for Community action is well established and has been exercised frequently enough to demonstrate a willingness to proceed to this level in the name of human rights. Since 1991 alone there have been numerous instances of the imposition of sanctions. Karen Arts identifies twelve countries subjected to some form of negative measure in the context of the Lomé Conventions.[159] But sanctions do not represent the only form of measure applied. At a less public level decisions made not to provide aid or to impose conditions on the assistance authorized *before* any aid relationship has been confirmed, can be an extremely effective means of pressure. The

---

[155] See Tomaševski in particular who has analysed the implications and effects of these policy initiatives, note 3 above.
[156] See note 74 above.   [157] Council Decision 2002/148/EC.
[158] Council Decision 2001/510/EC.   [159] Arts, note 132 above, at 422–6.

Commission has specifically announced that its development planning will take into account 'performance in the area of human rights (including economic, social and cultural rights) ... when deciding country allocations' under assistance programmes.[160] This imposes a heavy burden upon the developing states. Even though they might not breach civil and political standards, and even though Article 96 may not be engaged, they may still be subject to the most serious of sanctions. Nor need this process be subject to institutional dialogue under existing agreements. The Community has a free hand in its allocation of funds. Even auditors will find it difficult to analyse the many decisions made *not* to provide aid in specific circumstances. Consequently, the Community is possessed of a structured scheme of enforcement practices that is impressive in its potential to wield influence.

2.3 Conclusion

The long narrative of rights in development policy indicates a path towards a forceful and varied approach to human rights promotion and enforcement. From a silent base, rights have slowly assumed a crucial role that continues to be subject to refinement. The terminology of development now incorporates collective and individual understandings of human rights. The definition of those rights includes an appreciation of their universal, indivisible, and interdependent nature. A wide range of positive measures has been adopted to encourage the promotion of rights. And a detailed system of scrutiny and enforcement has been instituted that affects developing states at every level.

The policy constructed may be subject to criticism for hiding inconsistencies in its application from state to state but there is nevertheless a coherence in the willingness of the Community to become involved in ever more detail in defining human rights and ensuring their respect. Whether the Community's concern is a hollow one is perhaps an obvious critique. The ACP states have indeed always been quick to question the motivation for a continuing and blanket interference on rights issues, particularly where there is an absence of gross violations that normally provoke international attention. Accusations of neo-colonialism, the

---

[160] Communication from the Commission to the Council and the Parliament on 'The EU's Role in Promoting Human Rights and Democratisation in Third Countries' (2001) COM(2001) 252 final.

imposition of an ethnocentric world view, and a desire to justify a dominance and control through the language and surveillance of rights, all accompany the Community's development practice. They need not be rehearsed here but their relevance should be borne in mind when we return to consider the reasons for the Community's internal/external distinction in human rights policies.

Before addressing that latter issue the application of human rights in another vital external sphere must be examined. This will then answer whether development policy represents a special, even peculiar, place in the Community's approach to human rights outside its borders or whether it is indicative of a more general pattern of distinction.

3

Accession to the Community and Human Rights

Any exploration of the incoherence of the Community's human rights policies would be incomplete without consideration of the approach adopted in the enlargement process. In no other policy dimension is the contrast between the external and internal made quite so stark. For here, third party states on the cusp of entry to the European club experience a strange and ambiguous position. On the one hand they are subjected to human rights requirements and demands to ensure that their membership application proceeds and on the other they can view the prospect of being encompassed by a rights regime of a different hue once they achieve full entry to the Community. The nature of that difference tells a great deal about the extent of incoherence in the Community's policies.

To begin to explore the subject, the role of human rights in the process of accession to the Community is first placed in some historical context. The first part outlines the development of the human rights' dimension to the negotiation for membership by third states from early accession criteria to the present day. The second part then considers the key elements of human rights policy that currently mark the Community's approach. The meaning of human rights and the methods of scrutiny and enforcement applied to applicant states are analysed with a view to providing further detail for comparison with the internal condition.

3.1 A history of human rights in accession policy

3.1.1 *Membership and implicit conditionality*

From the Community's inception, the possibility of enlargement to encompass other states beyond the initial six was both contemplated and expected.

The EEC Treaty reflected this understanding. Article 237 envisioned *any* 'European state' applying to join the Community, thus embodying the founding members' belief in the desirability of an extended European family.[1] As with any exclusionary organization, however, such a desire was not unconditional. Any state applicant would, of necessity, have to accord with the Community's aims or, rather, the principles or values that delineated its 'Project' and upon which the Community was purportedly built.

Although the nature of the Project was always the subject of constitutional development and debate, the Preamble to the EEC Treaty did at least reflect some of the key understandings that might identify the conditions for membership. In particular, the original Contracting Parties resolved 'to preserve and strengthen peace and liberty' and called upon, 'the other peoples of Europe who *share their ideal* to join in their efforts' (emphasis added).[2] Identification and adherence to the values inherent in the Project, values that included the pursuit of 'liberty', could therefore have been imputed as prerequisites for full entry.

Consequently, any putative member of the Community would have had to demonstrate acceptance of these values or, at any rate, not display antipathy towards them, if it were to warrant approval for any entry application.[3] This was reinforced by the fact that any state seeking accession requires unanimous approval by all the existing Member States acting in the Council. It would be difficult to conclude that the approach represented anything more than a nascent or implied conditionality if only loosely based on human rights. But once the European Court of Justice (ECJ) and the other Community institutions had established that respect for human rights was a part of the general principles of European law (from 1969 onwards)[4] the discourse of rights began to infiltrate the very projections of the idea and ideals of the Project. The key requirements (albeit still implicit ones) for entry to the Community were thus more distinct. This was evident in the formulation of a notion of 'European identity'.

---

[1] The original Article 237 EC Treaty stated, 'Any European State may apply to become a member of the Community'. The TEU deleted this Article. Membership then became relevant in relation to joining the European Union, a matter that was covered by Article 49 (ex Article O) TEU.

[2] Preamble to the EC Treaty (emphasis added).

[3] See Article 49 (ex Article O) TEU. Article 237 EC Treaty contained a similar requirement.

[4] The story of the development of respect for human rights as a founding principle of the Community is considered in Chapter 6.

Prompted, perhaps not coincidentally, by the imminent accession to the Community by the United Kingdom, Ireland and Denmark, the Luxembourg Report of 1970 made a direct connection between identity and rights. It declared that a 'united Europe must be founded upon the common heritage of respect for the liberty and the rights of men, and must assemble democratic States having freely elected parliaments'.[5] The 1973 Copenhagen Declaration on the European Identity followed suit, specifying that '[t]he construction of a United Europe, which the Nine Member Countries of the Community are undertaking, is open to other European nations who share the same ideals and objectives'.[6] The ideals were given clearer expression in the Declaration and have been the subject of repetition ever since. In particular, the European Council's statement issued in Copenhagen in April 1978 reinforced the notion of qualification for entry to the Community. The Heads of State and Government not only 'expressed their determination to respect fundamental rights in pursuing the aims of the Communities' but also declared that 'respect for and maintenance of representative democracy and human rights in each Member State are essential elements of membership'.[7] The implication that any prospective entrant would also have had to abide by such an understanding prior to entry was a strong one and next to impossible to refute. Placed in the context of the Joint Declaration on Human Rights of 1977[8] and the other developments in the Community's discourse of rights up to that point, the implication becomes all the more tenable.

Despite the implied conditionality in operation, there was nevertheless little reluctance to allow '*selective* entry' for some of those European states that did not appear to satisfy the basic conditions of '*full*' entry.[9] By 'selective entry' I mean a practice of the Community that allowed access

---

[5] *First Report of the Foreign Ministers to the Heads of State and Government of the European Community's Member States* (27 October 1970) para 4. For a full text of this Report, see Press and Information Office of the Government of the Federal Republic of Germany, *Texts Relating to the European Political Co-operation* (1974) 18–25.

[6] Document on the European Identity, para 4, EC Bull 12-1973 at 118–22.

[7] Declaration on Democracy issued by the European Council, 8 April 1978, Copenhagen, EC Bull 3-1978 at 6.

[8] See Joint Declaration by the European Parliament, the Council and the Commission on Human Rights [1977] OJ C103/1.

[9] The term 'selective entry' is used to echo the notion of 'selective Exit' employed by Joseph Weiler in his article 'The Transformation of Europe' *Yale Law Journal* 100 (1991) 2403–83. For Weiler, 'Exit' suggested the ability of Member States to withdraw from the Community whereas 'selective Exit' indicated a practice of selective application of the Community's *acquis communautaire* by Member States.

by non-Member States to the economic and diplomatic spheres and operations of the Community without the benefits or demands of full membership. The use of trade and co-operation and association agreements, authorized by Articles 300 (ex Article 228) and 310 (ex Article 238) EC Treaty, demonstrated a willingness throughout the 1960s and 1970s to accord certain advantages of closer economic and political ties to countries despite their poor human rights records. Underpinning some of the association agreements was at least a suggestion of a promise that membership might eventually follow. It was only with the introduction of a 'human rights clause' in 1989 that such associations became subject to scrutiny on the basis of human rights considerations. Given the evolution of international human rights law it seems remarkable that it took so long for such a development to surface in the external arrangements of the Community.

However, with regard to the relationship of Spain and Portugal with the Community during the dictatorial regimes of Franco and Caetano respectively, human rights violations and the lack of democracy in these countries did not unduly hinder the formation of preferential trade agreements and continuing political dialogue. The agreement with Spain took effect in 1970 and that with Portugal in 1973[10] at a time when there were no discernible signs of the then current regimes undertaking any meaningful transformation. Admittedly, the nature of these relations could have been justified in accordance with the Community's express desire to 'strive to promote harmonious and constructive relations'[11] with third countries (as required under the emergent European Political Co-operation) but the partial engagement with those factors, which were so clearly expressed as being central to the creation of an external European Identity (in terms of represented values), indicated the presence of a fundamental distinction. Internally, it would have been inconceivable, given the rhetoric emerging from the Community on the subject of human rights, that the then operative regimes in Spain and Portugal could have been incorporated within the Community. Externally, however, even though the rhetoric of political co-operation was suffused with understandings concerning values and human rights, the political reality was that Spain and Portugal were inextricably linked with the common heritage to which the formative European Identity supposedly gave effect. As a consequence, even though these

---

[10] See Neill Nugent, *The Government and Politics of the European Union* (London: Macmillan, 1994) 32.

[11] See note 6 above, at para 9.

countries were controlled by regimes that significantly negated the values underlying such heritage, they continued to be the subject of dealings that recognized their putative membership or 'European' status.

An effective human rights policy as regards a selective entry for the Iberian countries was thus not apparent during the 1960s and early 1970s. Any efforts to deal with human rights concerns were rendered invisible or, at best, the subject of implication. Certainly, any implied human rights conditionality for full entry did not generally extend to selective entry at this time.[12] That area of external relations remained in the realm of a European political practice that seemed to pay scant attention to human rights.

It is not suggested, however, that the approach to external relations as regards selective entry was then peculiar to the Community in terms of international human rights promotion. The established international law doctrine was of non-interference in the domestic affairs of sovereign states (supported by Articles 2(4) and 2(7) of the UN Charter).[13] Thus any type of conditionality which sought to change the nature and character of a particular regime through direct economic or political means would have been difficult to sustain and would have opened itself to being declared politically and legally illegitimate.

The approach of non-interference remained a characteristic of international relations throughout the post-Second World War period until at least the mid-1970s if not beyond to the end of the Cold War. Given credence by international instruments such as the UN General Assembly's 1970 Declaration on the Principles of International Law Concerning Friendly Relations and Cooperation among States, which declared that, '[n]o state or group of states has the right to intervene, directly or indirectly, for any reason whatever, in the internal or external affairs of any other

---

[12] The exception was the freezing of the Greek Association Agreement during the regime of the colonels. Otherwise, trade and co-operation and association agreements did not involve human rights considerations until the European Parliament sought to apply a human rights conditionality on these formal relationships with the Community. For further consideration of this issue and the role of the Parliament see Barbara Brandtner and Allan Rosas, 'Human Rights and the External Relations of the European Community: An Analysis of Doctrine and Practice' *European Journal of International Law* 9/3 (1998) 468–90.

[13] Article 2(4) reads, 'All Members shall refrain in their international relations from the threat or use of force against the territorial integrity or political independence of any state, or in any other manner inconsistent with the Purposes of the United Nations'. Article 2(7) reads, in part, 'Nothing contained in the present Charter shall authorise the United Nations to intervene in matters which are essentially within the domestic jurisdiction of any state'.

State', the legal position against non-interference was extremely robust.[14] Consequently, there existed a powerful doctrine, which may well have impacted upon the Community's attitude to human rights in its external affairs.[15] Indeed, the Community's activities represented adherence to the norm.

Whether or not the principle of non-interference initiated or was only reflected in the Community's distinction between the role of human rights concerns in selective as opposed to full entry, its influence cannot be ignored. However, the doctrine did not generate the distinction. At most, it was a contributory factor, a legal influence that began to lose its credibility after the end of the Cold War if not sometime before.[16] Certainly the approach of the European Parliament (EP) has been to consider human rights concerns outside the exclusive preserve of any state since at least the early 1980s.[17]

Nevertheless, the instances of full entry achieved by Greece, then Spain and Portugal, saw no visible Community stance taken with regard to past violations and their possible repetition. The return of democracy seemed to be a sufficient guarantee. In the light of there then being no system whereby the new (or even longer standing) members of the Community could be the subject of direct action should the abuse of human rights on a large scale re-occur, these events of accession were either extraordinary acts of good faith or illustrations of the belief that those countries' essential 'Europeanness' and devotion to the European model of values would preclude such a development.

The absence of an explicit concern with human rights in the accession of the chosen states only began to change once the collapse of communist rule in Eastern and Central Europe occurred. Then, the concept of enlargement was altered radically amidst an avalanche of initiatives designed to ensure

[14] UNGA Res 2625 (XXV) (24 October 1970).

[15] For a consideration of this doctrine see Nigel Rodley, 'Collective Intervention to Protect Human Rights and Civilian Populations: the Legal Framework' in Nigel Rodley (ed), *To Loose the Bands of Wickedness: International Intervention in Defence of Human Rights* (London: Brassey's, 1992) 14–42.

[16] For a review of this sea-change see Lori Damrosch, 'Politics Across Borders: Non-Intervention and Non-Forcible Influence Over Domestic Affairs' *AJIL* 83 (1989), and C. Ellerman, 'Command of Sovereignty Gives Way to Concern for Humanity' *Vanderbilt Journal of Transnational Law* 26/2 (1993) 341.

[17] See, for instance, the European Parliament's annual reports on human rights in the world that first appeared in 1983. For a review of the Parliament's role in this regard see Reinhard Rack and Stefan Lausegger, 'The Role of the European Parliament: Past and Future' in Philip Alston *et al* (eds), *The EU and Human Rights* (Oxford: Oxford University Press, 1999) 801–37.

that the transformation of such ex-Soviet dominated countries was entrenched. The promise of entry to the Community became an incentive to maintain the move towards market economies and social systems that had abandoned soviet communist ideology. And it was at this juncture that human rights made a more direct appearance.

3.1.2 *European enlargement; the introduction of explicit conditionality*

(a) *The condition of the 'New Europe'*

The Community instituted a dramatic change in accession policy after the fall of the Iron Curtain at least in so far as the emergent 'democracies' in Central and Eastern Europe (CEE) were concerned. Once it became clear that Soviet dominance was at an end, the Community resolved to give effect to its rhetorical self-representation as *the* site for European development. The Agenda 2000 programme later applied a particular interpretation, or commemoration, of the recent past. It proclaimed that the 'end of the Cold War and the break-up of the Soviet Union opened up new horizons of international cooperation, and propelled the Union into a key role for promoting change and stability across Europe'.[18]

The impression that the Community was at last fulfilling its self-professed destiny whilst adhering to its core values, resonated throughout the subsequent initiatives that were inspired by the seismic shift in power. Immediate demonstrations of intent were provided through the significant financial assistance for economic transformation made available through the PHARE and the TACIS programmes to the CEE countries and the new independent states respectively.[19]

Amidst the euphoria induced by the end of the Cold War, the Community then rushed to develop a strategy that would establish it as the pre-eminent political as well as economic power base in the region, a model indeed for the 'New Europe'.[20] The sentiments expressed at the 1989 Strasbourg European Council captured the moment.

The Community's dynamism and influence make it the European entity to which the countries of Central and Eastern Europe now refer, seeking to establish close links. The Community has taken and will take the necessary decision

---

[18] Agenda 2000 'For a Stronger and Wider Union' EC Bull Supp 5-1997 at 11.
[19] These programmes were instituted by Council Regulation 3906/89 [1989] OJ L375.
[20] For a brief analysis of this period see Alan Mayhew, 'EU Policy Toward Central Europe' in Carolyn Rhodes (ed), *The European Union in the World Community* (London: Lynne Reiner, 1998) 105–25.

to strengthen its cooperation with peoples aspiring to freedom, democracy and progress and with States which intend their founding principles to be democracy, pluralism and the rule of law.[21]

An evident burgeoning desire to encourage the movement away from socialist ideology towards a liberal-capitalist model was not the only consequence of these sentiments. A resolve to embrace the emerging democracies into the Community's sphere of influence had also taken root. The Community was now in a position to fulfil its Project and potential whilst ensuring the security of its Member States and 'Europe' itself was not compromised. In this respect, the 'European model' that supposedly underpinned the Community would help define it as the 'cornerstone of a new European architecture and ... a mooring for a future European equilibrium'.[22] The only initial restraint was mentioned by the Strasbourg European Council, which cautioned that 'the changes and transitions which are necessary must not take place to the detriment of the stability of Europe'.[23]

It was in the context of trying to shape the future of the New Europe that human rights featured as an essential element both of the Community and the European model that it upheld. At a special meeting in Dublin in 1990, the Council declared that the 'process of change brings ever closer a Europe which, having overcome the unnatural divisions imposed on it by ideology and confrontation, stands united in its commitment to democracy, pluralism, the rule of law, full respect for human rights, and the principles of the market economy'.[24]

This was a defining moment for the Project. Indeed, developments in the East were used as political argument counselling greater efforts towards union within the existing Community structure. President Mitterand, in a speech to the European Parliament in 1989, suggested that internal constitutional developments would not only equip the Community with 'greater resources' but also enable the Community to 'exert a greater attraction on the rest of Europe'.[25] Here then lay the opportunity to establish a truly 'European' Community[26] one that would bring together those peoples with whom were shared 'a common heritage and culture'.[27] Within that concep-

---

[21] Strasbourg European Council, EC Bull 12-1989 at 12.
[22] Ibid. at 15.   [23] Ibid. at 14.
[24] Special Meeting of the European Council, Dublin, 28 April 1990, EC Bull 4-1990 at 7.
[25] EC Bull 10-1989 at 117.
[26] European in the sense that geographically the Community would stretch to its traditional perhaps racially (or racist) inspired limits.   [27] See note 24 above.

tion, human rights occupied, at least rhetorically, a vital role developing as a key element in the conditions attached first to the relations of 'association' with the ex-communist states and then those of potential 'accession'.

(b) The 'Europe Agreements' and the move towards enlargement

Initially, the relationship with the CEE states was understandably fluid. The dramatic institutional changes that were taking place in these countries at great speed inspired equally swift political responses by the Community. It was thus perhaps inevitable that policy would develop fitfully at first. Prior to 1989 the Community had already begun negotiating trade and co-operation agreements with Eastern European states largely on the strength of Mikhail Gorbachev's move to induce economic and political reform in the Soviet Union. The changing circumstances called for these initiatives to undergo development. In particular, human rights matters, which did not figure to any significant extent in the early (or so called 'first generation') agreements, became more apparent as negotiations with the new regimes progressed between 1989 and 1990.[28]

The approach was an ad hoc one to begin with, contingent on the identity of the state concerned and subject to negotiation. Charles Haughey, the then President of the Council, said in 1990 that the strategy was to be 'flexible' and 'tailored to respond to the political and economic situation in each country'.[29] In this spirit, human rights concerns became of some influence[30] but on the whole the rationale behind the co-operation agreements was the fostering of economic and political regimes committed to the adoption of a liberal-democratic, free market system.

Some structure to these burgeoning relationships then began to emerge in the first half of 1990. The Commission announced the general basis upon which the agreements were to evolve. They would *not*, 'include the

---

[28] For a review of the development of the agreements with CEE states during this period, see Toby King, 'The European Community and Human Rights in Eastern Europe' *Legal Issues of European Integration* 2 (1996) 93–125.

[29] Address to the European Parliament on the outcome of the Special European Council in Dublin, 28 April 1990, EC Bull 5-1990 at 140.

[30] See, for instance, the reference made in the Trade and Economic Co-operation Agreement between the EEC and Poland to the implementation of the provisions and principles of the Final Act of the Conference on Security and Co-operation in Europe (CSCE) and the Helsinki Final Act which incorporated the need to improve commitment to human rights by its signatories, [1989] OJ L-339. See also the suspension of negotiations for a trade and co-operation agreement with Bulgaria on the basis of 'concern about infringements of the rights of the Turkish minority' within that state as referred to by King, note 28 above, at 101.

objective of eventual accession to the Community',[31] but would represent, 'an incentive to Eastern European states to implement political and economic reforms'.[32] They would also protect the Community's own interests.[33] Even so, there was still an evident desire to alter qualitatively the relations with the CEE states.

It was in this context that the Commission introduced conditions for the resultant 'selective entry' available to such states.[34] The conditions were 'the introduction of the rule of law, the respect for human rights, the establishment of a multi-party system with corresponding free and fair elections and finally, the introduction of a market economy'.[35] The agreements that emerged applied slightly varying terminology and included different forms of clauses to enable the Community to suspend their operation in response to human rights violations but together they represented the first step of note on a path to enlargement.[36] This was evident from the way in which the agreements quickly became described as 'Europe Agreements', a change in nomenclature that was by no means without symbolic importance. A distinction had been created whereby the Community's intentions to discriminate between those associations that held little if any prospect of conversion to membership and those that were favoured to succeed in the transition, were made politically clear. The CEE states (along with certain other identified candidates such as Cyprus and Malta) were quickly encompassed within the latter category.

The 'Europe' epithet breathed new life into the mythic construction of a common heritage and common destiny, a theme present in the rhetoric applied to the CEE states. Once the communist aberration had been abandoned it was now possible to uncover the formative and 'true' sense

---

[31] Europe Information Service; European Report, 12 April 1990, External Relations no.1578, 8.

[32] Ibid.

[33] See King, note 28 above, at 103. Incentives took the form of financial assistance particularly through TACIS and PHARE, see note 19 above.

[34] The expression of these principles eventually found their way into the various agreements and arrangements concluded with non-CEE states as well. See Eibe Riedel and Martin Will, 'Human Rights Clauses in External Agreements of the EC' in Alston *et al*, note 17 above, at 723–54. See also Marise Cremona, 'Human Rights and Democracy Clauses in the EC's Trade Agreements' in Nicholas Emiliou and David O'Keefe (eds), *The European Union and World Trade Law* (Chichester: John Wiley & Sons, 1996) 62–77.

[35] See note 21 above.

[36] Later Europe Agreements explicitly referred to the institution of a 'framework for gradual integration' into the Community. See, for example, the Europe Agreement establishing an association between the Community and Lithuania [1998] OJ L51, 20 February 1998.

of community that lay underneath.[37] The values expressed as binding the Member States were ascribed historically to those peoples 'released' from the communist experiment and, as such, the countries they inhabited could be embraced by the Community as legitimate members of the European Project and incorporated as a valid extension to the European narrative.

The re-titling of the Agreements was both recognition of a fundamental alteration in the political contours of the continent *and* re-affirmation of the qualities of the Community that set it apart as a project of enduring importance. Consequently, the Community was able to substantiate its authentication as a site of governance for its existing and potential constituents as well as to legitimate its practices through binding the newly emerged regimes to the system of values that gave the Project its definition.[38]

The Commission outlined the potential scope of these values in 1990. It recommended that the Europe Agreements would *only* take effect, 'once certain basic conditions are fulfilled with regard to the rule of law and human rights, the setting-up of multi-party systems, the organization of free and democratic elections and economic liberalization'.[39] Even so, any clarity in definition of human rights in this context remained elusive. Vague references to 'common values' appeared in the Preambles to the Europe Agreements themselves[40] and there was a marked absence of any concrete measures to promote human rights *per se* or even to set out the scope of rights to be considered. This left the Community with the freedom to play out negotiations as it saw fit prior to any completion of a particular Europe Agreement. Even when those Agreements came to be signed rights were neither itemized nor promoted with any degree of specificity.

(c) From association to accession: towards full entry

By 1993, the Commission began to be explicit in suggesting that the Europe Agreements were a prelude to more ambitious goals. In its Communication with the Council in 1993 the Commission concluded that it was 'vitally important for the Community to give a clear, unambiguous signal of its

---

[37] Whether that sense of community extended to the case of Turkey is open to question.

[38] The themes of 'authentication' and 'legitimacy' are discussed in Chapter 6 where the role of human rights in the development of the Community is considered.

[39] Commission Communication to the Council EC Bull 7/8-1990 at 93.

[40] See, for example, the Europe Agreements establishing associations between the Community and Poland [1993] OJ L348, 31 December 1993, the Czech Republic [1994] OJ L360, 31 December 1994 and Lithuania [1998] OJ L51, 20 February 1998, which illustrate the consistency of language applied in this respect.

intention to forge closer political links with these countries [i.e. the CEE states] in a perspective of future membership'.[41]

The possibility of accession was at last countenanced as the objective of the relationships. Even so, the determination to identify specific states as potential members was still subject to constraints, a consequence of a certain wariness given the political and, more especially, the economic instability apparent in the East.[42] In the same Communication the Commission recommended that, 'the European Council should confirm, in a clear political message, its commitment to membership of the European Union for the associated countries of central and eastern Europe *when they are able to satisfy the conditions required*'.[43] The conditions were 'each country's capacity to assume the "acquis communautaire" and the competitive pressures of membership, its ability to guarantee democracy, human rights, respect for minorities and the rule of law, and the existence of a functioning market economy, as well as the [Community's] own capacity to absorb new members'.[44]

The Copenhagen Council in April 1993 built on the formula by confirming that membership was open to the now 'associated' states. Membership required each applicant to achieve 'stability of institutions guaranteeing democracy, the rule of law, human rights and respect for and protection of minorities, the existence of a functioning market economy as well as the capacity to cope with competitive pressure and market forces within the Union'.[45]

Here then was the formulation of the Copenhagen Criteria that has been the benchmark in accession negotiations ever since. From a human rights perspective, the criteria were particularly significant. The direct expression of a rights conditionality to be applied to the applicant states demonstrated a substantially more transparent policy for full entry to the Community, one that mirrored the application of the relatively new concept of 'good governance' in the field of development co-operation. Indeed, the Community's Copenhagen Criteria for membership fully embraced the good governance approach adopted by the World Bank and the

---

[41] Commission Communication on 'Towards a Closer Association with the Countries of Central and Eastern Europe' EC Bull 4-1993.

[42] See Hanns-D. Jacobsen, 'The European Union's Eastward Enlargement' *E.I.o.P.* 1/14 (1997) (available at http://eiop.or.at/eiop/texte/1997-014a.htm) for a review of this point.

[43] See note 41 above (emphasis added).   [44] Ibid.

[45] Conclusions of the Presidency at the Copenhagen Council 1993, EC Bull 6-1993 at 13.

international donor community, in which the Community occupied a major role.[46]

It also established the base from which the scrutiny of an applicant's human rights position could be put into effect. The European Council at Copenhagen instituted procedures by which such scrutiny and limited intervention could take place. These took the form of dialogue (rather than investigation) with an emphasis on 'meetings of an advisory nature' undertaken in parallel with the Europe Agreements.[47] The tone was therefore one of co-operation and assistance rather than forceful interference.

Successive Intergovernmental Conferences (IGCs) built upon the above foundation by considering the practical aspects of the proposed enlargement process. At Essen in December 1994 a pre-accession strategy was formulated that encouraged further efforts in the cross-border co-operation that had been instituted by the Europe Agreements and various related programmes.[48] In the following year, the Madrid European Council indicated that negotiations with the potential candidates for admission to the Community should commence within six months of the 1996 IGC. At the Florence European Council in 1996 a timetable for negotiations was established.

It was at this point that the Council also re-emphasized that the Commission should compile opinions and subsequent periodic reports on each of the applicant states paying particular attention to progress made towards complying with the Copenhagen Criteria. Although negotiations for entry would continue to be undertaken through constructive dialogue, the Community would only proceed once an in-depth, and on-going scrutiny of the political, and therefore human rights, considerations of the Criteria had been carried out.

The effect of this policy was to place human rights issues at the forefront of the accession process. It is arguable whether in practice they have remained so but certainly they have appeared as vital indicators throughout. Even up to the point of admission of ten of the thirteen applicants in 2004, the political criteria have continued to draw attention. Turkey's application in particular has stalled on these grounds. The attention paid to human rights should not then be underestimated even though the application of policy was not as diligent as it might have been.

---

[46] See World Bank Policy Paper, *Governance and Development* (1992).
[47] Copenhagen Council 1993, Conclusions of the Presidency, Annex II, EC Bull 6-1993 at 18.
[48] See, again, the PHARE and TACIS programmes, note 19 above.

3.2 The key aspects of human rights in accession policy

As with the Community's development policy three dimensions of human rights warrant examination in preparation for a comparison with internal policy: first, the definition and scope of rights applied in the accession process, secondly the methods of scrutiny employed, and thirdly the enforcement measures available that have been or may be deployed in this context. As there is often little to distinguish between measures of scrutiny and measures of enforcement in the accession process, these two aspects are considered in tandem.

3.2.1 *The definition of rights*

There is no one statement of principle produced by the Community that has satisfactorily established the full extent of its human rights concerns in the enlargement negotiations. Rather one must examine the directive texts (such as the Copenhagen Criteria) and the implementation of policy through the reports and partnership documents that have emerged.

These documents indicate that three categories of rights have been addressed: minority rights, civil and political rights, and economic, social, and cultural rights.

(a) Minority rights

On the face of it, the Copenhagen condition that institutions guarantee 'respect for and protection of minorities' appears wholly arbitrary in the Community context. There has been little evidence of the Community focusing previously upon this particular aspect of rights. As Barbara Brandtner and Allan Rosas have pointed out, the 'emphasis on minority rights is not anchored in any long-standing EC law tradition'.[49] M.A.M. Estébanez has also observed that no 'general policy with regard to minority protection within the borders of the Union' had been adopted prior to 1995.[50] Indeed,

---

[49] Barbara Brandtner and Allan Rosas, 'Human Rights and the External Relations of the European Community: An Analysis of Doctrine and Practice' *EJIL* 9/3 (1998) 21. The position was reiterated in Guiliano Amato and Judy Batt, *Minority Rights and EU Enlargement to the East: Report of the First Reflection Group on the Long-Term Implications of EU Enlargement* (European University Institute, RSC Policy Paper no 98/5, 1998).

[50] M.A.M. Estébanez, 'The Protection of National, or Ethnic, Religious and Linguistic Minorities' in N. Neuwahl and A. Rosas (eds), *The European Union and Human Rights* (The Hague: Kluwer Law International, 1995) 135.

the Commission's Report on the Action Plan against Racism (2000) admits that the field is one in which 'the Union needs to establish a coherent policy, at the level of its own Member States as well as the framework of enlargement'.[51]

Despite the ambiguity of the Community towards minority rights as a concept, Brandtner and Rosas have nevertheless attempted to justify the reference to minorities in the accession procedure. First, they suggest that the case of *Nold*[52] determined that when looking at the sources of human rights law the ECJ could take into account 'international treaties for the protection of human rights on which the Member States have collaborated or of which they are signatories'. This would include such provisions as Article 27 of the UN International Covenant on Civil and Political Rights, which declares that '*persons* belonging to ... minorities shall not be denied the right, *in community with the other members of their group*, to enjoy their own culture, to profess and practise their own religion, or to use their own language' (emphasis added).[53] Secondly, they also refer to Articles 13 (ex Article 6a) and 151(4) (ex 128(4)) EC Treaty, which aim to combat discrimination and promote the diversity of cultures respectively. However, the Community's approach to human rights has always focused on their individual application. Collective interests as such find little internal recognition. Consequently, both of Brandtner and Rosas' arguments serve to highlight the distinctive nature of this element of the Copenhagen Criteria. Certainly, a more consistent approach would have been to make the elimination of all forms of discrimination a key demand. That would have possessed significantly more force and identifiable content than the reference to minorities. The search for some kind of precedent in the Community's legal structure is therefore strained and fails to assist in understanding why minority rights received such specific attention as an entry requirement. Instead, we must look elsewhere for an answer to the prioritization of a distinct approach to rights that the Criteria installed.

A clue may be gleaned from another part of the 1993 Copenhagen Council conclusions. In considering France's proposal for a 'pact on stability in Europe' the Council found that such an initiative was 'directed towards assuring in practice the application of the principles agreed by European countries with regard to respect for borders and rights of

---

[51] Commission, *Report on the Action Plan against Racism* (2000) 22.
[52] *Nold v. Commission* Case 4/73 [1974] ECR I-491–516.
[53] Estébanez makes much the same point, note 50 above, at 158.

minorities'.[54] There can be little doubt that events in Europe, specifically in the former Yugoslavia, were a key influence behind the approach. The conflicts that erupted within the Balkans brought to life the very fears that manifested themselves soon after the collapse of communist rule in Central and Eastern Europe. The dangers resulting from a power vacuum, from the fragmentation of states, and from the prospect of conflict that might draw in Member States, were crucial concerns of the time.[55] In the case of the former Yugoslavia, the possibility of violence and oppression resulting from the emergence of independent states claiming legitimacy on the grounds of a nationalism founded in an ethnic identity was an attendant anxiety, echoing problems of the early 20th century. The potential 'victims' in this case were observed as those unfortunate enough to find themselves in the 'wrong territory' when the borders of these states were drawn or fought over. As such they were easily identifiable, or rather classifiable, as 'minorities'.

When the fighting flared in various parts of the former Yugoslavia in 1991 the primary political concern was to end the violence. That conflict was interpreted as akin to internecine strife whereby minorities were subjected to horrific persecution. 'Ethnic cleansing' became the motif that symbolized the nature of the violence. Given the appreciation of the conflict as emanating from the *disintegration* of a federation, a federation which attempted to draw together disparate cultures and ethnic groups, it is not difficult to understand the importance attached to establishing institutions that guaranteed democracy *and* respect and protection for minorities. It has even been suggested that the Community identified the conflict as a test of its own integration possibilities. Gow and Freedman comment that 'perhaps also it was embarrassing for the European Community to have an example close at hand of a failed experiment in federation. For those seeking closer integration within the Community, Yugoslavia was a poor advertisement, the obvious differences between the two notwithstanding'.[56] Certainly, the example of Yugoslavia may have presented an extreme version of the possibilities that followed the break-up of old communist and Soviet structures. The need to discourage such violence was a primary political aim for the Community.

---

[54] Conclusions EC Bull 6-1993 I.15 at 14.

[55] See James Gow and Lawrence Freedman, 'Intervention in a Fragmenting State: the Case of Yugoslavia' in Nigel Rodley (ed), note 15 above, at 93–132.

[56] See Gow and Freedman, note 55 above, at 98–9.

In the context of entry, the need to emphasize the respect for minority rights as a pre-condition for applicant states was therefore understandable. It was a requirement that had its roots in a policy designed to stabilize Central and Eastern Europe and thus reduce the threats that might directly affect the Community's members and the future realization of the European Project. As Lykke Friis and Anna Murphy suggest, 'the fear of internalising unresolved minority problems led to new policy instruments to address security issues along EU borders'.[57] This had the effect of recognizing and promoting a collective understanding of rights.

To clarify the Community's stance, Agenda 2000, which represented the Commission's response to the Council's call for a process of scrutiny of candidates, looked towards a 'number of texts governing the protection of national minorities' (including those adopted by the Council of Europe) for assessing the standards expected.[58] In particular, the Framework Convention for the Protection of National Minorities 1995 was identified as safeguarding 'the individual rights of persons belonging to minority groups'.[59] Although a number of Member States themselves had yet to sign and/or ratify the Convention this did not prevent the Convention from being recommended for applicant states.[60] This of course may well have sent contradictory messages to applicant states concerning the true value ascribed by the Community and its members to both minority rights in general and the specific international agreements in particular.

The subsequent application of Agenda 2000 indicates how extensive the Community's commitment to protecting minority rights has become. In the case of Estonia, for example, the 'integration of non-citizens'[61] was identified as a matter of concern that merited the demand for 'measures to facilitate the naturalisation process' including language training and financial support.[62] In Slovakia, the Commission noted in 1999 that the

---

[57] Lykke Friis and Anna Murphy, 'The EU and Central and Eastern Europe: Governance and Boundaries' *JCMS* 37 (1999) 211–32 at 221.
[58] See note 18 above.
[59] See Briefing no 20 on Democracy and Respect for Human Rights in the Enlargement Process of the European Union, 1 April 1998, PE 167.582 at 10.
[60] For details of signatories see http://conventions.coe.int/Treaty . Belgium only signed on the 31 July 2001, France, Belgium, Greece, Luxembourg, the Netherlands, and Portugal had yet to ratify by 2002.
[61] See Commission Opinion on 'Estonia's Application for Membership of the European Union' at 71, which focuses on the situation of Russian speakers within Estonia.
[62] Estonia Accession Partnership 1999 DG Enlargement Documents (available at http://europa.eu.int/comm/enlargement/estonia/ac_part_10_99_draft/index.htm4).

Hungarian minority had gained representation in government but that a bill for the 'use of minority languages in official contacts' had not been passed.[63] The Commission stated 'it is a measure which should be adopted at the earliest opportunity'.[64] In the case of Turkey, currently failing to meet the political conditions of the Copenhagen Criteria as we have seen,[65] the position of the rights of the Kurdish minority has been a particular concern. The Commission specified the measures it preferred to see introduced. They included 'the recognition of certain forms of the Kurdish cultural identity, greater tolerance *vis-à-vis* the means of expressing this identity, to the extent that this does not play into the hands of separation or terrorism'[66] (the last phrase perhaps indicating a certain wariness in case similar sentiments expressed *in* the Community would undermine the integrity of the nation-state).

The main target of concern has, however, been the situation of the Roma. Being a people possessing a presence across Central and Eastern Europe the Roma have become a symbol for minority rights. The Romanian Accession Partnership of 1999, for instance, required 'dialogue between the Government and the Roma community' to be strengthened 'with a view to elaborating and implementing a strategy to improve economic and social conditions of the Roma'.[67] It also called for 'adequate financial support to minority programmes' as a short-term priority. The fact that in 2002 the financial resources remained unavailable, and thus priority areas for action had only been partially met, is one particular reason for the delay in Romania's accession.[68]

Similar provisions regarding the Roma appeared in respect of many of the other candidate countries. For Bulgaria 'further efforts to integrate the Roma' were demanded in the first Accession Partnership.[69] This was followed by the requirement that a proposed Roma Framework Programme be implemented both in the short and medium terms.[70] In the *Regular Report*

[63] Communication from the Commission on 'Countering Racism, Xenophobia and Anti-Semitism in the Candidate Countries' COM(1999) 256 final.
[64] Ibid at 13.
[65] Commission, *Turkey Progress Report*, 8 November 2000 and Council Decision of 8 March 2001 on the Principles, Priorities, Intermediate Objectives and Conditions Contained in the Accession Partnership with the Republic of Turkey [2001] OJ L-85, 24 March 2001 at 13.
[66] Ibid at 14.
[67] Romania Accession Partnership 1999 DG Enlargement Documents (available at http://europa.eu.int/comm/enlargement/romania/ac_part_10_99draft/index.htm 4).
[68] *Regular Report on Romania's Progress Towards Accession 2002* SEC(2002) 1409 at 135.
[69] Bulgarian Accession Partnership, March 1998, para 4.1.
[70] Bulgarian Accession Partnership, November 1999, paras 4.1 and 4.2.

on Bulgaria's Progress Towards Accession 2002, the issue remained in view.[71] The Framework Programme had yet to be 'put into practice' and the suggestion was made that comprehensive anti-discriminatory legislation was necessary. There was no absolute requirement for action but the implication was clear. Action was expected, certainly by Bulgaria's proposed accession date of 2007.

The provision of financial support at national and local levels was also made a short-term priority for Roma assistance in the Czech Republic.[72] The Accession Partnership document in 2001 required that efforts to improve the condition of the Roma were continued.[73] Even so 'widespread discrimination' against the Roma continued to tax the Commission in its *Regular Report 2002*.[74] Again it called for comprehensive legislation in this field.

The attention paid to the plight of the Roma indicates the extent to which the Community is willing to intervene in the issues of minority rights. There appears to be a concerted attempt to recognize the problems and address them at every level, imposing standards and procedures on the applicants. This has rendered minority rights highly visible within the accession process and beyond. The issues raised and standards set provide precedents for all jurisdictions to follow. The collective nature of the rights involved have been reinforced and respected.

(b) Civil and political rights

The definitions of civil and political rights applied in the accession process have tended to concentrate on the basic provisions contained in the European Convention on Human Rights. The first Regular Report for Estonia issued in November 1998 raised the question of prison conditions, for instance. These, the Report demanded, required 'further improvement'. Although not an identified priority in the Accession Partnerships of 1998 or 1999 the issue was still the subject of enforcement through its very mention in the Report.

Prison conditions have also been a specific concern in the case of Turkey's application. Regularly upbraided for its lamentable standards in this regard, Turkey has been condemned for ill-treatment of detainees,

---

[71] *Regular Report on Bulgaria's Progress Towards Accession 2002* SEC(2002) 1400 at 32 *et seq*.
[72] Czech Republic Partnership, November 1999, para 4.1.
[73] Council Decision on the Principles, Priorities, Intermediate Objectives contained in the Accession Agreement with the Czech Republic (2001).
[74] European Commission, *Towards the Enlarged Union: Strategy Paper and Report* (2002) COM(2002) 700 final.

overcrowding, and the poor conditions of its juvenile offenders institutions.[75] Similarly, for Romania, great emphasis has understandably and consistently been placed upon the condition of children in care. The treatment of people with disabilities has also been an issue. The extent of the intervention in these respects is very broad. The short-term priorities established in the Accession Partnership 1999, for achievement by 2000, included a requirement to 'guarantee adequate budgetary provisions for the support of children in care and undertake a full reform of the child care system as well as of provisions for the treatment of children and adults with chronic diseases and handicaps'.[76]

In similar vein Bulgaria has been encouraged to improve community care services for children.[77] The UN Convention on the Rights of the Child has been specifically mentioned as the precedent in the country's child rights provision.

A whole range of other civil and political rights has been referred to across the accession process. Police misconduct, the fight against corruption, trafficking in women (in the case of Slovakia)[78] and various other matters have been the subject of comment and scrutiny. Consequently, there are no discernible areas where the Community will not tread in this field of rights.

(c) Economic, social, and cultural rights

Economic, social, and cultural rights may not have received the prominence accorded to the other rights issues mentioned above but nonetheless they still register a significant presence in the assessment of the political criteria for each applicant. Indeed, they appear under two sections, first, in their own right within the political criteria and second as elements of the *acquis communautaire* that is supposed to be adopted wholesale by the applicants. So, in the latter case, health and safety, employment rights, and consumer protection issues surface as matters to be addressed by the applicants where necessary.

It is under the political criteria that the widest scope of rights referred to appears. Thus, cultural rights attached to language, rights of equal

---

[75] *Turkey Progress Report*, 8 November 2000, at 16 (available at http://europa.eu.int/comm/enlargement/report_11_00/pdf/en/tu_en.pdf).

[76] See note 67 above.

[77] Council Decision on the Principles, Priorities, Intermediate Objectives and Conditions Contained in the Accession Partnership with Bulgaria [2002] OJ L-44/1.

[78] Commission, *Regular Report on the Progress Towards Accession by Slovakia 2000* (available at http://europa.eu.int/comm/enlargement/report_11_00/pdf/en/sk_en.pdf).

opportunities, rights of trades union, and rights of disabled people have all figured within the documents. The detail is perhaps less significant than the fact that these matters are subject to assessment and comment. In other words the Community, through the Commission's examination, has assumed responsibility for vetting a broad range of issues explicitly within rights terms. Merely ensuring that the *acquis* is adopted by the applicant states is not the only aim.

3.2.2 *Measures of scrutiny and enforcement*

The 1997 'Agenda 2000' document provided the basis for the institution for a scheme of scrutiny and enforcement that has been enthusiastically embraced by the Community.[79] In this influential document the Commission outlined 'in a single framework the broad perspectives for the development of the Union and its policies beyond the turn of the century'.[80] It noted the underlying principles that shaped the Community's approach to applicant states and suggested that enlargement would, 'promote the idea of European integration' and 'strengthen the European model'.[81] More particularly, the Agenda considered the political elements of the Copenhagen Criteria in tandem with the delivery of initial Opinions relating to ten applicants.[82] It created three thematic fields of enquiry: (a) democracy and the rule of law, (b) human rights, and (c) respect for minorities. The Commission's commitment to human rights as central to the political conditions to be scrutinized was re-affirmed.

Having established the general scope of investigation, Agenda 2000 then confirmed the grounds upon which that investigation would proceed. The Opinions attached to the Agenda both amplified the level of scrutiny and the methodology employed. The Commission approached each applicant state with a view to conducting a 'systematic examination of the main ways in which public authorities are organised and operate, and the steps they have taken to protect fundamental rights'.[83] The sources of information used were specified as:

---

[79] See note 18 above. [80] Ibid at 11.
[81] Ibid 'Impact Study' at 1.
[82] Those applicant states were (in alphabetical order): Bulgaria, the Czech Republic, Estonia, Hungary, Latvia, Lithuania, Poland, Romania, Slovakia, and Slovenia.
[83] This formula is repeated for all the initial Opinions. See for instance the Commission Opinion on Bulgaria's Application for Membership of the European Union, EU Bull Supp 13–1997 at 15.

- answers given to an initial questionnaire sent to the applicants in April 1996;
- bilateral meetings to pursue the results of the questionnaire;
- reports purportedly provided by the relevant embassies of the Community's Member States;
- assessments from international organizations including the Council of Europe and the Organisation for Security and Cooperation in Europe;
- reports made available by unidentified NGOs.[84]

The list was suffixed by an 'etc.' which presumably indicates other sources were employed although these were not identified.[85] Nonetheless, the sources specified suggest that the scrutiny was largely a paper-based process albeit incorporating direct dialogue between the Commission and representatives of each applicant state. Member State embassies might have been called upon to carry out specific reports on human rights conditions but it is more likely that normal reporting procedures were co-opted to supplement the information that the Commission may have unearthed itself.

The Opinions registered the results of the Commission's examination on the basis of the information acquired. However, the scrutiny did not, and was never intended to, cease there. It was deemed to be an on-going process that necessitated further annual reports on each country's progress towards satisfying the Copenhagen Criteria.[86] The Council later made clear that, 'the candidate countries are expected to address the issues'[87] presented in the reports even though Agenda 2000 may have concluded that all the then ten applicant states apart from Slovakia already satisfied the political criteria. Consequently, even a finding by the Commission that the human rights related criteria had been met has not prevented pressure being applied in order to effect change and/or improvement in human rights standards. The scheme of examination represented more than an exercise in data-gathering. The enforcement of specifically mentioned rights concerns was an underlying consequence of the strategy imposed.

---

[84] The list of sources was repeated in each of the Opinions regarding the applicant states. No amendment to the method of scrutiny has been indicated in subsequent country reports.

[85] Commission, *Composite Paper on Progress Made by the Candidate Countries Towards Accession 1998* indicates that the Commission may also draw on reports issued by the European Parliament. See EU Bull Supp 4-1998 at 6.

[86] The European Luxembourg Council 1997, para 29 established the regime for the delivery of 'regular reports'.

[87] Council, *EU Annual Report on Human Rights 1999* 11380/99 at 5.

Human rights conditionality, regardless of formal adherence to the Copenhagen Criteria, was given added force following decisions reached at the Luxembourg Council meeting in December 1997. The evolving pre-accession strategy was to be complemented by yet another instrument, the 'Accession Partnership'. Originally identified in Agenda 2000 by the Commission as a means to bring the different forms of pre-accession support within a single framework, the Accession Partnerships itemized the priority areas for further work referred to in each candidate's regular reports. The priorities were divided into short and medium term objectives and specifically included the political criteria for membership.[88] Failure to attend to these priorities, as well as satisfy the commitments under the Europe Agreements and the Copenhagen Criteria 'could lead to a decision by the Council to suspend financial assistance'.[89] Presumably, it would also stall the process of accession. The initial Accession Partnerships also provided a summary of recommendations for action extracted from the country Opinions. Each state was obliged to address *all* the issues raised as a condition of the Partnership document.

The sequence of scrutiny, and effective enforcement, was thus established. The Opinions issued for the applicant states in 1997 were each followed by Accession Partnerships produced in March 1998. The achievement of the objectives itemized within these Partnership documents was then assessed within the next regular country reports delivered in November 1998 and October 1999. These, in turn, gave rise to renewed Accession Partnerships in November 1999 and 2001 when priorities were reassessed and new objectives for each country put in place. The subsequent reports, delivered in the autumn of 2000, 2001, and 2002 determined the extent of compliance with those objectives.

How long this process of scrutiny followed by a call for action might continue is undefined. Presumably, it will depend on when the candidates are accepted as ready for accession and when the Community is ready to receive them. Given the possibility for regular renewal of the Accession Partnerships and the setting of new priorities, as well as the country reports, the process of scrutiny and intervention could conceivably continue for many years. The political determination that enlargement should proceed for ten of the candidates in 2004 is still only a potential cap upon the Community's action. There is no guarantee that further negotiations will not be required up to the very point of entry.

---

[88] See Commission Memo/98/21, 27 March 1998.   [89] Ibid.

The scrutiny and conditionality contained within this sequence has formed a forceful means by which human rights issues can be monitored and addressed and particular states 'persuaded' to act in accordance with the Community's directions if they wish to continue their application for membership. Even if a particular human rights concern is not translated into a priority in the Partnership Agreement, indeed even if the country reports continue to assert that the candidate fulfils the political criteria, that concern remains actionable. Such is the effect of the scrutiny and intervention strategy that the Community has instituted.

The above scheme has now become well established. As yet there is little sign that the process is waning. Rather, it would appear that for some countries at least (particularly Romania, Bulgaria, and Turkey) the scrutiny and enforcement will continue for some time. But how effective is it? A prolonged research programme would be required to answer this question but some tentative conclusions can be drawn from one example.

The case of Turkey perhaps presents the best indication of the impact of the accession process on human rights matters. Originally Turkey was an outcast from the European sphere. In 1989 the Commission concluded 'it would not be useful' to open negotiations for accession at that time.[90] Economic and political issues were cited as relevant to the decision, including the detrimental treatment of minorities. However, the Luxembourg European Council in 1997 determined that Turkey should be included in the discussions for enlargement and as a result the Commission's first Regular Report on the Copenhagen Criteria as applied to Turkey appeared in 1998. Specific causes for concern were noted in that report. Persistent cases of torture, disappearances, and extra-judicial killings, the failure to assure freedom of expression, the conditions in prisons, and the limitation of the freedoms of assembly and association were all highlighted.[91] Economic and social rights, such as those relating to trades union, education, and the restriction of the use of certain languages (Kurdish in particular) and 'major shortcomings in the treatment of minorities' were also identified.[92] The Commission demanded that all of these problems had to be resolved.

Little had changed when the Commission produced reports in the years 1999 and 2000. In the 2000 Report additional concerns about equal

---

[90] See *Regular Report on Turkey's Progress Towards Accession 1998* (available at http://europa.eu.int/comm/enlargement/report_11_98/pdf/en/turkey_en.pdf).
[91] Ibid at 15–16.   [92] Ibid at 21.

opportunities, children's rights, and the denial of cultural rights of the Kurds were noted.[93] The conclusion was that Turkey still did not meet the Copenhagen political Criteria.

The effect of this determination was to keep Turkey outside any possible enlargement process. However, the following years' Reports were able to conclude that significant progress had been made that would 'facilitate progress towards satisfying the Accession Partnership priorities'.[94] Various positive developments were reported: a moratorium on the use of the death penalty, the abolition of legislation restricting the use of minority languages, substantial prison reforms, reforms of the judicial system. Although Turkey still did not satisfy the Copenhagen political Criteria it was given encouragement to make further progress.

Whether the positive developments in the human rights situation can be put down to the interference by the Community through the Accession Partnership and its Regular Reports is impossible to conclude. However, the existence of the economic and political incentive for Turkey to join the Community suggests that the reforms and advances in human rights issues are connected. The opening of negotiations with Turkey seems to have engendered a response by the Turkish government in areas that have been devoid of improvement for decades. Large-scale reforms are underway. The reasonable assumption must be that the Community's accession strategy, its scrutiny and related enforcement through the dual process of the threat of exclusion and the promise of acceptance, has combined to apply considerable pressure on Turkey.

The level of scrutiny and possible sanction in respect of human rights matters discussed above demonstrates the development of a policy that is potentially highly interventionist. The pressures may be subtle, applied as they are through a system of dialogue and 'partnership', but they are no less forceful for all that. It would appear therefore that the Community's policy as regards the applicant states is to examine and alter the *systemic condition* of human rights in those countries. Particular aspects may provide a focus for the Community's concern but the scheme employed is nevertheless comprehensive in intent.

---

[93] *Regular Report on Turkey's Progress Towards Accession 2000* (available at http://europa.eu.int/comm/enlargement/report_11_00/pdf/en/tu_en.pdf).

[94] *Regular Report on Turkey's Progress Towards Accession 2001* (available at http://europa.eu.int/comm/enlargement/report2001/tu_en.pdf).

3.3 Conclusion

On the basis of the wide ranging approach to human rights issues, some elements of which have been discussed above, it can be seen that in matters of scrutiny, enforcement, and definition, the Community has developed a comprehensive scheme for assessing an applicant's human rights situation. By merely mentioning a particular issue, it impresses on the applicant that attention must be paid to that area. Even though many of the states are considered to have satisfied the political criteria of Copenhagen, this will not stop governments from concluding that there is still room for improvement. And in the absence of positive action the time to accession may be further prolonged.

The interconnected and comprehensive strategy thus imposed by the Community would seem to draw together a reporting mechanism with one of enforcement. The peculiar relationship between the Community and the applicant states provides that opportunity. The question to be addressed now is to what extent the external human rights policies, as adopted in development and accession, are distinct from the internal position. Chapter 4 addresses this issue.

4

The Scope of Internal-External Incoherence

The review of the Community's development and accession policies revealed three main areas of discursive and practical human rights activity: first, in the formulation of the definitions of rights, secondly, in the methods of surveillance adopted, and thirdly, in the powers of enforcement assumed. These components provide useful parameters for undertaking the comparison with the Community's internal policy. The extent of the alleged incoherence between internal and external affairs can then be mapped more accurately.

4.1 Distinctions in definition

To talk of 'human rights' as a recognized and established body of principles and concepts would be fallacious. The subject has been and remains contentious. The contents and meanings of the term are fluid and open to debate. Such has been the character of the international discourse for the past fifty years or more. Consequently, the fact that 'human rights' appears as a subject of policy and action by the Community in both the internal and external spheres does not necessarily mean that a uniform understanding is applied. Rather, it is in the discontinuities of definition evident from the Community's practices that the scope of incoherence first becomes evident.

The discussion, however, may at least commence with a suggestion of continuity that emanates from the Community. Rhetoric has been institutionally adopted that implies the Community adheres to a consistent interpretation of human rights principles regardless of context. The promotion of the principles of universality and indivisibility strongly infer that human rights are assumed to have a discernible content that will be applied uniformly in all spheres of activity.[1]

Internally, the language of universality and indivisibility may remain absent from the Treaties but there would nonetheless appear to be a consensus that it forms the bedrock of *all* Community human rights policies. The Council's *Annual Report on Human Rights 1999*, for instance, stressed adherence to the universality and indivisibility of human rights and their integration with 'peace and security, economic development and social equity'. The following year's Report also restated these principles, taking as its cue the universality concept promulgated at the World Conference on Human Rights in Vienna in 1993. It reported that the Community 'recognises the diversity of the world' but 'regardless of different cultures, social background, state of development, or geographical region, human rights are inalienable rights of every person'.[2] Similarly, the Commission has referred to the EU Charter of Fundamental Rights as evidence of the Community's overall commitment to the dual principles.[3] The Charter itself refers to the Community as 'founded on the indivisible, universal values of human dignity, freedom, equality and solidarity'.[4] One might surmise therefore that the human rights promoted externally would be of the same order and definition as those acted upon within the Community.

Whether or not this is in fact the case can be resolved by comparing two aspects: first, the sources of law relied upon to define human rights in the two spheres, and secondly, the concepts of rights accepted and promoted.

4.1.1 *Sources of law*

We have already seen in the analysis of development policy that the sources relied upon to define the meaning of human rights were extremely wide. The international instruments used as inspirations were largely products of the United Nations system although broader perspectives were also entertained. The application of the rights to development, the preference given to economic and social rights, and the linkage of rights with other concepts such as 'good governance' and security have been hallmarks of the language

---

[1] See Commission, 'The European Union and the External Dimension of Human Rights Policy: from Rome to Maastricht and Beyond' EC Bull Supp 3–1995 at 29.

[2] Council, *EU Annual Report on Human Rights* 2000 11542/00 at 8.

[3] Communication from the Commission on the 'Legal Nature of the Charter of Fundamental Rights of the EU, 20 November 2000, COM/2000/0644 final.

[4] EU Charter of Fundamental Rights [2000] OJ C-364/08.

adopted. Civil and political rights have also featured prominently and still form the basis for instigating negative measures of enforcement. Positive measures are not so constrained and thus from the General System of Preferences to development aid a whole raft of human rights can be said to be promoted.

In accession policy we have seen slightly more restricted sources applied. The European Convention on Human Rights (ECHR) has formed the basis for discussion but other instruments such as the Framework Convention for the Protection of National Minorities 1995 have been given prominence. Civil and political rights and economic, social, and cultural rights as well as specifically minority rights have also been the subject of scrutiny.

Internally, the sources of law that define rights that are the subject of Community action are somewhat different. The EU Charter of Fundamental Rights provides the latest expression of the Community's internal understanding. It claims to represent 'for the first time in the European Union's history, the whole range of civil, political, economic and social rights of European citizens and all persons resident in the EU'.[5] The preface states that 'the rights as they result, in particular, from the constitutional traditions and international obligations *common* to the Member States' (emphasis added) are reaffirmed.[6] It then lists as precedents 'the Treaty on European Union, the Community Treaties, the European Convention for the Protection of Human Rights and Fundamental Freedoms, the Social Charters adopted by the Community and by the Council of Europe and the case law of the Court of Justice of the European Communities and of the European Court of Human Rights'.

The reference to 'international obligations' therefore does not *directly* relate to a corpus of human rights texts applied by the global community. Rather, the obligations are only those 'common' to the Member States. Any international human rights instrument that does not find favour with one Member State by implication is excluded as a valid precedent for interpretation.

The European Court of Justice (ECJ) has in fact established a robust line of case law to substantiate the limitation. Since *Nold* it has held that '[i]nternational treaties for the protection of human rights *on which the Member States have collaborated or of which they are signatories*, can supply

---

[5] Preface to the Charter of Fundamental Rights of the European Union [2000] OJ C-364/01.
[6] Ibid at 8.

guidelines which should be followed within the framework of Community law' (emphasis added).[7]

The inference is that unanimity of collaboration or signature by the Member States is an absolute requirement for any international human rights treaty to form a source of law within the Community. Certainly, if the ECJ were faced with an international instrument that was adamantly opposed by one or more Member State, it would be hard to envisage that it would be treated as a viable precedent. One could imagine, for instance, a situation whereby moves to acknowledge a right to abortion would be fiercely resisted by countries such as Eire. In such a case, as *SPUC v. Grogan* might suggest through the ECJ's reluctance to rule on its substantive issues, the Court could find it extremely problematic to enforce a 'right' that was not universally recognized.[8] Consequently, although as Leonard Besselink submits, no 'obvious problems' have developed through Member States being parties to different treaties, difficulties might still arise.[9]

In passing it should be remembered that the *Nold* criteria was established with the ECHR very much in mind. That was the international instrument that held the attention of the ECJ at the time. The intention was not, therefore, to open the gates to the burgeoning library of human rights texts. It is unsurprising, therefore, that the ECJ's reference to other international instruments has been extremely limited.[10]

Externally the Community is not so bound. It may even adopt an approach to human rights that is founded on instruments to which third countries have not subscribed. In other words, the Community determines unilaterally those standards it wishes to make the basis for the scrutiny and enforcement of rights. Even though there is an element of negotiation in both development and accession policies through the drafting of agreements, it would be naïve to suppose that the Community did not determine the standards that apply.

By contrast, world or even regional standards may be suppressed internally where one or more Member State has decided to oppose (or at least not support) the expression of such rights. The fact that in accession policy reference may be made to the Framework Convention on National

---

[7] *Nold v. Commission* Case 4/73 [1974] ECR 491. See also *Opinion 2/94 on Accession by the Community to the ECHR* [1996] ECR I-1759 para 33.

[8] *SPUC v. Grogan* Case 159/90 [1991] ECR I-4685.

[9] See Leonard F.M. Besselink, 'Entrapped by the Maximum Standard: on Fundamental Rights, Pluralism and Subsidiarity in the European Union' *CMLRev* (1998) 629–80 at 652.

[10] Ibid.

Minorities when a number of Member States have yet to sign and/ or ratify the same suggests that the Community can even make an external requirement where there is no internal consensus. The latest example is in the 2001 Report on Turkey's application in which the candidate's failure to ratify the Framework Convention is noted with implicit disapproval.[11] This at a time when France similarly has failed to ratify. The result is the emplacement of a skewed approach to international human rights that could constitute a division in current or future human rights evolution.

On a similar note, the Preamble of the EU Charter refers to 'common values' and the Community's 'spiritual and moral heritage' as inspiring the Charter's construction. When talking of the 'preservation and development of these common values' respect is paid to 'the diversity of cultures and traditions of the *peoples of Europe* as well as the *national identities* of the Member States' (emphasis added). Although articles of the Charter relate to equality and the right not to be discriminated against,[12] (which undoubtedly seek to protect peoples not of Europe) the language adopted in the Preamble indicates a *preference* for promoting cultures and traditions that emanate *from* Europe not elsewhere. Despite their protection from abuse or discrimination, Europe's 'others' are effectively excluded within the very core of the Community's human rights creative and promotional rhetoric. The failure of the Charter to be all embracing from the outset therefore suggests an interior interpretation of human rights that is 'located' not 'universal'.

In this respect, the Charter follows the general parameters set down by the TEU and the ECJ. Article 6 (ex Article F) TEU determines that the Community shall respect fundamental rights as guaranteed by the ECHR 'and as they result from the constitutional traditions common to the Member States' and 'the national identities of its Member States'. As already indicated this includes international instruments but the parameters for interpretation are set. European texts are to govern European behaviour. There is no extension of the principle to the identities and principles that might have developed outside Europe even though a substantial proportion of Europe's inhabitants originated from other regions. What place then can Islamic cultures and traditions legal or

---

[11] See *Regular Report on Turkey's Progress Towards Accession* (2001) (available at *http://europa. eu.int/comm/enlargement/report2001/tu_en.pdf* at 29).

[12] See, for instance, Article 21 on 'Non-Discrimination', note 4 above, at 13.

otherwise, for instance, have within the rhetorical landscape that the Community's constitutional texts inscribe?[13]

In view of all the above it would seem ironic that the Commission should have decided to promote the EU Charter as a set of guiding principles for its external relations. In 2001 Chris Patten, Commissioner responsible for External Relations, stated that the Charter is 'an important' element in the European Union's efforts to ensure coherence between the internal and external human rights policy'.[14] But the means by which the Charter will achieve this objective are far from clear. If it is intended to identify those human rights that will be the concern of the Community in its development policy, for instance, then it singularly fails to emulate the definition of rights as putatively applied in that area. Specifically, the Charter contains no reference to collective rights, which is a particular interest in both development and accession policies. The absence of minority rights is key in this respect.

This brings us to the second element of definition: the conceptions of human rights that have emerged from the Community.

4.1.2 Conceptions of human rights

Human rights have been analysed as possessing historically three generations.[15] The first has been considered as the civil and political rights that characterized the French and American revolutions. The second are those economic, social, and cultural rights that were putatively represented in the Russian revolution. The third, notions of collective or 'peoples' rights' that have been the subject of increasing global discourse since the middle of the 1960s. Both of the first two 'generations' find expression by the Community internally *and* externally. It would be inaccurate to suggest otherwise. Although there may be some debate as to the extent of application by the Community in each sphere, and the emphasis that is placed on them, there is nonetheless a willingness to recognize their claims for respect regardless of policy area. Thus since at least the end of the Cold War both civil

---

[13] Silvio Berlusconi gave an indication of the type of rhetoric that might surface after the attacks on the World Trade Centre in New York on 11 September 2001. He reportedly spoke of the 'supremacy' and 'superiority' of Western civilization and called on Europe to recognize its 'common Christian roots'. See *Guardian*, 27 September 2001.

[14] Speech by the Rt Hon Chris Patten, European Parliament, Plenary Session, Strasbourg, 4 July 2001 (available at http://europa.eu.int/comm/external_relations/news/patten/sp04_07_01.htm).

[15] See Roland Rich, 'The Right to Development: A Right of Peoples?' in James Crawford (ed), *The Rights of Peoples* (Oxford: Clarendon Press, 1988) 39–54.

and political rights *and* economic, social, and cultural rights have found acceptance both internally and in the two external policies examined.[16] However, the situation is different for notions of collective rights. Indeed it is with regard to the appreciation of the third generation that the distinctions in definition become most evident.

Specifically, the analysis of development and accession policies revealed that the Community was intent on promoting the rights of minorities and the right to development (and rights *in* development). These collective or group rights have been central to the Community's discourse and practice in the two external policies covered. But can the same be said for the internal condition?

(a) Minority rights

Little has occurred over the Community's history to suggest it is willing to promote minority rights interests as ardently within its internal sphere as it does externally. Bruno de Witte goes so far as to suggest that the Community's concern in this field is for export only.[17] Condemnation or official sanction in relation to problems of the integration of and discrimination against minorities within the Member States has been largely absent at Community level. Only the European Parliament has paid any great attention to the issue with various resolutions produced since 1981.[18] Even these fail to register any significant disapproval of the situation of minorities in particular Member States. Thus, there has been a general silence and inaction with regard to, for example, Germany and its treatment of Turkish migrant workers,[19] to the situation in Greece in relation to the institutional discrimination applied to the Turkish minority,[20] and as

---

[16] Chapters 2 and 3 illustrate the broad range of rights pursued externally. For a brief review of the breadth of rights covered internally see Christiane Duparc, *The European Community and Human Rights* (Brussels: European Commission, 1993) 14–18.

[17] Bruno de Witte, *Politics Versus Law in the EU's Approach to Ethnic Minorities* (EUI Working Paper, RSC no. 2000/4, 2000).

[18] The first of these was Resolution on a Community Charter of Regional Languages and Cultures and on a Charter of Rights of Ethnic Minorities [1981] OJ C-287, at 106.

[19] See Human Rights Watch, *'Foreigners Out' Xenophobia and Right-Wing Violence in Germany* (1992) and *'Germany for Germans' Xenophobia and Racist Violence in Germany* (1995). For further discussion on this and related topics, see also Michael Spencer, *States of Injustice: A Guide to Human Rights and Civil Liberties in the European Union* (London: Pluto Press, 1995). See also the European Parliament's Committee on Civil Liberties and Internal Affairs, *Report on Respect for Human Rights in the European Union in 1994* (1996) A4-223/96.

[20] See Human Rights Watch, *The Macedonians of Greece* (1994) which examines the situation of ethnic Macedonians in northern Greece and Human Rights Watch, *The Turks of Western Thrace* (1999) which condemns the Greek government's attitude to the Turkish minority in the region.

regards Belgium and its widespread failure to deal with racism at all levels. In the latter case, the European Commission against Racism and Intolerance (ECRI) reported in 2000 that 'problems of racism and intolerance still exist in Belgium'. It concluded that the 'widespread exploitation of racism in politics by extreme right-wing political parties' and 'racism and intolerance on the part of some law enforcement officials' was of particular concern.[21] More generally, since the 11 September 2001 attacks Amnesty International and ECRI have noted the up-surge in both popular and institutional antipathy and violence directed against Muslims in the Member States.[22] Still the Community has steadfastly avoided interfering directly in such matters.

This is not to say that attempts have not been made to address issues of racism and xenophobia through various initiatives. Indeed Article 13 EC Treaty introduced by the Treaty of Amsterdam has been touted as providing the impetus for action at a Community level. Even so, significant questions over the provision's efficacy in countering racism in the ways that are possible externally remain. In particular the methods chosen to apply Article 13 demonstrate an institutional hesitancy about treading on the toes of the Member States. Two directives, one to combat discrimination in the labour market on *all* grounds referred to in Article 13 (except for sex) and one to combat discrimination on grounds of racial and ethnic origin in areas beyond employment, and an Action Plan setting out a programme of action 'in particular by enabling exchanges of experience and good practice between the Member States' provided the framework for action.[23]

The very choice of form for these measures is problematic. By adopting directives rather than regulations the Commission again fell foul of treating the Member States with undeserved deference in a matter that is supposed to be core to the Community's human rights policies. In the Ninth Report of the UK Parliament's Select Committee on European Union, a Commission spokesperson is quoted as admitting that 'in respect of both the principle of subsidiarity and proportionality it is better to address the issue on a very broad, objective basis while leaving for Member States a lot

---

[21] See ECRI, *Second Report on Belgium*, adopted 18 June 1999, CRI(2000)2, Executive Summary.

[22] See *Amnesty International Report 2003* and *ECRI Annual Report 2002* CRI(2003) 23.

[23] See Council Directive 2000/78/EC establishing a general framework for equal treatment in employment and occupation, Council Directive 2000/43/EC implementing the principle of equal treatment between persons irrespective of racial or ethnic origin, and Council Decision 2000/750/EC establishing a Community action programme to combat discrimination (2001 to 2006).

of margin of manoeuvre to adapt their legislation in response to their specific cultural diversity'.[24]

Such sensitivity may be welcomed by the Member States (as it was by the Select Committee on the whole) but it is hard to square with the statements of fundamental principle that are otherwise presented. The fact that by mid-2003 the Commission was compelled to issue a press release condemning the failure of 'most Member States' to transpose the Racial Equality Directive into their national laws serves to reinforce the point.[25]

The scope of the directives, in any event, indicates the limited nature of the ambition of the Community to confront the Member States constitutionally on the issue of racism. Why cannot there be a direct, unfettered, and uncomplicated constitutional acceptance that any form of race discrimination is contrary to Community law? The failure to address the matter in such direct terms undermines the Community's internal narrative on racism and as a result its commitment to acknowledge the importance of minority rights as an independent construct.

But what of the Community's practical initiatives, the secondary legislation, soft law, and the work conducted by the institutions? On one level, the changes to the EC Treaty with regard to racism and discrimination do at least enable one to suggest that such matters are no longer considered to be the sole preserve of the Member States. Some of the Community's practice over the past decade or so would even suggest that the divide between Community and Member State on this issue is being slowly eroded.

Since at least the 1986 Joint Declaration by the Parliament, Council, and Commission, the Community has attempted to carve out a role for itself. In the context of a growing realization that Europe continued to be a home for racist political parties and extreme violence against ethnic minorities, the Declaration claimed that 'respect for human dignity and the elimination of forms of racial discrimination are part of the common cultural and legal heritage of all the Member States'.[26] The statement is suspect in the extreme and was itself undermined by the contemporary widespread acts of racial discrimination and violence that if anything poured doubt on the true common heritage that the Member States embodied.[27] Nevertheless,

[24] Select Committee on European Union, *Ninth Report 1999*, Part 5 para 30.
[25] Press release IP/03/1047 'Commission concerned at Member States' failure to implement new racial equality rules'.
[26] European Parliament, Council, Commission, Declaration against Racism and Xenophobia [1986] OJ C-158/01.
[27] For a brief review of the acts of racism recorded in the Member States see the many reports issued by such bodies as the European Commission against Racism and Intolerance.

the Declaration condemned 'all forms of intolerance'[28] and stressed the 'importance of adequate and objective information and of making all citizens aware of the dangers of racism and xenophobia, and the need to ensure that all acts or forms of discrimination are prevented or curbed'.[29]

Fine intentions, of course, but no scheme for action was promoted through the Declaration. Wider initiatives emerged with the establishment of the Vienna Monitoring Centre on Racism and Xenophobia in 1997.[30] However, this institution only has as its primary aim, 'study, data collection and problem analysis' not the recognition and enforcement of any collective rights that might be asserted.[31]

The contrast with the Community's approach particularly in accession policy is acute when we examine the situation of the Roma. As Chapter 3 details, the plight of the Roma throughout Eastern and Central Europe occupies considerable attention in the accession process. A difficult example of institutional discrimination that transcends national boundaries is recognized by the Community and serious attempts have been made to encourage, if not enforce, change. The treatment of the Roma within the Community is no less a cause for concern. The Roma possess a significant presence in some of the Member States. The European Parliament's Committee on Civil Liberties and Internal Affairs in 1994 has acknowledged both the size of the Roma minority in the Community and the extent of the racism and discrimination that they suffer.[32] It continues to draw attention to the problem.[33] Organizations such as the European Roma Rights Centre (ERRC), have also highlighted significant discrimination within Member States, in particular Austria, fiercely condemned for introducing legal and administrative measures that gave rise to 'systemic exclusion of Roma'.[34] Italy too has been criticized in reports by the UN Committee on the Elimination of Racial Discrimination (CERD) in 1999

---

[28] Declaration, note 26 above, at para 1.
[29] Ibid at para 5.
[30] Council Regulation 1035/97 [1997] OJ L-151/1.
[31] Conor A. Gearty, 'The Internal and External "Other" in the Union Legal Order: Racism, Religious Intolerance and Xenophobia in Europe' in Philip Alston *et al* (eds), *The EU and Human Rights* (Oxford: Oxford University Press, 1999) 325–58.
[32] See *Report on the Situation of the Gypsies in the Community* A3-0124/94 quoted in Spencer, note 19 above, at 139.
[33] *Report on Countering Racism and Xenophobia in the European Union* A5-0049/2000, Preamble para T9.
[34] ERRC, *Divide and Deport: Roma and Sinti in Austria* (1996) (available at http://errc.org/publications/reports/austria.pdf at 5).

and by the ERRC in 2000. The ERRC Report, for instance, concludes '[t]he will to expel Roma from Italy has grown ... Aggressive and abusive raids by police and other authorities have continued apace. Italian politicians have publicly offered hate and been rewarded by public support'.[35]

The Report further points to a cloak of silence over the country's record stating '[r]esponse by other European countries has been close to non-existent; while Europe has shunned Austria since the xenophobic Freedom Party entered the Austrian government, there has been little to no response to the rise of racial hate in Italy'.[36]

Despite such revelations, recognition, and the existence of Article 13 EC Treaty, no legally binding framework for direct institutional intervention in the affairs of the Member States on minority rights has been constructed in the name of the Community. Some support for Roma is provided through initiatives in education and culture[37] but little has been done to combat the serious issues of institutional discrimination and racism identified internally.

The position of both the Commission and the Council in this respect appears to have been articulated in replies given to two European Parliamentary questions raised at the end of the 1990s.

First, Jan Wiersma in 1999 enquired as to the Commission's knowledge of the plight of the Roma in the applicant states and also asked whether the Commission had any facts about problems relating to Roma resident within the Member States.[38] Mr Verheugen on behalf of the Commission replied first that the 'Commission closely monitors the initiatives by the applicant states to improve the Roma situation'. Secondly, he stated simply that the 'situation of Roma minorities in the Member States is monitored by the Council of Europe'. In contrast to the approach to applicant states, the Community is not concerned internally with monitoring the treatment of the Roma. That is left to the Council of Europe, of which significantly all the applicant states are now members.

Secondly, in 1997 Eva Kjer Hansen asked the Council whether it was 'reasonable that the Union requires more from the future Member States

---

[35] ERRC, *Campland: Racial Segregation of Roma in Italy* (Country Report Series no 9, October 2000) (available at http://errc.org/publications/reports/italy.pdf at 93).

[36] Ibid.

[37] See, for example, Resolution of the Council and the Ministers of Education, meeting within the Council, 22 May 1989, on School Provision for Gypsy and Travellers Children [1989] OJ C-153/3.

[38] Written Question E-2815/99 by Jan Wiersma (PSE) to the Commission (18 January 2000) [2000] OJ C-280E, 3 March 2000, at 137.

from Eastern Europe, when it comes to the protection of minority rights, when the Union has made no legislative effort in that field for the minority groups within the Union'.[39] She also asked whether the Council planned 'any legislative measures for the protection of minority groups in the Union'. The Council responded:

The specific question to which the Honourable Member refers does not fall within Community competence. However, the Council recalls that Article F(2) of the Treaty on European Union states that the Union shall respect fundamental rights, as guaranteed by the European Convention for the Protection of Human Rights and Fundamental Freedoms signed in Rome on 4 November 1950 and as they result from the constitutional traditions common to the Member States, as general principles of Community law.

The use of issues of competence to avoid dealing with the problem and the deflection of responsibility on to other organizations is in direct contrast to the external approach. The accession process in particular could easily adopt the same line given that all applicants are members of the Council of Europe. But the Community chooses to embrace fully the need to address matters of racism and discrimination against the Roma in the applicant states.

The legal position of minority rights is equally ambiguous in the ECJ. Indeed, the notion of group rights does not figure within its reasoning. When deciding its understanding of those rights that must be respected as 'an integral part of the general principles of law' of the Community,[40] it has confined itself almost entirely to those individual rights protected by the ECHR. Even when faced with a possible group right in the shape of a people's language in *Groener v. Minister for Education* it avoided the discourse of rights altogether. Instead, it concluded that the 'EEC Treaty does not prohibit the adoption of a policy for the protection and promotion of a language of a Member State' whilst adding the proviso that 'the implementation of such a policy must not encroach upon a fundamental freedom such as that of the free movement of workers'.[41] It did not frame the issue in terms of rights at all. This is in direct contrast to the position adopted externally. Council Regulation 975/ 1999, which sets out the objectives for Community operations in development co-operation policy, states that

---

[39] Written Question E-1621/97 by Eva Kjer Hansen (ELDR) to the Council (14 May 1997) [1998] OJ C-82/13.

[40] *Internationale Handelsgesellschaft v. Einfuhr- und Vorratsstelle fur Getreide und Futtermittel* Case 11/70 [1970] ECR II-1125–55. For a review of this history see Chapter 6.

[41] *Groener v. Minister for Education* Case 379/87 [1989] ECR 3967.

support for minorities and promoting and protecting 'the right to use one's own language' are two items worthy of receiving aid.[42]

Niamh Shuibhne may suggest that there is scope for the Community, and thus the ECJ, to develop its 'visibility' in the language rights field but acknowledges that attaining influence over 'minority language rights protection within its Member States is a more problematic concept'.[43] The ambition may be present but the competence and perhaps will are less evident in rights terms.

The idea that there exists a lack of will has been given credence by the most blatant failure to address the question of minority rights in the drafting of the EU Charter of Fundamental Rights.[44] No mention is made of minorities in that text, a fact that may be tempered by anti-discrimination rhetoric but which nevertheless misses the very point assumed by the Community in its relations with third countries in general and applicant states in particular. Group rights require recognition and promotion to ensure that institutionalized and widespread discrimination and racism is to be countered. Internally, the Charter indicates a total absence of minority rights as a separate rights construct. It has been criticized by the Assembly of the Council of Europe for that reason, which stated:

the Assembly also regrets that the draft Charter makes no express reference to the rights of persons belonging to ethnic, religious or linguistic minorities or indeed to the right to local and regional self-government—rights which are protected by Council of Europe instruments such as the Framework Convention for the Protection of National Minorities and the European Charter of Local Self-Government.[45]

The Charter therefore directly countermands the Commission's own suggestion in 2001 that the Charter should 'promote coherence between the EU's internal and external approaches' on minority rights.[46] It is indicative of a Community approach that externally is keen to promote those rights

---

[42] Council Regulation 975/1999 [1999] OJ L-120/1.

[43] Niamh Nic Shuibhne, 'The European Union and Minority Language Rights' *MOST Journal on Multicultural Societies* 3/2 (2001) (available at www.unesco.org/most/v13n2shui.htm para 4.2).

[44] EU Charter, note 4 above.

[45] Report of the Parliamentary Assembly of the Council of Europe adopted by Resolution 1128(2000) at 3.

[46] Communication from the Commission to the Council and the European Parliament on 'The European Union's Role in Promoting Human Rights and Democratisation in Third Countries' COM(2001) 252 final at 3.

on a collective basis and internally is reluctant to even discuss them in such a fashion. The very concept of rights in this context is therefore subject to a fundamental distinction.

(b) Development rights and the right to development

The Community's promotion of the right to development was discussed in Chapter 2. Suffice to say that although the Community has maintained a stance that emphasizes a right to development that 'embraces the notion that every individual has the right to take part in the development process'[47] it also supports collective interests within the concept. It may not endorse more radical approaches but its promotion of the rights of persons with disabilities, minorities, and indigenous peoples, as well as the initiatives that are designed to alleviate poverty, all acknowledge as much.[48] The Community's practice through its general aid programme over the years has also supported economic, social, and cultural rights in preference to (at least monetarily) civil and political rights. Consequently, development policy has now become centrally entwined with human rights principles that purportedly govern the Community's practice. This has been enforced by Article 177(2) (ex Article 130u) EC Treaty, which confirms that Community development policy 'shall contribute to the general objective of ... respecting human rights and fundamental freedoms'.

Of equal significance is the Community's related advocacy of the principle of 'good governance'. The Commission has described this as 'implicit in a political and institutional environment respecting human rights, democratic principles and the rule of law'.[49] Again respect for human rights appears as an indispensable component. Human rights have also been incorporated into the review of developing countries' public governmental management. The Commission suggests that 'equity and the primacy of law in the management and allocation of resources call for an independent and accessible judicial system that guarantees all citizens basic access to resources by *recognising their right to act against inequalities*' (emphasis added).[50]

---

[47] Overview of the 57th Session of the UN Commission on Human Rights, 19 March–27 April 2001 at 69, (available at http://europa.eu.int/comm/external_relations/human_rights/doc/uncom57.pdf).

[48] Ibid.

[49] Commission Communication to the Council and Parliament on 'Democratisation, the Rule of Law, Respect for Human Rights and Good Governance: the Challenges of the Partnership Between the European Union and the ACP States' COM(98)146 at 8.

[50] Ibid.

It continues to demand that 'government and civil society must be able to implement an equitable development model and guarantee the judicious use of all resources in the public interest'.[51]

Although the discourse of a *right* to development does not appear in the internal sphere, the concept of development does possess an important presence within the Community's regional policy. It does not, however, embody any cultured understanding of human rights. Joanne Scott reveals that 'Community law in relation to regional development operations incorporates a narrow vision of "development" and one which is closely linked to economic growth'.[52] The Community's concern is quantitative rather than qualitative development. Economic issues are paramount and are not interrupted by any concerns about human rights of an individual or collective nature. This can be differentiated in particular from the short-term requirements placed on Turkey by the 2000 Accession Partnership.[53] As an element of the priorities in respect of the political criteria, Turkey was required to 'develop a comprehensive approach to reduce regional disparities, and in particular to improve the situation in the south-east, with a view to enhancing economic, social and cultural opportunities for all citizens'. The notion of development constructed around rights was reflected in the political rather than economic criteria within which this demand was placed.

The dissimilarity with the external dimension is further apparent when assessing the conditionality applied in determining the extent of development funds that may be provided by the Community. Internally, the provision of aid under the Structural Funds[54] to achieve economic and social cohesion is dependent on Member States satisfying certain economic criteria. Few if any requirements are made on the basis of human rights considerations of whatever hue. By contrast, funds provided to states seeking accession are subject to both economic *and* political criteria, which as we have seen include human rights as a crucial factor.[55]

This distinction undermines both the concept of development *and* of rights. By placing rights at the centre (if only rhetorically) of an externally

---

[51] Ibid.
[52] Joanne Scott, *Development Dilemmas in the European Community: Rethinking Regional Development Policy* (Buckingham: Open University Press, 1995) 49.
[53] Incorporated in Council Decision 2001/235/EC [2001] OJ L-85/13.
[54] See Articles 158–162 (ex Articles 130a–130e) EC Treaty.
[55] For a comprehensive review of the issue see Joanne Scott, 'Regional Policy: An Evolutionary Perspective' in Paul Craig and Gráinne de Búrca (eds), *The Evolution of EU Law* (Oxford: Oxford University Press, 1999) 625–52.

applied policy at the same time as ignoring them in the internal context suggests that rights do not assume equal importance in the two spheres. Even if an assumption were made that all relevant rights were respected in the Member States there is no reason why their importance in development could not be reiterated. However, the internal narrative of development steadfastly denies any rights element, which runs wholly counter to the rhetoric of the right to development that the Community is so keen to promote. Consequently, the adherence to a common understanding about established rights and rights still undergoing formation is made impossible. The Community's approach is entirely relativist, fundamentally contradicting its own adopted universalist principles.[56]

Having considered both the sources of law applied and two examples of rights practice, the argument may be made that the concept of universalism is an ambiguous construct in the Community's hands. It is constantly subject to a basic distinction in application. For whatever reason, internal rights are not affected by the same considerations and approaches as the external. The Community's choices as to which human rights it promotes, scrutinizes, and enforces in each sphere are subject to different understandings and criteria. It draws dissimilar boundaries for action and interference that belie the very meaning of the universal. In particular, there is a willingness externally to embrace a collective conception of rights that finds little expression internally. Individuals are the holders of rights within the Community legal order not groups or peoples. *Van Gend en Loos*[57] has been a guiding principle in that regard, determining that Community law 'not only imposes obligations on individuals but is also intended to confer upon them rights which become part of their legal heritage'. The internal discourse of rights has followed that rubric. The scope of distinction in definition described above has emanated from this central feature.

4.2 Distinctions in scrutiny

Turning away from matters of definition to matters of practice, one may observe from the analysis of development and accession policies that a

---

[56] Other examples will present themselves. Gráinne de Búrca maintains that certain rights issues such as cultural rights, 'which have gained importance within general human rights discourse have not acquired that status or been discussed in those terms in Community legal vocabulary and instruments, even where those issues fall within Community competence'. See 'The Language of Rights and European Integration' in Jo Shaw and Gillian More (eds), *New Legal Dynamics of European Union* (Oxford: Clarendon Press, 1995) 38.

[57] *Van Gend en Loos v. Nederlandse Administratie der Belastingen* Case 26/62 [1963] ECR I-55.

structure of human rights scrutiny has been created that possesses considerable breadth. Processes have evolved that are intrusive and extensive. By drawing on various international sources of information as well as its own contacts, the Community has been able to institute a system that of necessity needs to be expansive. If it were not, the very procedure for determining whether applicant states fulfil the criteria for entry or developing states are worthy of receiving aid would become suspect. Even though Philip Alston and Joseph Weiler suggest that there is an 'absence of any systematic approach to monitoring and reporting'[58] in the Community's external relations, the evidence from accession and development policy is that the practice adopted is sweeping in nature.

By contrast it was noted in 1999 by a *Comité des Sages* report entitled *A Human Rights Agenda for the European Union for the Year 2000* that the Community 'currently lacks any systematic approach to the collection of information on human rights' within the Community.[59] On the face of it there would therefore appear to be a significant distinction between the external and internal practices in this respect.

To examine the extent of this element of distinction the internal condition must be considered in a little more detail. To do so another distinction, between scrutiny of the Community institutions themselves and scrutiny of the Member States by the Community, needs to be made.

4.2.1 *Scrutiny of Community actions*

Despite decades of debate the Community as a political entity has never become a member of an international human rights regime. The ECJ's *Opinion 2/94*[60] ensured that from a legal standpoint accession to the ECHR could not be undertaken without Treaty amendment. The Member States would have to agree unanimously to such a step, something they steadfastly refused to countenance for decades. Only with the demand for a constitutional treaty has the issue become one for serious intergovernmental decision.[61] In the absence of accession the Community and its institutions

---

[58] Philip Alston and J.H.H. Weiler, 'An "Ever Closer Union" in Need of a Human Rights Policy: The European Union and Human Rights' in Alston *et al* (eds), note 31 above, at 13.
[59] See Alston *et al* (eds), note 31 above, Annex 922.
[60] *Opinion 2/94 on Accession by the Community to the ECHR* [1996] ECR I-1759.
[61] Article I-7(2) of the Draft Constitutional Treaty of 2003 proposed that the Community 'shall seek accession' but inserts no timetable or other requirement for the completion of the process.

remain devoid of external scrutiny by organizations with the power or authority to review decisions and practices in human rights terms.

Historically this has been a source of concern for both commentators and national constitutional courts alike. The Community's development of the principle that 'fundamental rights form an integral part of the general principles' of Community law assuaged some of the criticisms.[62] The ECJ has been empowered to review the acts of Community institutions to ensure they are compatible with the standards discussed above. However, it does not have the power to monitor or scrutinize institutional practice on an on-going basis.

The European Ombudsman, however, *is* specifically authorized to oversee Community acts under Article 195 (ex Article 138e) EC Treaty. Individuals who are citizens of the Community or legally resident within it are entitled to bring complaints. The Council has also recognized that the Ombudsman's role should be 'to examine alleged cases of maladministration in the actions of the Community institutions or bodies [and] to undertake investigations on his own initiative' that might 'relate to questions of human rights, particularly freedom of expression and non-discrimination'.[63] In practice, the Ombudsman's investigative role is piecemeal and prompted by specific information and complaints received against the Community's institutions. In no sense can it claim to provide comprehensive or regular coverage of human rights issues.

The European Parliament has acknowledged the lacunae in scrutiny that exists and has attempted to rectify the position. Its Committee on Citizens' Freedoms and Rights, Justice and Home Affairs noted that:

it is the particular responsibility of the European Parliament (by virtue of the role conferred on it under the new Article 7(1) of the Treaty of Nice) and of its appropriate committee to ensure (in cooperation with the national parliaments and the parliaments of the applicant countries) that both *the EU institutions* and the Member States uphold the rights set out in the various sections of the [EU Charter on Fundamental Rights] (emphasis added)'.[64]

Article 7(1) (ex Article F.1) TEU as amended by the Treaty of Nice gave the Parliament the discretion to determine 'that there is a clear risk of a

---

[62] The story of this development and its importance is explored in detail in Chapter 6.

[63] Council, note 2 above. See also Article 9 of the Decision of the European Ombudsman adopting implementing provisions (1997) (available at www.euro-ombudsman.eu.int/lbasis/en/provis.htm).

[64] Committee on Citizens' Freedoms and Rights, *Justice and Home Affairs Report on the Situation as regards Fundamental Rights in the EU* (2000) A5-0223/2001.

serious breach by a Member State' of respect for human rights as contained in Article 6(1) (ex Article F) TEU. The institutions are not mentioned in this provision. It is therefore questionable authority for examining the institutions' human rights record.

Nevertheless, the Parliament has taken it upon itself to undertake a process of monitoring the Community using the EU Charter of Fundamental Rights as its guide. Although this is an innovative move it fails to match the processes available in external policies in two ways.

First, by now focusing on the provisions of the Charter it does not provide the means for examining the Community's work in rights outside that instrument. Group rights, as we have seen, are thus largely excluded as relevant issues for scrutiny.

Secondly, the Parliament is almost entirely reliant upon other sources for its information. Individual communications, reports from NGOs, and publicly available data from international organizations such as the Council of Europe provide the material for assessment. It does not have the facilities to undertake a continuous assessment of human rights issues. The Rapporteur for the year 2000, Thierry Cornillet, was pained to admit 'the lack of resources available'.[65] He pointed out that there 'is no dedicated service within the European Parliament dealing with fundamental rights in the Union capable of helping the rapporteur either to gather useful source material for verification during the year or to draw up the report itself'.[66]

Such an admission is fundamental to the efficacy of the Parliament's monitoring role. The position is no better with regard to scrutiny of human rights in the Member States.

4.2.2 *Scrutiny of Member States by the Community*

From a political point of view it has been the approach of the Community that 'the protection and promotion of human rights is primarily a matter for the Member States of the Union, in accordance with their own judicial systems'.[67] Equally, the ECJ has made clear 'no Treaty provision confers on the Community institutions any general power to enact rules on human rights'.[68] Member States have given no indication that they would appreciate a change in this approach. Rather, the Community has generally relied upon the argument that, being signatories to the ECHR and numerous

---

[65] Ibid at 24.   [66] Ibid.   [67] Council, note 2 above, at 11.
[68] *Opinion 2/94*, note 60 above, para 27.

international human rights instruments and procedures, Member States are already subject to a rigorous system of scrutiny by outside agencies.

Despite these arguments and restrictions, the Community has recognized the need to adopt some kind of approach that would bring its internal activities into line with the external. It has therefore touted a number of processes as instituting a monitoring scheme. Three are particularly relevant.

(a) European Parliament reports

First, as already mentioned, the European Parliament has embraced the role of monitor for both institutions *and* Member States alike. Since 1993 it has produced general reviews on the situation within the Member States as well as the Community institutions.[69] However, whether or not the Parliament has been constrained by lack of resources (as intimated above) reports of difficulties in Member States are invariably covered sketchily if specified in any detail at all. Even the information produced by the assigned rapporteur is couched in such vague terms that the notion of scrutiny is difficult to discern from the process.

Reports delivered at the end of the 1990s and into the new millennium attempted to place more pressure on Member States to live up to the similar values espoused externally. There has been explicit recognition that 'if the promotion of human rights outside the Union is to be credible, we must begin by examining the human rights situation at home. Numerous reports remind us that there is not always complete congruence between the ideals as they are printed in international Conventions and national Constitutions vis-à-vis the situation experienced by citizens and residents in Member States'.[70]

Nonetheless, the vagueness of the reports continues to undermine the Parliament's intentions. Similarly, the fact that the Parliament operates independently of the Commission and Council weakens the effect of its actions. Externally, the whole weight of the Community is behind its practice. Politically and economically it is imbued with a severe authority, whatever cynical view of the Community's presence in the world one may

---

[69] See, for instance, *Annual Reports on Respect for Human Rights in the European Union 1993* A4-124/94, *1994* A4-0223/96, *1995* A4-0112/97 etc. See, generally, R. Rack and S. Lausegger, 'The Role of the European Parliament: Past and Future' in Alston *et al* (eds), note 31 above, at 801–37.

[70] Committee on Citizens' Freedoms and Rights, Justice and Home Affairs, *Annual Report on Respect for Human Rights in the European Union (1998–1999)* (2000) A5-0050/2000 at 20.

have. Scrutiny by the Parliament simply does not possess that capacity. The Parliament recognizes as much. It has called for an integrated and dialogic approach to monitoring that is already applied in development and accession policies.[71] Little perceivable headway has been made to realize the Parliament's demands. Its scrutiny continues to be fundamentally deficient in comparison with the external processes examined.

(b) The Council's Annual Reports

Secondly, the Council has instituted *Annual Reports on Human Rights*, the first of which was delivered in October 1999. The expressed aim was to 'enhance the transparency of the Union's human rights policies'.[72] But the Report then went on, almost perversely, to state that it 'concentrates on the EU's external relations'.[73] The only concession to the charge of inconsistency was to acknowledge that 'the picture would be incomplete without at least making a reference to EU action related to developments in the EU area'.[74] The one matter subjected to internal scrutiny was that of racism.

Such a startling decision to focus almost entirely upon external human rights activities only served to enhance the condition of incoherence. The attention paid to racism fell into the category of cliché in that it was the exception that proved the rule. Rather than tackling one element of distinction as an illustration of an overall intention, the Report became an exercise in reiterating that scrutiny on human rights was reserved almost exclusively for those *outside* the Community.

The 1999 Report was criticized at the first European Human Rights Forum of November/December 1999 for its failure to consider the internal dimension.[75] As a result the *European Union Annual Report on Human Rights 2000* amended its approach.[76] It included a 'substantial section devoted to human rights within the European Union'.[77] It even conceded that the 'European Union is aware that it must begin by applying to itself the principles for which it stands'.[78] A belated admission it has to be said and not entirely without a sense of begrudging acceptance but the possibility presented itself that the Community was finally responding to the conditions of incoherence on the question of scrutiny.

---

[71] See ibid at 24–5.   [72] *EU Annual Report on Human Rights 1999* 11380/1/99 at 1.
[73] Ibid.   [74] Ibid.
[75] Human Rights Discussion Forum, 30 November–1 December 1999, at 29, ironically available on the Community's website under external relations (see http://europa.eu.int/comm/external_relations/human_rights/conf/forum1/report.pdf).
[76] Council, note 2 above.
[77] Ibid at 5.   [78] Ibid.

A brief examination of the 2000 Report and its treatment of the internal and external policies, however, suggests that a sense of irony hangs over the exercise. The Report *again* made clear in its introduction that 'its contents are primarily focused on the external activities of the European Union and its role on the international stage'.[79] Internal human rights matters were reviewed only on a thematic basis, racism once again taking the lead, with individual Member States *not once* receiving any critical mention. In contrast, external matters were peppered with references to actions taken against third countries. Common positions adopted under the Common Foreign and Security Policy, the issuance of *démarches* and declarations, the institution of political dialogue, and the activation of human rights clauses in various external trade and co-operation agreements, all specified those countries subjected to criticism for their human rights failures.

On the face of it, therefore, the 2000 Report contributed to the entrenchment rather than the dispersal of the conditions of incoherence. When the Report restated the legal bases for the Community's human rights policies it reiterated the universality of rights and confirmed that 'the principle of respect for national sovereignty should not be used by governments to absolve them from their obligations to respect human rights and fundamental freedoms'.[80] It then proceeded to set out the legal authority for Community action in relation to human rights. Article 2 TEU was quoted confirming that one of the objectives is to 'strengthen the protection of the rights and interests of the nationals of its Member States'. Article 6(1) and (2) TEU were mentioned as establishing the founding principle of respect for human rights and committing the Community to respect 'fundamental rights'. Article 7 TEU, it said, laid down 'a procedure to monitor respect for human rights and fundamental freedoms by Member States'.[81] Article 13 EC Treaty was referred to as specifically enabling the Community to 'take appropriate action to combat discrimination'.

And yet the final proviso stated by the Report that has the effect of negating much of all the precedents cited, provided the official explanation for the difference in internal/external approaches. It stated '[n]onetheless, the protection and promotion of human rights is primarily a matter for the Member States of the Union, in accordance with their own judicial systems'.

'Nonetheless'. 'Primarily'. These words could easily be missed or discounted and yet they signify so much. They summarize the sense of

---

[79] Council, note 2 above.   [80] Ibid at 8.   [81] Ibid at 9.

contingency applied in practice with regard to the respect and promotion of 'universal' human rights. They infer that despite all the eloquent descriptions of the Community's need to be involved in human rights matters its actions have no place with regard to its Member States. In effect they confirm the abrogation of the Community's responsibility (a responsibility acknowledged in international law terms as the Report confirms)[82] with regard to its own constituent states. They also make quite plain that even where the Community may be involved internally its role is always a subsidiary one. The sentence establishes in effect that even the European Court of Justice is *not* the site for determining questions of human rights. That is reserved for the Member States' own judicial systems.

In making these statements the Community effectively identified the conditions and dimensions of incoherence rather than addressed them. For externally, the provisos outlined have much less application. Indeed, it is a constituting principle of foreign affairs that the Member States and the Community will act in concert, rather than allow the Member States to hold the 'primary' position. More importantly, as Chapters 2 and 3 have shown, the Community has *assumed* a leading role in significant areas of external human rights policies. Practice therefore has determined that the notion of primary actors occupies little time for the Community in the external human rights realm.

The 2001 and 2002 Reports did nothing to alter the situation. Instead, being the third and fourth of their kind, they appeared to be taking on a consistent, institutional form. Their layout now appears to be settled and the arguments presented unchanged. They remain steadfastly focused on 'the EU's external relations and on its role on the international stage'.[83] Internal 'themes' are considered, with racism again being first on the list but no mention is made of individual Member States in these respects. The only change is the reference to a policy of 'mainstreaming' human rights into all aspects of policy, whether internal or external, a meaningless, objectionable, institutional term that speaks of management not principle, of bureaucratic niceties not fundamental changes in approach. Without the requisite definitions and coherent institutional conditions for scrutiny that can shape and direct the application of human rights throughout all

---

[82] Ibid. The Report states that the 'EU is committed to continuing to work in the UN and within the European framework to improve the implementation of the principles enshrined in human rights instruments, notably the Universal Declaration of Human Rights and the core human rights covenants and conventions'.

[83] Council, *EU Annual Report on Human Rights* 2001 12163/01 at 5.

manifestations of Community and Member State activity the idea of 'mainstreaming' remains vapid and insulting to the intelligence of all concerned observers.

(c) *European Monitoring Centre for Racism and Xenophobia*

Clearly the issue of racism has taxed the Community for some time. It has been identified as a key area of concern internally as well as externally. At the European Council in Florence in June 1996 a European Monitoring Centre for Racism and Xenophobia (EUMC) was accepted in principle as a necessary first step to provide a process of scrutiny *within* the Community on the issue. The following year a Council Regulation was adopted for the establishment of such a centre.[84] It was charged with monitoring the 'development of racism, xenophobia and anti-Semitism in the European Union', with providing 'up-to-date information to EU institutions, the Member States and political representatives, and to prompt them to take concrete political action'.[85] The resulting organization has been presented as a possible template for similar action in other rights fields.[86]

The basic premise of the EUMC was to monitor the condition of racism and xenophobia in Member States and to provide information on the subject. It has instituted a European Racism and Xenophobia Information Network (RAXEN), has established a website, has organized conferences on specific themes related to racism, has begun to commission research on the subject, has constructed a documentation centre, and has commenced the process of publishing annual reports on its findings.

On first view, therefore, it would appear that the external processes of scrutiny have been surpassed in this one important area. Indeed, the EUMC's first Annual Report gave an indication of the organization's promise. It provided a survey of the manifestations of racism and xenophobia in the Community, analysed the sociological and political and economic context, and reviewed the action taken to combat the problems by Member States and the Community alike.

However, a deeper analysis of the work of the EUMC and the methods it employs suggests that it is flawed as a precedent for addressing divergent standards of scrutiny. It may even be argued that the EUMC bolsters the

---

[84] Council Regulation 1035/97.

[85] EUMC, 'Giving Europe A Soul: Setting up the European Monitoring Centre on Racism and Xenophobia', *Annual Report* (1998) Part 1 at 14.

[86] See in particular Alston and Weiler, note 58 above, in which they refer to the EUMC as a valuable precedent for creating a general human rights monitoring agency (at 55–9).

continuing existence and influence of incoherent human rights policies. It represents part of the problem as well as potentially part of the solution.

The first issue of note relates to its official terms of reference. The Council Regulation bringing the EUMC into being reveals that the primary objective of the Centre is 'to provide the Community and its Member States, more especially within the fields referred to in Article 3(3), with objective, reliable and comparable data at European level on the phenomena of racism, xenophobia and anti-Semitism in order to help them when they take measures or formulate courses of action within their respective spheres of competence'.[87]

Article 3(3) states:

The information and data to be collected and processed, the scientific research, surveys and studies to be conducted or encouraged shall be concerned with the extent, development, causes and effects of the phenomena of racism and xenophobia, particularly in the following fields:
(a) free movement of persons within the Community;
(b) information and television broadcasts and the other media and means of communication;
(c) education, vocational training and youth;
(d) social policy including employment;
(e) free movement of goods;
(f) culture.

However, the scheme introduced does nothing to suggest that the EUMC's work will possess any force within the Community system. There is no mechanism for the Community institutions to pay any regard to the findings of the Centre, to consider its recommendations, to institute dialogue with or action against any Member State under Articles 6 or 7 TEU, or to evaluate or alter any subsisting laws or policies that are criticized on discriminatory or racist grounds. The EUMC is thus devoid of a framework within which its work might have a practical impact. It is entirely dependent on the Community and/or the Member States both taking note of its findings *and* acting upon any recommendations should the Centre be bold enough to make any. Because of these shortcomings the European Parliament has respectfully requested that the EUMC should have:

as its focus the investigation of discrimination as defined in Article 13 TEC deriving from national and European laws, policies and practices, and the

---

[87] Council Regulation 1035/97 Article 2.

drawing up of proposals designed to amend or abolish the latter for use by EU and national institutions; a duty under Article 2(b) and 2(e) of its founding regulation to monitor, evaluate and report regularly on developments concerning racism, xenophobia and anti-Semitism in all Member States and candidate countries, to draw specific attention to any related breach of the commitment to respect human and fundamental rights in Article 6 TEU and to advise on action under Article 7.[88]

Neither the Council nor the Commission has responded effectively to this request. The potential impact of the EUMC thus remains largely unfulfilled.

Even within its limited role there is evidence that the EUMC is further constrained. With regard to its investigatory functions the Centre is only charged with the acquisition of data. It is not empowered to take any action. Indeed, it has been given only a diplomatic role that requires a sensitive approach to the Member States. The result has so far been one of delicate manoeuvring whereby information about racism and discrimination is handled almost obliquely. In its first Annual Report, the EUMC confirmed that the information it provided by way of an overview of racism and xenophobia in the Member States was 'neither comprehensive nor complete'.[89] Given the limited ambition of the EUMC's initial activities this is none too surprising. But the means by which it acquired the data that *has* been revealed undermines even the limited nature of the Centre's preliminary aims. Five types of sources are identified by the EUMC as being used to prepare its reports:

(1) personal contributions provided by the members of the Management Board of the EUMC;
(2) official documents produced by national public bodies;
(3) country reports by the UN Committee for the Elimination of Racial Discrimination;
(4) country reports filed by the European Commission against Racism and Intolerance; and
(5) documents produced by specialist NGOs and press coverage.[90]

---

[88] *European Parliament Report on Countering Racism and Xenophobia in the European Union* final A5-0049/2000, para 8 at 14.
[89] EUMC, 'Looking Reality in the Face: the Situation regarding Racism and Xenophobia in the European Community', *Annual Report* (1998) Part II at 6.
[90] Ibid.

The indication from this list is that the EUMC is entirely engaged in a co-ordinating role. It does not *intrude* on Member States. Other than the faintly amateurish notion of 'personal contributions' it relies on publicly available information. In its Second Report in 1999, which uses the same sources, the Centre even acknowledges that:

at present there is a lack of uniformity and common definitions in the Member States for the purposes of data collection on the subjects of racism, racial violence or even racial/ethnic minorities. The way the acts of racism and discrimination are monitored and registered varies considerably from one Member State to another ... The EUMC therefore lacks the complete set of tools to measure and monitor racism effectively at a European level.[91]

The implication is twofold: first, the EUMC is heavily reliant on the Member States' reporting to ascertain the scope of the issues under consideration, and secondly, its powers are severely restricted at the most basic level, that of definition.

Together, therefore, the lack of an institutional mechanism for the Centre's work to be embraced and acted upon by the Community *and* the restrictive nature of its investigative practice suggests that, although a positive development, the EUMC does not in its present form represent a working precedent for Community schemes to address the incoherence that can be observed in the scrutiny of human rights. It remains to be seen whether the EUMC will advance its influence and redraw its terms of reference to become an agent for change.

The various initiatives described above do little to alter the systemic condition of incoherence. The problems are acknowledged but they remain in place. However, one further dimension of human rights practice needs to be considered, that of enforcement.

4.3 Distinctions in enforcement

The argument against the involvement of the Community in the internal human rights affairs of its Member States focuses mainly on questions of competence and jurisdiction. Direct involvement in such internal matters might be 'an invitation to a wholesale destruction of the jurisdictional boundaries between the Community and its Member States'.[92] However,

---

[91] *EUMC Annual Report 1999*, Summary at 2 (available at www.eumc.eu.int/publications/ar99/AR99S-EN.pdf).

[92] Alston and Weiler, note 58 above, at 23.

the Council itself is not shy in explicitly recognizing the 'relativity of the principle of non-interference'.[93] At Luxembourg, in 1991, it maintained that, 'different ways of expressing concern about violations of rights, as well as requests designed to secure those rights, cannot be considered as interference in the internal affairs of a State'.[94] The imposition of various forms of human rights conditionality, including that applied in the pre-accession strategy, has thus received formal and legal approval. The apparent contradiction between the arguments raised at the internal level and the practices at the external could not be clearer.

We have already witnessed in the scope of rights addressed and the scrutiny methods adopted that the approach to external states differs markedly from that applied internally. The possible enforcement of rights by the Community in respect of its Member States is of equal relevance. The failure, for instance, to acknowledge that collective rights (in the form of minority rights) are applicable within the Community will clearly have an impact on the legal and political ability or desire to enforce those rights.

Nonetheless, there are issues relating to enforcement internally that need to be analysed if the full extent of incoherence is to be determined. We have already seen that in the accession process, for instance, the system of enforcement is made explicit.[95] The Accession Partnerships impose a conditionality for entry and assistance on the basis of improvement and continuing respect for specific and general human rights issues. The threat has ensured that applicant states have changed practices and adhered to the human rights demands of the Community. If only at the level of rhetoric and law, applicants have responded to the Community's calls.[96] Those states that have failed to respond sufficiently, specifically Romania and Turkey, have remained firmly on the periphery, cast as regimes unworthy of entry for the present. In development policy also there has been a clear statement of possible graded measures that may be applied.[97] From positive measures to sanctions a wide range of action may be taken. Of particular note is the Commission's acknowledgement that a state's human rights

---

[93] Commission Communication to the Council and the European Parliament on the 'European Union and the External Dimension of Human Rights Policy: From Rome to Maastricht and Beyond,' COM(95) 567, at 10.

[94] Declaration on Human Rights, Luxembourg European Council 1991, quoted ibid at 10.

[95] See Agenda 2000 'For a Stronger and Wider Union' EC Bull Supp 5-1997.

[96] For a short review of the impact on rhetoric of applicant states, see Iver B. Neumann, 'European Identity, EU Expansion, and the Integration/Exclusion Nexus' *Alternatives* 23 (1998) 397–416.

[97] See Resolution of the Council and of the Member States, EC Bull 11-1991 122–3.

performance '*including economic, social and cultural rights*' (emphasis added) will be taken into account when deciding the quantity of funds to be made available under the development co-operation programmes.[98]

What comparable internal measures does the Community possess? Prior to the Treaty of Amsterdam the position was fairly plain. The internal condition of human rights was generally outside the jurisdiction of the Community. Only where actions by Member States were undertaken within the scope of Community law would the ECJ intervene. *Wachauf* first held that the possible intervention of the ECJ was in relation to Member States in the implementation of a Community provision.[99] *ERT* extended this to include circumstances when Member States derogated from a Community measure.[100]

That this extended principle has been subject to some amplification by the ECJ has not seriously undermined the expressed restriction on intervention reiterated by the EU Charter of Fundamental Rights. Article 51 ensures that the provisions of the Charter are addressed to Member States 'only when they are implementing Union law'. A fundamental restriction on enforcement action is thus inherent within the Community's legal structure. The fact that there 'are many, many areas where [Member States] face Community generated negative constraints or must respect positive prescriptions'[101] does not change the fact that the ECJ remains only vaguely involved in human rights cases. As Armin von Bogandy mentions, 'there seems to be a mismatch between the range and depth of the EU activities and the tiny number of human rights cases involving EU intrusion brought'.[102] Judicial enforcement is therefore highly restricted in practice. Indeed, A.G. Toth highlights the possibility that the standard required for human rights protection by an applicant state is greater than that demanded to remain a member once admitted, by noting, 'if the status quo continues the Court of Justice will not be in a position ... to ensure compliance with ... a whole range of vitally important human rights issues

---

[98] Communication from the Commission to the Council and the European Parliament on the 'EU's Role in Promoting Human Rights and Democratisation in Third Countries' COM(2001)252 final at 12.

[99] *Wachauf v. Germany* Case 5/88 [1989] ECR 2609.

[100] *ERT v. DEP and Sotirios Kouvelas* Case C-260/89 [1991] ECR I-2925.

[101] Giorgio Sacerdoti, 'The European Charter of Fundamental Rights: From a Nation-State Europe to a Citizens' Europe' *Columbia Journal of European Law* (2002) 37–52 at 48.

[102] Armin von Bogandy, 'The European Union as a Human Rights Organization? Human Rights and the Core of the European Union' *CMLRev* 37 (2000) 1307–38 at 1321.

(e.g. oppression of ethnic and other minorities) simply because they fall outside the scope of Community/Union competence'.[103]

The Treaty of Amsterdam might be said to have tried to alter the tendency to maintain the jurisdictional divide. The introduction of Article 7 (ex Article F.1) TEU seems to indicate a response for an enforcement mechanism that might correspond to that employed externally. As Manfred Nowak observes, the requirements for suspension set out, 'are, of course, even more stringent' than the accession criteria we have already encountered.[104] Koen Lenaerts further suggests that it is 'not very probable that the sanction mechanism as it now stands will easily be applied'.[105] This was confirmed with the strange case of Austria in 1999/2000.

The matter has been well covered by Heather Freeman and only the basic facts need to be revisited here.[106] In the aftermath of the assumption of power by the Freedom Party following the Austrian 1999 elections the Community was supposedly faced with the position of a potentially unsavoury regime taking control of one of its Member States' government. As an institution it possessed no authority to take any action. Article 7 TEU had not been breached. There may have been a prospect of the Freedom Party matching alleged racist rhetoric with practical initiatives but there was no evidence of a 'serious and persistent breach' of human rights having taken place. It was therefore left for the fourteen remaining Member States to institute their own sanctions. Official contacts were suspended, Austrian candidates seeking election in international organizations were not supported and Austria's ambassadors in the Member States' capitals had their status reduced.[107]

The 'sanctions' introduced had little impact. The Austrian government made various solemn statements of principle regarding respect for human rights and slowly Austria was welcomed back into the Community fold. Many were vexed, however, by the apparent impotence of the

---

[103] A.G. Toth, 'The European Union and Human Rights: the Way Forward' *CMLRev* 34 (1997) 491–529 at 529.

[104] Manfred Nowak, 'Human Rights Conditionality in the EU' in Alston *et al*, note 31 above, at 694.

[105] Koen Lenaerts, 'Fundamental Rights in the European Union' *EL Rev* 25/6 (2000) 575–600 at 587–8.

[106] Heather Berit Freeman, 'Austria: the 1999 Parliamentary Elections and the European Union Members' Sanctions' *Boston College International and Comparative Law Review* (2002) 109–24.

[107] Ibid at 118.

Community's institutions when faced with such a situation. A report was commissioned. The recommendation that emerged focused on an amendment to Article 7.[108] Preventive and monitoring procedures were necessary so that such an event 'would be dealt with within the EU from the very start'.[109] The suggestion was taken up and a revised Article 7 was agreed in the Treaty of Nice. The European Parliament immediately acted as though it was in force.

Article 7 now provides that the Commission, Council, or Parliament may determine whether there is a clear risk of a serious breach of human rights and if so can make 'appropriate recommendations' to the state concerned. In extreme circumstances the Council may then, acting by a qualified majority, decide to suspend certain rights available under the Treaty. By doing so it must, however, take into account the possible consequences of such a suspension on the rights and obligations of natural and legal persons. There is no mention of a systematic and continuing monitoring process. Nor is it clear what may amount to a serious breach.

Consequently, even the revised Article 7 is by any interpretation vastly more limited in scope and application than those measures adopted for putative Members in the pre-accession process or states receiving development assistance. The range of political and economic sanctions available to the Community to enforce human rights externally compared with that available internally is extensive. Politically, the publication of the results of the Commission's scrutiny process of the applicants and its 'consultation' with states under the Cotonou Agreement is a well-tested form of enforcement in itself. For instance, in respect of Haiti, Cote d'Ivoire, and Zimbabwe, the Community's demands for talks and its public identification of current rights problems have all been measures of enforcement in themselves.[110] The ability to 'name and shame' has been significant in international human rights practice since the United Nations developed its various reporting systems. In Europe the reporting process adopted under the European Convention on the Prevention of Torture is considered a key enforcement strategy.[111] But the Community has not adopted

---

[108] Report by Martti Ahtisaari, Jochen Frowein and Marcelino Oreja, 8 September 2000 (available at www.eumc.at/general/report-A/report-en.pdf).
[109] Ibid at 34.
[110] See Council Decisions 2001/131/EC, 2001/510/EC and 2002/148/EC respectively.
[111] For a recent review of the Convention's activities, see Jim Murdoch, 'The European Convention for the Prevention of Torture and Inhuman or Degrading Treatment or Punishment: Activities in 2000' Supp *EL Rev* 26 (2001).

a scheme internally to match these measures. The European Parliament's attempts to fill the void do not compare favourably with the external approach. They are neutered by the fact that they are not supported by the powers of enforcement or persuasion available to the Commission. Institutional dialogue, economic assistance (or its withdrawal), and ultimately the threat of exclusion are reserved for external states producing a highly persuasive package that can operate to change human rights conditions.

This is the key point. The conjunction of strategies open to the Community is simply unparalleled internally. The highly unlikely event of interference in the affairs of Member States on human rights issues except in the most extreme situations only serves to emphasize the distinction. One only has to look at the absence of any involvement in the practices of the United Kingdom in Northern Ireland in the 1970s, for instance, or the current racist tendencies in various Member States to which I have referred, to see that interference has always been and presently remains outside the Community's concern. It is difficult to predict what it would take for the Community to become so involved. It is even more difficult to conceive how the Community would react given its historically constrained approach to internal affairs.

4.4 Conclusion

The scope of the distinctions between the external and internal policies underlines the scale of incoherence in the Community's practices. But why has this state of affairs arisen? Several standard explanations have emerged from European commentators. Chapter 5 examines these accounts with a view to determining whether they provide a satisfactory and adequate analysis of the condition.

5

Explaining Incoherence: the Orthodox Arguments

The previous chapter makes the case that incoherence between the Community's internal and external human rights practices and policies is both significant and deeply imbedded. Although the full extent of the distinction might rarely, if ever, have been acknowledged institutionally or academically there has been a willingness to accept that some disparity exists. As a consequence, various arguments can be constructed from what is a highly limited literature on the subject to explain the condition. However, few if any of the commentaries have sought to acknowledge, let alone look deeply into, the incoherence phenomenon. Nonetheless, the purpose of this chapter is to explore these extracted interpretations and to consider their contribution to aiding our understanding of the issue.

The arguments evident from miscellaneous sources tend to revolve around four interconnecting propositions. They can be usefully characterized as follows.

First, incoherence is the result of a legal delineation of competence that has seen human rights acquire a much more significant presence externally than they do internally. Accordingly, the Community, constrained by its legal framework, has adopted different practices and policies to mirror its distinct interior/exterior authority.

Secondly, in an effort to preserve the Council of Europe and European Convention on Human Rights (ECHR) system, one fondly regarded as a successful provider of human rights protection within Europe, a conscious decision has been made to leave the established regime unchallenged, at least in respect of the Community's Member States. Externally, where the ECHR possesses limited application, the Community is not constrained by such sensibilities. It can and should act as a promoter of human rights in its capacity as a collective manifestation of Western European concern. Distinct approaches have arisen as a reflection of this difference in legal and political emphasis.

Thirdly, political reality dictates that the condition of human rights in the Community as a whole and Member States individually is far superior to that experienced in other less developed parts of the world. Whilst on the one hand there may be little need to waste resources or legislative time on adopting a Community-led approach to internal human rights issues, on the other the Community has a duty to act externally as an effective ambassador and advocate for human rights. In this capacity it can complement the work of organizations such as the United Nations and the International Labour Organisation. There is little surprise therefore that, at least in terms of enforcement and scrutiny, action taken by the Community will follow these separate political motivations.

Fourthly, the tenets of governmental rational choice dictate that providing the Community with unlimited authority to act on human rights matters internally would be tantamount to serving up all vestiges of national sovereignty to the European project. This would be politically unpalatable. To avoid such an eventuality, internal powers need to be restricted. Externally, the concerns are less obtrusive. In some fields, such as the foreign affairs of Member States, there may be concern over interference by the Community but generally the political cost of Community activity abroad is negligible. Hence, a distinct, or rather incoherent, approach is the product of a rational decision to distribute powers in such a way as to reflect the position most acceptable to the Member States.

All of these arguments might be mustered either individually or in association with each other to justify the development of an internal/external human rights policy distinction. Each warrants further analysis in order to see how far they take us in determining whether they do indeed explain, or merely describe, the condition.

5.1 Legal competence

It would not be an undue distortion to suggest that the foremost argument advanced by commentators for the distinction between the Community's human rights activities centres on the issue of competence. Essentially, the powers invested in the Community have always been a matter of dispute and negotiation. Indeed, the theme of competence is likely to remain a point of contention for some time to come with human rights as a discrete and live subject within that debate.[1] Nevertheless, for our purposes the argument is straightforward. The Community has simply never been provided with the authority or competence to act on human rights with legislative or practical impunity. Those powers it has acquired or been granted have emerged over time, have resulted from progressive negotiation between actors (as well as some careful jurisprudence), and have developed along incoherent patterns accordingly. Such is the understandable, even predictable, result of policy constructed through intergovernmental bargaining in reaction to the needs of governments, institutions, and political actors.

As a consequence of this haphazard approach to human rights decision-making, emanating from the original silence on the subject in the Treaty of Rome, the orthodox argument suggests there have evolved different streams of competence. Externally, the authority to develop a human rights presence was assumed, as we have seen, particularly in the histories of accession and development policies, as the Community's general activities in external affairs became more sophisticated. With occasional reinforcement of those acquired powers through the Treaties and the institutions making proclamations of one kind or another,[2] the position became more concrete. Article 11 (ex Article J.1) TEU, for instance, maintained that a common foreign and security policy shall include the objective of developing and consolidating 'democracy and the rule of law, and respect for human rights and fundamental freedoms'. Article 6(2) TEU generally required the Community to respect rights as guaranteed by the ECHR and 'as they result from the constitutional traditions common to the Member States as general principles of law'. We have also seen that in development policy and in trade relations the Community has either been authorized to operate in relation to human rights issues or has assumed these powers over time.

The ability or competence of the Community to act in the field of human rights was specifically supported by the adoption of Council Regulations 975 and 976 of 1999.[3] Although a response to *United Kingdom v. Commission*[4]

---

[1] It was a key issue for the Convention on the Future of Europe and the 2003 Draft Constitutional Treaty. For the latter, see http://european-convention.eu.int/bienvenue.asp?lang=EN&Content=

[2] For a prime example, see the Commission's Communication to the Council and the European Parliament on the 'European Union and the External Dimension of Human Rights Policy: from Rome to Maastricht and Beyond' (1995) EC Bull Suppl 25–41.

[3] Council Regulations 975/1999 [1999] OJ L-120/1 and 976/1999 [1999] OJ L-120/8.

[4] *UK v. Commission* Case C106/96 [1998] ECR I-2729.

so as to provide an authority for significant expenditure for otherwise non-specifically sanctioned activities, these regulations had the effect of formalizing competence for the Community to operate in human rights promotion with respect to development co-operation and Community co-operation policy *vis-à-vis* third countries respectively.

Internally, explicit and implicit competence has been deliberately kept under tight control. In the areas of judicial interpretation, Treaty design, and in institutional rhetoric there has been a concerted effort to restrict the Community's ability to develop a co-ordinated human rights policy. Actions have thus been confined to individual initiatives usually authorized by specific Treaty provisions.[5]

The argument for the internal/external divide may thus derive on one level from a positive law perspective. Competence is determined by the legal basis for action. That basis has developed, for whatever reason, so as to provide the Community with restricted powers internally and vastly more liberal authority externally. Hence the incoherence that can now be observed. Of course, this is a simplified interpretation but the literature that has emerged on human rights competence rarely goes deeper than a description of powers assigned to the Community in law. Even the EU Charter of Fundamental Rights was drafted so as to ensure the balance of competence was undisturbed. The Charter provided that it did not 'establish any new power or task for the Community or the Union, or modify powers and tasks defined by the Treaties'.[6]

The position was affirmed and even extended in the Draft Constitutional Treaty (DCT) issued in May-June 2003.[7] Article II-51(1) DCT provided that the institutions and Member States shall 'respect the rights, observe the principles and promote the application [of the provisions of the Charter] in accordance with their respective powers and respecting the limits of the powers of the Union as conferred on it in the other Parts of the Constitution'. Article II-51(2) also stated that the Charter 'does not extend the field of application of Union law beyond the powers of the Union or

---

[5] See, for instance, the Racial Equality Directive 2000/43/EC designed to implement aspects of Article 13 EC Treaty introduced by the Treaty of Amsterdam. Some commentators have suggested these provide evidence of the Community's willingness to engage in select human rights issues. See, for instance, Leo Flynn, 'The Implications of Article 13 EC' *CML Rev* 36 (1999) 1127–52 and for a more optimistic reading Siobhan McInerney, 'Bases for Action Against Race Discrimination in EU Law' *EL Rev* 27 (2002) 72–9.

[6] Article 51 EU Charter of Fundamental Rights.

[7] For the text of the DCT, see note 1 above.

establish any new power or task for the Union, or modify powers and tasks defined in the other Parts of the Constitution'.

The workings of the Convention on the Future of Europe also confirmed the robust stance taken in devising this form of words.[8] There can be little doubt, therefore, that the status quo on human rights policy competence was intended to remain firmly controlled.

Joseph Weiler and Sybilla Fries have argued that notwithstanding the assumed nature of competence, the Treaty structure does provoke a reading that could enable the Community institutions to develop their internal rights presence more proactively.[9] They suggest a combination of three potential strategies. First, specific legal authorities provided by the Treaties, such as Articles 13 (ex Article 6(a)) and 141 (ex Article 119) EC Treaty, as well as clear human rights aspects of policy areas within the Community's exclusive or shared competence, provide liberty to instigate action. Indeed, they have already generated important human rights initiatives.[10] Secondly, Article 95 (ex Article 100a) EC Treaty might well sustain broader application in the search for the approximation of laws. By arguing that a failure to harmonize certain human rights standards would adversely affect the free movement principles of the Treaties, the Community would have the legitimate power to intervene in the relevant affairs of Member States. Thirdly, Article 308 (ex Article 235) EC Treaty might be interpreted in such a way as to encourage greater Community involvement in human rights matters within the strict application of Community law. This might extend into the internal dimension as well as the external. Provided the Community 'respected the current institutional balance', Weiler and Fries maintain, 'which avoided formal accession to the ECHR, which left intact the definition of the material contents of rights and their Community autonomy and which, critically, scrupulously remained within the field of Community law' it would be legally entitled to develop its human rights initiatives if it so chose.[11]

The Draft Constitutional Treaty of 2003 may well give further ammunition for Weiler and Fries' central suggestion that the Community could

---

[8] Working Group II had charge of the issue. For a reflection on these discussions see Andrew Williams, 'EU Human Rights Policy and the Convention on the Future of Europe: A Failure of Design?' *EL Rev* 28 (2003) 794–813.

[9] Joseph Weiler and Sybilla Fries, 'A Human Rights Policy for the European Community and Union: the Question of Competences' in Philip Alston *et al* (eds), *The EU and Human Rights* (Oxford: Oxford University Press, 1999) 147–65.

[10] For instance the directives that have emanated from Article 13 EC Treaty.

[11] Weiler and Fries, note 9 above, at 160.

adopt a more creative and thus more interventionist approach to human rights competence. Article I-2 DCT states that the 'Union is founded on values of respect for human dignity, liberty, democracy, the rule of law and respect for human rights'. Article I-3(1) DCT then holds that the 'Union's aim is to promote *its values* and the well-being of its peoples' (emphasis added). *Ergo* the new Union should be empowered to promote human rights regardless of context and across the interior/exterior divide.

Such a syllogistic reading can be supported by a number of statements made by the Community institutions in recent years. For instance, the Council's *Annual Report on Human Rights 2002* made the case that the 'protection and promotion of human rights constitute not only defining principles of the EU, but also form part of Community legislation'.[12] It went on to suggest that human rights were 'explicitly incorporated into and stated as common European objectives in the TEU' a step that represented 'a significant strengthening of human rights as a priority issue for the EU in its internal as well as external policies'.[13] Similarly, the Council's Athens Declaration 2003, which accompanied the Accession Treaty to admit ten new states to the Community in 2004, included the commitment to 'uphold and defend fundamental human rights, both inside and outside' the Community.[14]

Whether the linked provisions of the DCT, coupled with the encouraging rhetoric, would really overhaul the position adopted on competence, so explicitly determined by the DCT itself through its amendments to the EU Charter of Fundamental Rights, must be open to significant doubt. Indeed, the Council has recognized as much on a number of occasions. In its Legal Service's celebrated Opinion on legislation proposed to authorize Community action on human rights in external affairs, Gráinne de Búrca suggests it presented Community competence 'as an essentially negative set of standards to be judicially enforced rather than as a positive basis for political action'.[15] More recently, in its *Annual Report on Human Rights 2002*, the Council reprised previous statements that 'protection and promotion of human rights within the Member States of the Union are primarily a concern of the States themselves with due regard to their own judicial

---

[12] Council, *EU Annual Report on Human Rights 2002*.   [13] Ibid.

[14] Athens Declaration made at the Athens Informal European Council, 16 April 2003 (available at www.eu2003.gr/en/articles/2003/4/16/2531/index.asp?).

[15] See Gráinne de Búrca, *Setting Constitutional Limits to EU Competence* (Working Paper 2001/2, Francisco Lucas Pires Working Paper Series on European Constitutionalism). De Búrca's comment was based in part on Weiler and Fries' analysis, see note 9 above.

systems and international obligations'.[16] Equally, the emphasis placed on the application of the principle of subsidiarity is likely to restrict any radical interpretative move.[17] Nonetheless, the scope for argument that the Community's competence on internal human rights issues may have been widened, the position as advocated by Weiler and Fries, does seem to have been given some much needed assistance.

Notwithstanding this hopeful and imaginative interpretation, the fact remains for present purposes that incoherence is displayed as a product of negotiated powers reflecting competing interests and concerns and changing priorities. No doubt any Constitutional Treaty that finally emerges after 2004, with its likely attachment to different levels of competence depending on policy area, will give credence to this view.[18]

But does the competence argument rehearsed above really explain the incoherence outlined in this book? Certainly it describes the condition. By pointing to the constitutional dispositions it succeeds in portraying the internal/external divide as a legal construction. But fundamentally it fails to determine *why* the edifice of distinction should have arisen in the first place, why each of the multiple decisions that have led to the current position were made. Neither does it explain the reasons why the Community should be so relatively free in its acquisition of external authority, as opposed to its highly restricted internal approach. By failing to address these questions the argument ignores the political choice(s) that lay at the root of the legal and constitutional framework that continues to be assembled. It also perpetuates the understanding that human rights activities are subjugated to other interests rather than holding a central and principled position in the Community's affairs. Arguing that the general distribution of competences reflects the desire to preserve national identity by maintaining the Member States' 'leeway for responsible decisions'[19] does not address the core problem. After all, what aspect of national identity is truly challenged when human rights are portrayed as part of the European heritage and possessed of universal character?

---

[16] See note 12 above, at 13.

[17] For a review of issues of subsidiarity and human rights in the Community, see Leonard Besselink, 'Entrapped by the Maximum Standard: On Fundamental Human Rights, Pluralism and Subsidiarity in the European Union' *CML Rev* (1998) 629–80.

[18] The DCT of 2003 envisaged three fundamental levels of competence: exclusive, shared, and complementary measures. However, human rights receive no specific mention in these designated areas. See Articles I-11 to I-17 DCT, note 1 above.

[19] Udo di Fabio, 'Some Reflections on the Allocation of Competences Between the European Union and its Member States' *CML Rev* 39 (2002) 1289–301 at 1294.

In failing to explain satisfactorily why the incoherence has developed as it has we are left with an incomplete appreciation of the phenomenon. Whether the position can be rectified with reference to the other arguments considered below remains to be seen.

5.2 Legal reverence

The second argument can perhaps best be characterized as a form of legal reverence. It is based on a belief that the Community's interference in the human rights affairs of its Member States, beyond that which is possible under existing competence structures and within the realm of Community law, has been intentionally restricted so as to preserve the integrity of the Council of Europe and ECHR human rights system. As this regime has achieved something of an iconic status over the past half century, with the role of the European Court of Human Rights (ECtHR) in particular representing for many a vital contribution to human rights, any transference of authority to the Community might undo decades of important advances in human rights promotion. As Antonio Cassese suggests, 'no one can deny that the [ECtHR] is playing a pivotal role in Europe ... contributing to the creation of an extensive region ... where arbitrary or discriminatory action by governments is being strongly curtailed'.[20] There is small wonder that jurists and human rights activists might not want to see the ECHR system undermined or challenged by the Community.[21]

Such an argument presupposes that any greater involvement by the Community in the human rights affairs of its Member States would be unlikely to complement the ECHR system. Rather, it might be at best a distraction or worse a dilution of standards and practices refined over the past half-century. This negative impression emanates from a well-established body of critique levelled against the approach in particular of the ECJ to human rights. J. Coppel and A. O'Neill, in their seminal article, made the case that fundamental human rights were subordinated to the demands of economic integration.[22] The latter being the Community's focus, its 'fundamental priority', the language of human rights protection

---

[20] Antonio Cassese, *International Law* (Oxford: Oxford University Press 2001) 367.

[21] See, for instance, Francis Jacobs, *The European Convention on Human Rights*, 2nd edn (Oxford: Clarendon Press, 1996).

[22] J. Coppel and A. O'Neill, 'The ECJ: Taking Rights Seriously' *Legal Studies* 12 (1992) 227–45.

can be seen as 'no more than a vehicle for the Court to extend the scope and impact of European law'.[23] Although subject to counter-argument, there is little dispute that the economic and political interests operating in the Community are by far a more overt influence on human rights development than apparent in the ECHR regime. Consequently, should the Community adopt an intrusive stance with regard to human rights in the Member States without restriction, the more 'pure' form of rights assessment offered by the ECHR might be threatened, particularly if the Community develops as an alternative rather than complementary system.

The chance of a challenge through the Community's involvement would be particularly irksome for those who have viewed the ECHR regime as a sophisticated framework that has benefited from massive moral and legal investment over the last 50 years. So much legal time and effort has been applied towards the development of the ECHR system, the operation and reform of the ECtHR, and the development of a pan-European forum for new human rights standards formation, that any move that would undermine its efficacy and authority would be highly dispiriting. The ECHR system remains for some a beacon of virtue amidst an otherwise discredited global failure to develop functioning and effective human rights regimes. It is even promoted as worthy of replication beyond Europe. Hence, a number of voices have been raised warning of the 'loss' that would be experienced should the Community and its Member States 'go their own way in protecting human rights'.[24]

The legal arguments for maintaining the Community's restricted involvement in the internal affairs of the Member States have been reflected, to some extent, in the debate incited by the Laeken Declaration and the Convention on the Future of Europe. A key question posed was whether or not the Community should accede to the ECHR. The Working Group assigned to examine the question summarized the case for accession in three parts: first, so as to 'give a strong political signal of coherence between the Union and the "greater Europe" reflected in the Council of Europe and its pan-European human rights system';[25] secondly, to provide citizens with protection against acts of Community institutions; thirdly, to promote 'harmonious development of the case law of the two European Courts in

---

[23] Ibid at 245.
[24] H.G. Schermers, 'The New European Court of Human Rights' *CML Rev* 35 (1998) 3–8 at 6.
[25] *Final Report of Working Group II* (2002) CONV 354/02 at 11–12.

human rights matters'.[26] In recommending that the Community should be provided with the authority to negotiate accession, the working Group made it quite explicit, however, that there would be no extension to the Community's competences 'let alone to the establishment of a general competence of the Union on fundamental rights' as a result.[27] Whilst clearly supporting the position on the distribution of competences reinforced by the DCT, the recommendation also echoed the concern to maintain the moral and legal predominance of the ECHR system. The restricted internal human rights mandate for the Community was to be preserved constitutionally, particularly when read in conjunction with Article 51 of the EU Charter of Fundamental Rights.

Whether or not this is a realistic stance to take, given the expansion of Community law into so many areas of activity and thus the *de facto* increase in competence for the Community, the argument for a curtailed internal presence to preserve the ECHR system remains alive. Of course, this does not provide any justification for similar limitations being placed on the Community's external human rights affairs. In that context the ECHR system is not generally viewed as under threat from the Community's actions. Its preservation is not therefore an obstacle to the development of a meaningful policy in foreign matters. Hence the understandable disparity in the powers and methods adopted by the Community.

The logical interpretation offered above starts to become strained when we examine the one area of external matters where the ECHR has assumed an important presence, namely in the accession process. As we have seen, applicant states are required to accede to the ECHR as a precondition for entry. Even so, becoming a signatory has never been seen as sufficient. A tacit recognition is made that the ECHR system does not represent the pinnacle of human rights protection. It provides an important series of norms and human rights interpretations but further procedures and schemes to promote human rights in practice have always been deemed essential. If the ECHR system is considered sacrosanct and worthy of conservation why is it not assigned a similar position on the margins of entry? The simple answer is that the ECHR system has never been considered sufficient for safeguarding human rights in Europe. It is an important precedent and provides a judicial focus. But it does not, and perhaps is incapable of, installing an effective human rights regime alone. That task is left to individual Member States in the Community, to civil

[26] *Final Report of Working Group II* (2002) CONV 354/02 at 11–12.   [27] Ibid at 13.

society in general, and to other agencies such as the United Nations. From a strategic perspective, therefore, the argument that reverence for the ECHR system has induced a reticence for the Community to assume greater responsibility for human rights matters internally is inadequate. It does not explain why such a distinction can be drawn between Members and applicants. It does not explain why the Community, which possesses the capacity to provide an important contribution to the development of a human rights protective scheme in Europe, should be constrained internally and encouraged externally. It does not explain the sheer depth of incoherence that is now manifest.

5.3 Distinct conditions

The third argument is a simple if not simplistic one. Paul Craig and Gráinne de Búrca rehearse it very briefly by pointing to the suggestion that incoherence results from an appreciation that 'there are more severe and more fundamental human rights problems occurring outside the EU than within'.[28] In other words, in the external sphere conditions are qualitatively and even quantitatively different from that experienced inside the Community. Consequently, the scale and breadth of action in the affairs with third states is of necessity a response to a perceived human rights 'reality'. Internally the problems are of a different order. Less in scale and, it might be inferred, less worrying, they demand a much more restrained response, one that pays due regard to Member States' 'autonomous human rights regimes, given their crucial function in the national legal orders and political cultures'.[29]

There are two main dimensions to this position, both of which suggest the argument is flawed as a satisfactory argument for incoherence.

First, a general assumption is made that underpins the central argument, namely that external conditions invariably and axiomatically warrant greater concern. To support such a position one only need cite the well-known examples of genocide and mass human rights abuses that have occurred outside the Community since the 1970s. From Uganda under Amin, Cambodia under Pol Pot, Chile under Pinochet, to the regimes of

---

[28] Paul Craig and Gráinne de Búrca, *EU Law: Text, Cases and Materials*, 3rd edn (Oxford: Oxford University Press 2003) 355.

[29] Armin von Bogandy, 'The European Union as a Human Rights Organization? Human Rights and the Core of the European Union' *CML Rev* 37 (2000) 1307–38 at 1319.

apartheid in South Africa and the dictatorial rule of Saddam Hussein, Mobutu, Banda, and numerous others, the list is nauseously and tragically long. Few would thus deny the noble intentions expressed by the Community, particularly since the end of the Cold War, to intervene in these and similar situations using whatever influence and power it can muster. The fact that not every country or regime outside the Community is afflicted by horrific human rights conditions is irrelevant. Rather, the weight of these and other extreme examples justify the determination that the Community's 'one boundary is democracy and human rights' and that it has a moral obligation to intervene.[30]

The flip-side to this position is the belief that no mass human rights abuses have taken place within the Community since its formation. After the horrors of the Second World War those states who became Members of the Community embraced regimes that respected and promoted human rights within their borders. Consequently, any internal replication of the powers and methods of scrutiny and enforcement used externally would be redundant and unnecessarily interventionist. The condition of human rights in the world simply dictates that different approaches should be applied.

There is, of course, a clear hypocrisy in such a position. It is based on the false premise that the condition of human rights within the Community is not worthy of scrutiny because the dangers of abuse are restrained. Such an underlying assumption is both dangerous and short-sighted. Although evidence of human rights violations on the scale of the examples cited above is absent, this hardly warrants any complacency within the Community. There are many areas where the records of Member States are dubious to say the least. A prime example relates to the problem of racism. Despite years of initiatives and pronouncements designed to combat the problem Europe still suffers acutely from endemic racism. The European Commission against Racism and Intolerance (ECRI) reported in 2002 that the 'persistence of racial discrimination, which is closely linked to the lack of effective anti-discrimination legislative provisions in most Member States, is a fundamental problem in Europe'.[31] Amnesty International similarly reported in 2003 that discrimination against ethnic minorities was rife in Europe, identifying France, Belgium, Spain, and the United Kingdom

---

[30] See Declaration of the Laeken Council (available at http://european-convention.eu.int/pdf/LKNEN.pdf).

[31] *ECRI Annual Report 2002* (available at www.coe.int/T/E/human_rights/Ecri/1-ECRI/1-Presentation_of_ECRI/4-Annual_Report_2002/Annual_Report_2002.asp#TopOfPage).

amongst other Community states, as particular offenders.[32] Even if the Community has taken it upon itself to make an exception of racism vis-à-vis its intervention in internal human rights matters, by having as a starting assumption that Member States should remain autonomous in dealing with these problems provokes a sense of moral disengagement for the Community. One can see that the ambivalent position undermines those initiatives it promotes. In 2003, for instance, the much heralded racial equality directive,[33] designed to give partial effect to Article 13 EC Treaty, was threatened by the lack of interest in its introduction seemingly displayed by Member States. The Commission claimed it was 'deeply concerned that Member States have so far failed to write new EU rules on racial discrimination into national law' thus missing the deadline of 19 July 2003.[34]

Any blanket presumption of innocence to the extent that it precludes effective monitoring and methods for intervention at an early rather than an acute stage must therefore represent a dangerous position to adopt.

The second dimension of the 'distinct conditions' argument also generates cause for concern. This focuses on the appreciation that Member States should have their individual cultures and legal structures respected, even in the application of Community law, in partial acknowledgement of the general ethos of 'unity in diversity'. Although 'human rights' as a collective concept binds all the Member States together, there is a wide range of interpretations that requires individual autonomy. Any central attempt to apply a universal strategy for all rights across all countries and in all situations would jeopardize what is otherwise an acceptable and even indispensable aspect of the Community ethos. A generous margin of appreciation needs to be preserved if diversity is to have any meaning in the new European construct. Should the Community develop a centralizing and harmonizing policy approach internally the resulting resistance would be divisive.

This is not to say that a margin of appreciation is not recognized externally as well. Undoubtedly the Community is not concerned with minor differences in human rights conditions in specific countries. It reserves its high profile external interventions for situations of gross human rights violation. But this only reflects human rights activity at one level, that of

[32] *Amnesty International Report 2003* (available at http://web.amnesty.org/report2003/index-eng).
[33] Racial Equality Directive 2000/ 43/EC.
[34] European Commission Press release IP/03/1047 (available at http://europa.eu.int/rapid/start/cgi/guesten.ksh?p_action.gettxt=gt&doc=IP/03/1047|0|RAPID&lg=EN&display=).

the extreme position. What it does not explain is the scope of incoherence. Both the different interpretations placed on the meaning of human rights that are propounded to be universal and the Community's breadth of interventions in external human rights matters go far beyond the extreme. In terms of its methods of scrutiny and monitoring, in terms of its measures of enforcement and in terms of its promotional activities, the Community intervenes regularly, with purpose and across the human rights spectrum. It does not restrict itself to the 'gross' or extreme position. If Armin von Bogandy's suggestion that third states should only be the subjects of intrusion to counter 'grave human rights violations' were adopted, the principle of non-interference that underpins the approach to Member States would at least be consistently applied.[35] The fact is the Community takes no such stand. It may well reserve its most severe measures for particularly gross human rights positions (although by no means applied consistently) but it continues to adopt policies that move far beyond such instances. The previous chapters outlining human rights in development assistance and accession policies indicate strongly the breadth of issues that are the subject of concern and regular interference.

There is little here that therefore takes us beyond a description of incoherence. We are left to surmise why basic assumptions are made in favour of the Member States and why the Community feels capable of imposing increasingly interventionist strategies across the external human rights plain.

5.4 *Realpolitik*

The final argument is in essence a representation of *realpolitik*. Three forms present themselves, all of which are interwoven.

First, the general political critique that the path of integration represents an unwholesome trend towards European centralization has particular application to human rights. Those who view the Community with scepticism, preferring to emphasize the economic aspects of the Project, oppose any further encroachment into the political and social realms that human rights inhabit. Any attempt to construct a union that would interfere with such sensitive issues as human rights would inevitably be opposed as an unnecessary incursion into national sovereignty. Given the high levels of

---

[35] von Bogandy, note 29 above, at 1319.

political and public opposition to the European Project as a whole in various Member States,[36] there is little wonder that a significant political decision to subject national authorities to analysis by a bureaucratic centre leading to possible high-profile public disputes on the imposition of values, would be considered undesirable. Externally, it is doubtful that the Community's involvement in purely human rights matters would attract such political opposition, even though the restriction of individual Member States' ability to operate autonomously in external affairs when deemed of national interest certainly provokes a similar political backlash. Rather, the notion of collective or centralized action in the face of human rights violation abroad is likely to receive substantial popular support, making sense as it does to optimize the impact and sweep of action.

Secondly, it may also be argued that Member States cannot justify further including the Community in the systems of multiple internal scrutiny and enforcement that are already in place. From the national institutions to the ECHR system, from the Community law aspects to the United Nations treaty system, sufficient coverage of human rights matters is already assured. Expanding the interference of the Community would be hard to excuse. It would not only entail more report writing and investigation but it would be the Member States who would have to foot the bill. In external affairs the situation is different. By co-ordinating monitoring and enforcement strategies amongst the Member States through the Community, costs can be shared and procedures rationalized.

Thirdly, criticism of governments in relation to human rights matters can be politically highly embarrassing. It creates tensions that are difficult to deflect, particularly when the criticisms emanate from an external source like the Community. Having an acute moral dimension, human rights are endowed with a peculiar force that other concepts perhaps do not own. In Joseph Weiler's terms they are 'part of social identity about which people care a great deal'.[37] Their violation can be accompanied by severe and sustained political and public outrage. The difficulties are enhanced when the Community's own terms are applied. At a time when the promotion of diversity is encouraged, when national identity is recognized as worthy of preservation, when conflict over human rights issues might constitute a divisive factor, removing human rights from the Community's internal

---

[36] See, for instance, the analysis provided in M. Franklin, M. Marsh, and L. McLaren, 'Uncorking the Bottle: Popular Opposition to European Unification in the Wake of Maastricht' *JCMS* (1994) 455–72.

[37] J.H.H. Weiler, *The Condition of Europe* (Cambridge: Cambridge University Press, 1999) 102.

political scene would seem to make sense. Thus, beyond the rhetoric a practical response is called for that dictates a severely restricted approach to human rights within the Community. In external matters the only embarrassment is likely to arise when examining any complicity in violations attributable to Member States' actions. But on those occasions, witness the involvement of the United Kingdom and Spain in the invasion of Iraq in 2003, criticism is generally avoided.

These intertwining rationales suggest that the incoherence between the Community's internal and external human rights policies and practices are the product of a political pragmatism. The application of *realpolitik* has encouraged the distinction to appear and imbed itself into the Community structure, fulfilling the needs of all governments to protect their popular appeal and stave off any destructive criticism of their administrations.

Although these political arguments are persuasive they do not explain sufficiently why, on the one hand, the Community can present itself as an entity that respects and promotes a universal notion of human rights, and on the other maintains fundamental distinctions of definition and practice that undermine that position. Nor do they explain why there should be such sensitivity in the first place given the fundamental and non-negotiable nature of human rights that the Member States and the Community suggest determines their action. Why has the Community been so unwilling to establish any strategic involvement in the internal affairs of Member States *and* external scrutiny of its institutions that could match that which it applies beyond its borders? Why should a powerful new force in human rights for the European sphere be so unpalatable? Is the embarrassment factor really that strong across the European plane?

The *realpolitik* explanation is insufficient alone to answer these specific questions as well as those wider issues of human rights definition raised in the previous chapter.

5.5 Conclusion

Individually, the orthodox explanations for incoherence rehearsed above fail to provide a satisfactory understanding of the condition. The question remains, however, whether together they are both persuasive and comprehensive.

Undoubtedly, they do possess a cumulative force that analysts might rely upon to explain the development of diverging approaches. Even with their individual flaws, highlighted in each case above, when treated in sum they appear to cover a wide range of relevant legal and political dimensions. Why then might they be collectively unsatisfactory?

First, none of the suggested arguments have been constructed with an appreciation of the full extent of the incoherence revealed so far in this book. They have roots in the context of the more visible distinctions but do not tackle the deeper elements. They do not, for instance, help explain the institutional commitment to universality on the one hand and the application of unjustified disparities of definition on the other. Equally, they do not countenance the scope and depth of the distinction that has evolved. None succeed in fully explaining the progressive nature of the Community's external powers. They might indicate why internally there has been reticence in allowing the Community to adopt an interfering agenda but they do little to establish why such a relatively disproportionate assumption of powers and strategies has been encouraged externally. As pointed out several times already, this disjunction has been brought to the fore with the process of enlargement. Having established a regime of definition, scrutiny, and enforcement in relation to the applicant states, which will fall away once they have gained entry, the prospect of a dramatic loss of control over human rights development in those countries is acute.

Similarly, none of the explanations satisfy any demand for a critical inquiry into the condition. They ignore any deeper interpretations of the history of incoherence or any appreciation of the underlying beliefs and prejudices that might have had a hand in its development. The failure to read these elements means that the explanations, such as they are, are at best partial.

There is ample reason, therefore, to seek a different analytical approach to incoherence, to subject it to examination with a view to understanding the condition and its implications for the future of the Community. The succeeding chapters attempt to do just that. By looking closer at the undercurrents that have produced the institutional narrative of rights in the Community and re-examining familiar interpretations of its development, a deeper appreciation may be provided. Only then can constitutional changes be constructed to address the position.

6

The Invention of Human Rights in the Community

The failure of existing analyses to grasp the extent of the incoherence in human rights policies as well as its long-term significance is quite startling. Despite the rich vein of subject matter and the interdisciplinary attention paid separately to both human rights and the Community we are still faced by a relatively underplayed hand when it comes to considering the two topics together. Specifically, as suggested in the previous chapter, the attempts to explain the current condition are highly limited in their scope. A more intrusive examination is therefore sorely needed.

In order to provide such an investigation we need to return to some fundamental questions. Why did the notion of human rights come to be embraced as a part of the Community's project in the first place? By what means and in what form have human rights become embedded in the Community's constitutional structure? And what have been the implications of these developments? This chapter analyses these distinct questions in three parts.

First, it considers the role of human rights in the Community's search for legitimacy. In the political and moral climate of the post-Second World War world human rights were identified as a prerequisite for the establishment of the Community as an 'authentic' polity capable and authorized to involve itself in the affairs of its constituents and the international community. Legal arguments concerning its competence to act in certain fields did not provide sufficient justification for this assumption of powers. Rather, even though the Community was originally presented as an economic entity, its wider ambitions required that a human rights discourse be deployed as a necessary ideological addition to its 'proto-constitution'. In conjunction with other concepts, such as democracy and the rule of law, the discourse of human rights was identified as providing both the ethical direction for the Community's actions and the constraints upon its interference in the sovereignty of its Member States. The language of human rights was thus used to authenticate the Community as a site of governance.

Secondly, the question of how the Community has rhetorically and legally addressed the need for authentication through human rights is examined. An evolved narrative is traced to show that the identification of respect for human rights enshrined as a founding principle of the Community, was a mythic construction, a retrospective account that imputed values into the original design of the Community. This myth depended on the 'invention of a tradition' purportedly establishing the Community as an authentic guardian and successor of a West European approach to human rights.

Thirdly, the chapter concludes by suggesting the mythic narrative created the base condition from which a *'bifurcation'* of human rights policies materialized, rather than simply an incoherence or even inconsistency. In other words, by relying upon vague notions of rights and imprecise means of employing them in the Community's decision-making processes, human rights and the principles that would govern their relevance were left indeterminate and open to interpretation. The possibility for differing influences deciding policy depending on *where* they were applied thus became instituted. As the first part of this book has shown, the distinction has manifested itself along the internal/external fault-line.

6.1 Human rights as institutional authentication

6.1.1 *Legitimacy and authentication*

Since its creation, many of the debates concerning the form and substance of European integration have focused upon the legitimacy of the Community. Should it acquire the powers of governance that have been pressed upon it? Should the Member States see their sovereignty reduced through the transfer of powers? What, indeed, should be the extent of the Community's jurisdiction and competence? And what are the legal ramifications of these issues? Such questions have been present throughout the Community's political development. Both internal discussion and external critique have analysed the issue either with a view to finding solutions for any perceived lack of legitimacy or to forming arguments to support resistance to any further transmission of powers to the Community.

Much of the attention has concentrated upon the 'democratic deficit' apparent in the Community's decision-making processes.[1] However, as Joseph Weiler has noted, legitimacy and democracy are not interchangeable concepts. He suggests that 'a non-democratic government or political system in the West could not easily attain or maintain legitimacy, but it is still possible for a democratic structure to be illegitimate—either *in toto* or in certain aspects of its operation'.[2]

Furthermore, legitimacy can be divided into two components: first, formal or legal legitimacy looks to the observance of the law 'in the creation of the institution', which in the Western model inevitably identifies democracy as a central part of that process;[3] secondly, social legitimacy, which 'connotes a broad, empirically determined, societal acceptance of the system'.[4] Again, democracy amounts to a necessary if not sufficient condition in the Western context, although as Weiler confirms, such legitimacy might be more generally engendered through a government's commitment and active guarantee of 'values that are part of the general political culture.'[5]

Other authors have attempted to define the concept of legitimacy in similar terms. Andreas Føllesdal, for instance, suggests that laws and authorities need to satisfy three requirements to be deemed politically legitimate: first, they will be considered 'legally legitimate in so far as they are enacted and exercised in accordance with constitutional rules and appropriate procedures'; secondly, they will be, 'socially legitimate if the subjects actually abide by them', and finally, they will be 'normatively legitimate in so far as they can be justified to the people living under them, and impose a moral duty on them to comply'.[6]

Both Weiler's and Føllesdal's conceptions, as with similar analyses of political legitimacy,[7] have been informed by liberal democratic traditions

---

[1] For recent analyses, see Larry Sidentop, *Democracy in Europe* (London: Allen Lane, 2000) and J.H.H. Weiler, 'European Democracy and its Critics: Polity and System' in *The Constitution of Europe* (Cambridge: Cambridge University Press, 1999).

[2] See J.H.H. Weiler, 'The Transformation of Europe' in *The Constitution of Europe* (Cambridge: Cambridge University Press 1999) 79.

[3] Ibid at 80. [4] Ibid. [5] Ibid.

[6] Andreas Føllesdal, 'Democracy, Legitimacy and Majority Rule in the European Union' in Albert Weale and Michael Nentwich (eds), *Political Theory and the European Union: Legitimacy, Constitutional Choice and Citizenship* (London: Routledge, 1998) 36.

[7] See David Beetham and Christopher Lord (eds) *Legitimacy and the European Union* (London: Longman, 1998).

that relate to the creation and development of states in the Western mode. When such conceptions are applied to the Community, however, a distinction needs to be made. Whatever else it might be, it is not a state. Nor is it simply an international organization or agreement between states. Rather a different kind of polity has emerged, one that operates with, on, and beyond states, acting internationally if not supranationally.

The multi-faceted nature and possibilities of the Community placed it outside familiar polity patterns. Consequently, it has not been easy for the Community to attain a form of ready made *prima facie* legitimacy by mimicking other legitimated polities. Instead it has had to address a test that precedes any specific questions of legitimacy, one more concerned with political geography than political activity. In other words, the Community embarked on a process of 'authenticating' itself as a site of governance before turning to justify the way in which it exercised any assumed power.

The process of authentication entailed the conjunction of a three-fold discourse. First, the Community needed to represent itself as an *authentic* institutional site of governance so as to authorize the making of decisions and laws that were to bind the Member States and their citizens and to intrude politically and legally on their lives. Secondly, the Community had to justify its claim to represent its constituency beyond its borders. And thirdly, the Community had to authenticate its right to act as a 'locale' of power internally and externally.[8] In all three areas, the issue of competence has been of key importance. It has vexed courts and commentators alike raising questions of international law and constitutionalism as we saw in the previous chapter.

The European Court of Justice (ECJ) has had a pivotal role to play in this respect and its interventions to pace out the parameters of authority for the Community and its law have been fundamental for the development of a 'new legal order' that has constitutional pretentions. The ECJ summed up its own view in *Opinion 1/91 (Re the EEA Agreement)*:

the EEC Treaty ... constitutes the constitutional charter of a Community based on the rule of law. As the Court of Justice has consistently held, the Community Treaties established a new legal order for the benefit of which the States have limited their

---

[8] 'Locale' in this sense follows Anthony Giddens definition as 'circumscribed arenas for the generation of administrative power'. The arenas, he acknowledges, can range from 'cities to nation-states and beyond'. It therefore seems appropriate in the context of the Community. See Anthony Giddens, *The Nation-State and Violence: Volume Two of a Contemporary Critique of Historical Materialism* (Cambridge: Polity Press, 1985) 13.

sovereign rights, in ever wider fields, and the subjects of which comprise not only the Member States but also their nationals. The essential characteristics of the Community legal order which has thus been established are in particular its primacy over the law of the Member States and the direct effect of a whole series of its provisions which are applicable to their nationals and to the Member States themselves.[9]

Internally, the cases of *Van Gend en Loos*[10] and *Costa v. ENEL*[11] laid down the central principles of supremacy and direct effect respectively and thus clarified the conditions under which the Community could assert authority over its constituents. Crucial in this respect was the finding that the process captured individuals as well as states.

In the external sphere the Community's legal competence was also developed by the ECJ. The EEC Treaty may have provided specific powers, for instance to associate with overseas countries and territories[12] and to act in the field of commercial policy,[13] but the ECJ also introduced a notion of implied external powers. As a result the Community expanded its competence so that it could truly portray itself as possessing an authority to act in a broad range of external areas.[14]

The parallel stories of the principles of supremacy and direct effect on the one hand, and the establishment of external competence on the other, have been told frequently enough.[15] They have been crucial in the Community's negotiation of legal authority vis-à-vis the Member States. However, such matters of law could not hope fully to satisfy any perceived need for social and political authenticity in both the internal and external spheres. As the integration of powers at Community level began to infringe increasingly on the sovereignty of the Member States and the Community developed its presence on the international stage, the problem of authenticity grew more acute. The Community thus looked to factors that would unify states and peoples alike rather than merely satisfy relatively arcane legal requirements developed by the ECJ. The law might have possessed significant political value for the Community in acquiring acceptance but

[9] *Opinion 1/91 (Re the EEA Agreement)* [1991] ECR 6079 para 21.
[10] *Van Gend en Loos v. Nederlandse Administratie der Berastingen* [1963] ECR 1.
[11] *Costa v. ENEL* [1964] ECR 585.
[12] See Articles 182–188 (ex Articles 131–136a) EC Treaty.
[13] Article 133 (ex Article 113) EC Treaty.
[14] See I. Macleod, I.D. Hendry, and Stephen Hyett, *The External Relations of the European Communities* (Oxford: Oxford University Press, 1996) 37–74.
[15] See Marise Cremona, 'External Relations and External Competence: the Emergence of an Integrated Policy' in Paul Craig and Gráinne de Búrca (eds), *The Evolution of EU Law* (Oxford: Oxford University Press, 1999) 137–75.

on deeper socio-psychological levels it was not sufficient in itself. For integration and union to be recognized in hearts and minds as well as to capture political territory, other means were required. In Weiler's terms Europe needed an 'ethos and telos to justify ... the constitutionalism it has already embraced'[16] and, for that matter, the constitutionalism it had and continues to have in mind.

6.1.2 *Human rights discourse and the search for authenticity*

It is in the search for an authenticity and thus an ethos that the discourse of human rights has become of particular constitutional importance. This is not to imply that other means of authentication and legitimacy have not been deployed. The principle of democracy has had an equally prominent rhetorical role in the authenticating process. Cases can also be made out for more specialist arguments. The possibility of increased efficiency, consumer protection, more effective governance in matters such as environment and competition policy, may all justify the Community's existence and those actions carried out in its name. However, few of these warrant the label of fundamental condition that human rights have acquired. Working alongside the rhetoric, if not practice, of democracy, the rule of law, and the free market, the language of respect for human rights has developed into an essential precondition promoted by the Community for its claim to be an authentic and legitimate institution of governance. Whatever the audience, internal or external, human rights have been deployed to acquire authenticity.

Why might this be so? Two crucial and interconnected aspects of the discourse of human rights are relevant for the Community's institutional narrative. First, the status of international human rights discourse has acquired such a position of symbolic pre-eminence in the post-Second World War world that turning to human rights as a means of authentication for any polity would be both logical and inevitable. Secondly, a regional discourse of rights (one focused on Europe) fulfils a similar function but more specific to the European stage. In both respects, the language is fluid and variable. The recognition of specific rights and the articulation of their meaning and scope are not subject to any exact scheme of definition. Rather, we are dealing with a symbolic construct the power of which

---

[16] J.H.H. Weiler, 'Does Europe Need a Constitution? Reflections on Demos, Telos and Ethos in the German Maastricht Decision' in Peter Gowan and Perry Anderson (eds), *The Question of Europe* (London: Verso, 1997) 265–94 at 266.

transcends the specific. It is this power that provides the authenticity described. It is subtly different in the two aspects mentioned.

(a) Authentication in the international sphere

In the global field, the story of an evolved international human rights discourse is a familiar one.[17] It is not a story that needs to be rehearsed here. Suffice to say that the Universal Declaration of Human Rights, the foundation of the United Nations, and the seemingly constant production of international human rights instruments over the past sixty years have underpinned the development of a universally promoted language, a sort of 'political Esperanto'[18] or 'sociolect'.[19] As the World Conference on Human Rights in Vienna in 1993 declared, '[t]he universal nature of human rights and freedoms is beyond question'.[20] Even though it is subject to constant refinement and dispute, the discourse has become entrenched within the global network, acting as a foundation for the assessment of a regime's acceptability on the international stage.[21] Equally, the words 'respect for and promotion of human rights' have served as a mantra for those seeking ready international recognition if not assistance. In both cases, the representation of human rights may appear only through rhetoric, hiding practices that pay lip service to respect for human rights. But the power of the discourse provides the basis for determining the legitimacy of any particular state or political entity operating internationally. Moreover, by referring to the range of human rights instruments produced by the United Nations or regional intergovernmental organizations there has been

---

[17] See Henry Steiner and Philip Alston, *International Human Rights in Context: Law, Politics, Morals* (Oxford: Clarendon Press, 1996).

[18] Boaventura de Sousa Santos' term could be interpreted as both descriptive of the current state of rights discourse and a suggestion of how it might fulfil an emancipatory potential. It could also be an ironic comment upon the inability of the discourse to find any permanent roots. See B. de Sousa Santos, *Toward a New Common Sense: Law, Science and Politics in the Paradigmatic Transition* (London: Routledge, 1995) 348–9.

[19] See Upendra Baxi, 'Human Rights: Suffering Between Movements and Markets' in Robin Cohen and Shirin Rai (eds), *Global Social Movements* (London: Athlone Press, 2000) 34.

[20] See Kevin Boyle, 'Stock-Taking on Human Rights' in David Beetham (ed), *Politics and Human Rights* (Oxford: Blackwell, 1995) 79–95 for a review of the conference and extracts from the declarations.

[21] As Yash Ghai observes '[t]here has even been an attempt by the Organization for Security and Co-operation in Europe to make respect for human rights, especially of cultural minorities, a condition of the recognition of states': Yash Ghai, 'Universalism and Relativism: Human Rights as a Framework for Negotiating Interethnic Claims' *Cardozo Law Review* 21 (2000) 1095–140 at 1095.

an apparent checklist against which any polity can be judged, at least at the level of ratification or signature if not observance. The language of human rights, therefore, offers a universal formula that provides the first step towards modern political institutional authentication.

Admittedly, the process of univeralization, inferred from the above, is by no means uncontested.[22] Within the term itself lurks a self-sustaining and self-reflexive ideology that denies alternative. In many respects therein lies its discursive power. The precept of the universal does not admit fundamentally distinct approaches. It denies that there are other perspectives and other cultures that might view the notion of rights in a wholly distinct way and have equal social and political validity. The imposition of a universal view has therefore been criticized for being a product of Western dominance and neo-colonialism. By some accounts, adherence to the discourse of universal human rights has amounted to the pedalling of a 'global morality' that has been 'bound up with the global manufacture of the independent western nation-state'.[23]

Even with the potential neo-colonial subtext, the concept of universalism possesses significant international credibility. It is portrayed as a non-negotiable fundamental principle against which states will be judged. It can hardly be surprising, therefore, that the Community should look towards the discourse as part of its search for authentication. Whatever the critique, the international language of human rights is a powerful tool for providing an institution with a recognizably acceptable ethos. As Gráinne de Búrca has suggested the 'international status of human rights had become such that no state and no developed political entity, especially not such an ambitious emerging supra-national order [as the Community] could afford to eschew its language or its values'.[24]

The implication for the Community was that in order to acquire credibility on the world stage it had to embrace human rights.

(b) Authentication in the regional sphere

At a purely European level, a parallel and interrelated projection has developed. In the aftermath of the horrors of the Second World War, the

---

[22] Arguments against a universal conception of human rights have raged for many years. For an introduction to the debate, see Steiner and Alston, note 17 above, 166–255.

[23] Gustavo Esteva and Madhu Suri Prakash, *Grassroots Post-Modernism* (London: Zed Books, 1998) 114.

[24] Gráinne de Búrca, 'The Language of Rights and European Integration' in Jo Shaw and Gillian More (eds), *New Legal Dynamics of the European Union* (Oxford: Clarendon Press, 1995) 40.

Holocaust, and the excesses of nationalism, human rights assumed a position of central concern to Western European democracies. Within West European states the traditions of liberal democracy and human rights were acknowledged as representing the values that could counter National Socialism and safeguard against extremism of all kinds. Those nations that had seen the overthrow of fascist regimes saw to it that rights formed a central constitutional position post-1945, thus protecting against possible resurrection of any politically extreme tendencies. Equally, in the external sphere, human rights provided a defining language for challenging the Soviet system and *its* claims to authenticity as a means of political and social organization. In particular, the European Convention on Human Rights (ECHR) acquired an almost iconic status of ethical 'purity' during the Cold War and symbolized the values that finally 'triumphed' after the collapse of the Iron Curtain.

As a moral bulwark against a past filled with violence and abuse and a present threat from other dictatorial regimes, the ECHR therefore became a moral text that provided basic conditions for any system within the region. It provided a symbolic construct that could form the basis for talking about human rights in the European context. The rush to become members of the Council of Europe and to sign up to the ECHR by the Central and Eastern European states showed its political and diplomatic significance after 1989.[25] Even before that, the fact that the Community was concerned to debate on a number of occasions the possibility of it becoming a signatory to the ECHR was testament to the Convention's influential status.[26]

Beyond the ECHR, the responses to the demand for rights in particular states' constitutions after the War also served to place human rights at the heart of political authenticity in the region. Indeed, as will be seen below, that position gave rise to the forceful reaction of the constitutional courts of West Germany and Italy to the principle of supremacy that the ECJ had put in place. The idea that a continental institution such as the Community could ride roughshod over basic rights by taking actions that

---

[25] We have already seen the significance attached to the ECHR in relation to states seeking accession to the Community in Chapter 3.

[26] See the studies prompted by the Commission in 1976, *The Report of the Commission on the Protection of Fundamental Rights as Community Law* EC Bull Supp 5–1976 and 1979, *Memorandum on the Accession of the European Communities to the Convention for the Protection of Human Rights and Fundamental Freedoms* EC Bull Supp 2-1979 6–21 and the ECJ's consideration of the issue in *Opinion 2/94 Re: Accession by the Community to the ECHR* [1996] ECR I-1759.

might compromise their protection without challenge or review by constitutional courts was always likely to be a concern.

The general and specific notions of rights at the international and European level respectively therefore became heavily interlinked with the Community's need to acquire authenticity. Economic arguments for the Community's existence would never suffice legally or politically in such an environment. The gradual infiltration of human rights language into the Community was a natural consequence of these conditions. For this reason human rights became a vital concern for the Community and could not be ignored as it developed. How the institutional narrative of human rights in the Community then evolved and formed the base from which incoherence or, in my terms, a bifurcation eventually emerged is the concern of the next section.[27]

6.2 The myth of human rights as a founding principle of the Community

6.2.1 *The creation of the Community and the silence on human rights*

Perhaps ironically, given the later significance attached to the subject, the narrative begins with an acknowledgement of a protracted silence. Indeed, consensus has been reached between commentators and institutions alike that the founding Treaties contained no explicit reference to human rights. Nor did they incorporate a constitutional requirement that the Community's constituents (the Member States and the various Community institutions) should respect human rights in their activities under the Treaties.

Joseph Weiler comments that '[n]either the Treaty of Paris nor the Treaty of Rome contained any allusion to the protection of fundamental human rights'.[28] Peter Neusse goes further to suggest that '[t]he founding Treaties of the European Communities did not foresee any human rights provisions'.[29] Others have been perhaps more cautious. Christiane Duparc

---

[27] It should be borne in mind throughout that the subtle differences between the international and European human rights discourses drawn on in the search for authenticity may well have contributed to the eventual development of incoherence and/or bifurcation.

[28] J.H.H. Weiler, 'Fundamental Rights and Fundamental Boundaries: On the Conflict of Standards and Values in the Protection of Human Rights in the European Legal Space' in *The Constitution of Europe* (Cambridge: Cambridge University Press, 1999) 107.

[29] Peter Neusse, 'European Citizenship and Human Rights: An Interactive European Concept' *Legal Issues of European Integration* (1997) 54.

concludes only that no explicit reference to human rights based on international texts was made in the EEC Treaty.[30] Rudolph Bernhardt, in his report made to the Commission in 1976, merely acknowledges that nothing in the way of a catalogue of rights was provided or indeed intended.[31]

Such interpretations are not confined to commentators on European integration. They are acknowledged institutionally by the Community. In particular, the ECJ specifically pronounced in *Opinion 2/94* that '[n]either the EC Treaty nor the ECSC or EAEC Treaties makes any specific reference to fundamental rights'.[32] It is thus widely accepted that the Treaties failed to provide either a catalogue of rights (or even any specific rights *per se*) or a statement of principle regarding the respect and promotion of human rights within its constituting framework.

Patrick Twomey suggests that the original silence is not surprising. The Community was originally economic in character. The possibility of human rights (as widely recognized in Western Europe in the 1950s) being affected by the new arrangement was considered remote.[33] Equally, the field of human rights remained captured in any event by either nation-states alone (under the principle of non-interference in the internal affairs of sovereign states) or potentially by other international fora such as the Council of Europe[34] (and its human rights mechanisms) and the United Nations.[35]

Perhaps of greater immediate significance, however, was the failure of the European Defence Community and a European Political Community,

---

[30] See Christiane Duparc, *The European Community and Human Rights* (Luxembourg: European Commission, 1992) 11.

[31] Rudolf Bernhardt, 'The Problems of Drawing up a Catalogue of Fundamental Rights for the European Communities', Annex to *Report of the Commission on the Protection of Fundamental Rights as Community Law* EC Bull Supp 5-1976 8–69.

[32] See, *Opinion 2/94*, note 26 above, para III.1.

[33] See Patrick Twomey, 'The European Union: Three Pillars without a Human Rights Foundation' in David O'Keefe and Patrick Twomey (eds), *Legal Issues of the Maastricht Treaty* (London: Wiley Chancery Law, 1994) 121–2. Twomey quotes from Bernhardt's report to the Commission (see note 31 above) in which it was opined that 'the essentially economic character of the Communities...makes the possibility of their encroaching upon fundamental human values, such as life, personal liberty, freedom of opinion, conscience etc, very unlikely'.

[34] Article 1(b) Statute of the Council of Europe 1949 affirms that the Council's aims will be pursued through, *inter alia*, 'the maintenance and further realization of human rights and fundamental freedoms'. See David de Giustino, *A Reader in European Integration* (London: Longman, 1996) 53.

[35] Article 1(3) Charter of the United Nations 1945 states one of the purposes of the United Nations is 'to achieve international cooperation...in promoting and encouraging respect for human rights and for fundamental freedoms for all without distinction as to race, sex, language, or religion'.

which in the latter case included statements recognizing the need to respect human rights, to emerge from the creation of the European Coal and Steel Community in the early to mid-1950s. The political opposition to these proposals in France in 1954 led to 'sober utilitarian considerations' taking precedence when it came to drafting the EEC Treaty.[36]

Despite the cumulative reasons for the absence of human rights principles from the originating Treaties, the fact of that absence called into question the authenticity of the new Community as an institution worthy of power. Over time the institutional response has been to deny the importance of, if not explain, the acknowledged silence. The Community has proclaimed that it is and always has been founded on a respect for human rights. The institutional narrative is retroactive and owns a 'live' genealogy. It has been composed, and continues to be so, in strata through the gradual accumulation of rhetorical and legal expressions and re-interpretations of texts that purportedly demonstrate the Community's original commitment to human rights as a constitutional imperative. Two important texts in particular have framed the narrative.

First, the Treaty on European Union as amended by the Amsterdam Treaty confirms the Member States' 'attachment to the principles of liberty, democracy and respect for human rights and fundamental freedoms and of the rule of law'.[37] More significantly, Article 6(1) (ex Article F.1) TEU establishes that the EU 'is *founded* on the principles of liberty, democracy, respect for human rights and fundamental freedoms, and the rule of law, principles which are common to the Member States' (emphasis added).

Secondly, the EU Charter of Fundamental Rights 2000 makes clear at its outset that '[c]onscious of its spiritual and moral heritage, the Union is founded on the indivisible, universal values of human dignity, freedom, equality and solidarity'.[38]

Together, these provide important statements of constitution. Unlike Article 6(2) TEU[39] they are not a collective expression of intent on the

---

[36] Manfred Dauses, 'The Protection of Fundamental Rights in the Community Legal Order' *EL Rev* 10 (1985) 399.

[37] See third recital of the Preamble TEU.

[38] Charter of Fundamental Rights of the European Union, Preamble para 2 [2000] OJ C-364/08.

[39] Article 6(2) TEU states 'The Union shall respect fundamental rights, as guaranteed by the European Convention for the Protection of Human Rights and Fundamental Freedoms signed in Rome on 4 November 1950 and as they result from the constitutional traditions common to the Member States, as general principles of Community law'. It does not indicate any retroactivity.

question of human rights promotion or recognition. Rather, they form a declaratory statement of interpretation, an interpretation of what was, and has ever since been, a fundamental precept underpinning the whole European Project and the institutions that have given it form.[40] Unsurprisingly they have been embraced wholesale by the Draft Constitutional Treaty of 2003 (DCT), a late attempt to set in text all those precepts that have purportedly governed the Community throughout its existence.

Article 6(1) TEU and Article I-2 of the DCT, which states the 'Union is founded on the values of [inter alia] ... human rights', in particular as constitutional provisions, represent the latest examples in a long line of a developing history of imputation. Faced with the undeniable fact that the Treaties founding the Community contained no statement of principle on the question of human rights the Community forged a retrospective institutional account of its own formation. The account maintained that human rights were not only within the minds of the 'founding fathers', or 'European saints' as Alan Milward calls them,[41] but also buried subtly within the Treaties themselves. They were *imputed* over time into the very structure of the Community, into the core of its Project.

The genealogy of the narrative construction has two fundamental interweaving strains. First, through institutional rhetoric, the Community has evolved a discourse that suffuses it with a set of values, including respect for human rights, with increasing vigour over the years. Secondly, the Community has succeeded in establishing the motif of founding principle within its legal order thus imbuing the discourse with the force of law and all that that implies for constituting legitimacy and authenticity. The two cross-referential themes have worked together to form an institutional narrative (essentially mythic in nature) that has been employed as a central means of authentication.

6.2.2 *Constituting authenticity through rhetoric: the foundation of a myth*

One function of myth can be to establish, in Roland Barthes' words, 'a natural and eternal justification ... a clarity which is not that of an

---

[40] The fact that reference is made to the Union only could suggest a limited retrospective interpretation. However, given the narrative that has been constructed, it would be disingenuous to suggest that the Communities were not also subject to this statement of founding principle. Indeed, it is inconceivable that an argument would be raised that the Community or any part was not founded on respect for human rights.

[41] Milward refers to Monnet, Schuman, Adenauer, de Gasperi *et al* as the European saints in the process of integration after the Second World War: Alan Milward, *The European Rescue of the Nation-State* (London: Routledge, 1992).

explanation but that of a statement of fact'.[42] The myth may be a 'cruel deceit', as Ian Ward suggests in relation to 'the whole idea of European integration',[43] but this is not necessarily its purpose. The Community's early construction of a story about the role of human rights in its own formation was more about establishing *its* interpretation of the purpose behind the European Project.

Initially, the narrative construction emerged through a rhetoric that ignored the lack of reference to a human rights ethos within the founding Treaties. Instead, reliance was placed on a history that looked beyond and beneath the available texts. Rather than be constrained by the patently obvious economic design and early practice of the Community, actors drew, in particular, upon two latent sources of authority.

(a) The 'spirit of the Treaties'

The first related to the hidden meanings that lay within the initiating texts. What was frequently termed the 'spirit of the Treaties' was invoked to justify their interpretation so as to incorporate the designs of the 'founding fathers'. The Commission was intent on adopting the theme. In 1961, for instance, it advocated an awareness of a 'Community spirit' in all aspects of the Member States activities.[44] In 1967 it commented that '[i]n accordance with the spirit of the Treaties, [the Commission] will therefore continue to base its action on the necessary convergence of social and economic exigencies, so as to contribute, by all the means in its power, to the welfare of the peoples of the Community'.[45]

Although human rights were absent, the recollection of a spirit associated with a people's welfare provided a basis for future rhetorical developments. It also suggested the presence of values and ambitions that could be uncovered even though they were not explicit textually.

Equally, when celebrating the achievement of the Customs Union in 1968, the Commission recalled the aim of a 'political Europe', evoking the designs of Schuman, Adenauer, de Gasperi and the like and emphasizing that 'Europe is not only customs tariffs . . . [i]t must also be the Europe of the peoples'.[46] By thus calling upon the 'human aspect' of the European

---

[42] Roland Barthes, *Mythologies* (London: Vintage, 1993) 143.
[43] See Ian Ward, *The Margins of European Law* (London: Macmillan Press, 1996) 51.
[44] See *Fourth General Report on the Activities of the Community* EC Bull 5-1961 at 14.
[45] EC Bull 3-1968 at 29.
[46] Declaration by the Commission on the Occasion of the Achievement of the Customs Union, 1 July 1968, EC Bull 7-1968 at 5.

Project,[47] it became possible to lend more credence to the Community's involvement in the wider realm of European affairs. In alluding to the underlying spirit and intention it was then open for the institutions to move into political and social spheres that might otherwise lie out of its legally constituted boundaries.

Within the developing narrative, one can infer the presence of human rights as one of the possible sets of underlying values attributed to the founding fathers. Indeed, Walter Hallstein, when President of the Commission, maintained from an early stage '[o]ur Community ... is entirely based on freedom. The spirit of freedom imbues every provision of our Treaty, our regulations, our decisions and all our acts of our Institutions'.[48]

The reference to 'freedom' surely cannot be restricted to a purely technical interpretation, one focusing on the four freedoms (of movement of goods, workers, services, and capital) that the Treaty of Rome specified. Rather it symbolized something far greater, socially and politically, in which the language of human rights would not be alien. The EEC Treaty itself provided some justification for taking such a view. The Preamble referred to the resolution to pool resources to 'preserve and strengthen peace and liberty'. Admittedly, however, the freedoms that appeared explicit in the text remained fixed on the economic aspects of European affairs. The free movement provisions, the prohibition of discrimination on the grounds of nationality, and the equal pay provisions, were all 'in the nature of fundamental rights'.[49] These were essential for the completion of a common market and had little if any relevance to the human rights discourse as discussed above, at least as regards their inclusion in the Treaty.

Consequently, the imputation of a spirit within the Treaties, reasonably enough assumed to substantiate the political designs of the institutional actors, required some extra ballast if it were to contribute to the search for authenticity beyond the economic. The response was to allude to another spirit, a spirit of Europe, a far deeper and older concept that entailed the adoption of a rhetoric of tradition and common heritage that was incorporated into the European enterprise by implication.

---

[47] See Jean Rey's introduction to the Commission's Declaration on the Occasion of the Achievement of the Customs Union, 1 July 1968, EC Bull 8-1968 at 7.

[48] See Hallstein's contribution to the debate in the European Parliament on the Berlin Situation, EC Bull 11-1961 at 11.

[49] Dauses, note 36 above, at 399.

(b) The spirit of Europe: an invented tradition

At the Bonn Conference in July 1961 the Heads of State and Government issued a communiqué that affirmed the *'valeurs spirituelles'* and *'traditions politiques'* that formed a common inheritance between the Member States.[50] The references to tradition echoed similar rhetoric that imbued other European attempts at international co-operative ventures after the Second World War. The 1948 Brussels Treaty, for example, committed its signatories to 'fortify and preserve the principles of democracy, personal freedom and political liberty, the constitutional traditions and the rule of law, which are their common heritage'.[51] It also reaffirmed faith in 'fundamental rights, in the dignity and worth of the human person and in the other ideals proclaimed in the Charter of the United Nations'. The Statute of the Council of Europe equally referred to the aim to 'achieve a greater unity between its members for the purpose of safeguarding and realizing the ideals and principles which are their common heritage'.[52]

The fact that the EEC Treaty did not also include a similar statement is telling in itself but this did not preclude the Community from imputing retrospectively the sentiments expressed in other international instruments. Human rights were assumed part of a 'common heritage' that had been inherited by the Community by reason of its geographical and political location. The Luxembourg Report,[53] commissioned by the Heads of Government at the 1969 Hague Conference, confirmed the construction. The overall framework of a united Europe was envisaged as 'founded upon the common heritage of respect for the liberty and the rights of men'.

Was this discovery of human rights in the foundations of the Community a mythic construction? If one adopts the perspective of myth as 'a transforming signifier capable of re-ordering the "radical imaginary" of the European polity'[54] then the subsumption of human rights within a notion of common heritage did have mythic qualities. It was not evident that human rights, the 'rights of men' or other general concepts of liberty and freedom were guiding forces behind the construction of the Community.

---

[50] EC Bull 7/8-1961 37–9.
[51] See de Giustino, note 34 above, at 47, paras 1, 2 respectively.   [52] Ibid at 53.
[53] *First Report of the Foreign Ministers to the Heads of State and Government of the European Community's Member States*, 27 October 1970. See Press and Information Office of the Government of the Federal Republic of Germany, *Texts Relating to the European Political Co-operation* (1974) 18–25.
[54] James Henry Bergeron, 'An Ever Whiter Myth: The Colonization of Modernity in European Community Law' in Peter Fitzpatrick and Bergeron (eds), *Europe's Other: European Law Between Modernity and Postmodernity* (Aldershot: Ashgate, 1998) 4.

The concept of the underlying influence of human rights relied upon a *belief* that they were fundamental. Its adoption signified a transformation of the text from the functional to encompass a spiritual dimension. In this sense, the embrace of human rights acted as a means of making explicable and authenticating not only past events and decisions but also present activities and future intentions. This returns us to the role of narrative and myth in establishing origins and justifying behaviour of an institution. On that basis the story told so far has all the hallmarks of a myth in the making.

The notion of 'invented tradition' advocated by Eric Hobsbawm and Terence Ranger supports this analysis.[55] According to them an 'invented tradition is taken to mean a set of practices ... which seek to inculcate certain values and norms of behaviour, which automatically implies continuity with the past'.[56] They serve a number of purposes including 'establishing or symbolising social cohesion or the membership of groups, real or artificial communities' and 'establishing or legitimising institutions, status or relations of authority'.[57] The reference to the tradition of human rights by the Community achieves a similar result. It is invented in the sense that the tradition is deployed rather than evoked with the aim of establishing some kind of Community cohesion. It is also a tool that is utilized to authenticate and thus legitimate the Community and its assumption of powers. The fact that the tradition is marked more by its abuse than respect in modern European history suggests the invention is based on myth and not just fiction.

However, the early rhetoric employed should not be read in isolation. The parallel developments undertaken through law and the ECJ are of vital importance in the creation of the myth.

6.2.3 *Constituting authenticity through law: the contribution of the ECJ*

It was the ECJ that began to make *explicit* the re-interpretation of original intent as regards human rights. As many authors have pointed out, this aspect of the story has been subjected to intense scrutiny by commentators and the institution alike and has certainly been well rehearsed over time.[58]

---

[55] Eric Hobsbawm and Terence Ranger (eds), *The Invention of Tradition* (Cambridge: Canto, 1992) 1–14.
[56] Ibid at 1.   [57] Ibid at 9.
[58] See Weiler, note 28 above, at 102–29, and Andrew Clapham, *Human Rights and the European Community: A Critical Overview* (Baden-Baden: Nomos, 1991), vol I.

Despite the wealth of literature, however, a brief review of the Court's involvement in the textual and rhetorical (re-)construction of the formative period is warranted. It will, of course, cover familiar ground. That is to be expected when dealing with the construction of an authorized version appearing as an institutional narrative.

The initial aspects of the story were recorded succinctly by the Commission in its 1976 *Report on the Protection of Fundamental Rights as Community Law*.[59] A three-stage sequence was identified. First, the Report recalled initial judgments of the ECJ, which 'held that it was not competent to examine the legality of acts of the Community institutions according to the yardstick of national fundamental rights'. Secondly, it referred to the cases of *Stauder*[60] and *Internationale Handelsgesellschaft*[61] as displaying 'a new attitude in the jurisprudence of the Court', which insisted that respect for fundamental rights were in fact an integral part of the general principles of law that the ECJ would apply. Thirdly, it interpreted the case of *Nold*[62] as in effect cementing the new approach to human rights, taking 'one step further ... towards a sort of optimum standard of fundamental rights'. In so doing the ECJ drew explicit inspiration from international human rights treaties and the 'constitutional traditions common to the Member States' as sources of law.

Although the three stages identified by the Commission's Report do not accord with some commentators' opinions on the development of the ECJ's approach,[63] they do represent a clear attempt to compose the story of human rights as founding principle.

(a) The ECJ and human rights: stage one

The initial reaction by the ECJ to applicants seeking to challenge the legitimacy of Community acts on the basis of a breach of fundamental rights contained in the national constitutions of individual Member States was to retreat into the rhetoric of competence. The possibility of human rights as a foundational principle of the Community was largely ignored.

---

[59] EC Bull Supp 5-1976 8–9.
[60] *Stauder v. City of Ulm* Case 29/69 [1969] ECR 419–30.
[61] *Internationale Handelsgesellschaft v. Einfuhr- und Vorratstelle fur Getreide und Futtermittel* Case 11/70 [1970] ECR II-1125–55.
[62] *Nold v. Commission* Case 4/73 [1974] ECR I-491–516.
[63] For instance, Dauses preferred to separate consideration of the cases of *Stauder* and *Internationale*, suggesting that they represented distinct developments. Such a distinction does not add to (or, for that matter, detract from) the analysis proffered here. Nevertheless, cf. Dauses, note 36 above, at 398–419.

Rather, a strict interpretation was applied to the Treaties. This was demonstrated by *Stork*,[64] in which it was held that '[u]nder Article 8 of the [ECSC] Treaty the High Authority is only required to apply Community law. It is not competent to apply the national law of Member States ... Consequently the High Authority is not empowered to examine a ground of complaint which maintains that, when it adopted its decision, it infringed principles of German constitutional law'.[65]

The ECJ thus restricted the extent of its own authority by a rigid reading of the Treaty wording. Any flexible interpretation of the text was eschewed in favour of a strict depiction of the ECJ's competence. That the issue involved questions of the application of rights enshrined in a Member State's constitution was merely incidental.

As if to re-emphasize the absence of human rights principles in the ECSC Treaty, which was the extent of the ECJ's concern at that time, *Stork* was closely followed by a more explicit rejection of any such contrary contention in the case of *Ruhrkolen*.[66] The ECJ ruled 'Community law, as it arises under the ECSC Treaty, does not contain any general principle, express or otherwise, guaranteeing the maintenance of vested rights'.[67]

Even though this definitive and accurate reading only applied to the ECSC Treaty, the ECJ adopted the same approach, at first, in respect of the EEC Treaty in a number of cases during the mid-1960s.[68] Nevertheless, the distinctions that existed between the form and content of the two treaty documents offered the scope for a more flexible interpretation made increasingly necessary given the noises made in certain constitutional courts within the Member States.

(b) The ECJ and human rights: stage two

G. Federico Mancini has made the point that as 'Community law came to govern diverse and sometimes unforeseen facets of human activity, it encroached upon a whole gamut of old and new rights with both an economic and a strictly "civil" content'.[69]

The ECJ's stance as represented by *Stork* had little chance then of placating national constitutional courts concerned at the possible erosion of rights through the activities of the Community.

[64] *Stork v. High Authority* Case 1/58 [1958–59] ECR 17–40.   [65] Ibid at 27.
[66] *Ruhrkolen-Verkaufsgesellschaft mbH v. High Authority* Case 40/59 [1960] ECR 423–62.
[67] Ibid at 439.
[68] See *Sgarlata v. Commission* [1965] ECR 215 and *Van Eick v. Commission* [1968] ECR 329.
[69] G. Federico Mancini, 'The Making of a Constitution for Europe' *CMLR* 26 (1989) 595–614 at 609.

The challenge, in particular in West Germany and Italy, to the unfettered principle of supremacy was of great moment for the establishment of the narrative of human rights in the Community. The growing disquiet felt at the possibility that the application of Community law could result in the contravention of national constitutional rights threatened to undermine the 'new legal order'. The prospect of consistent findings by national courts that Community law was incompatible with constitutional rights would make a mockery of the notion of supremacy. Lars Krogsgaard has suggested that it was 'the Court's fear that this principle would be endangered rather than philosophical considerations of a humanitarian kind that led to the introduction of the concept of fundamental rights'.[70] M.H. Mendelson also called it an 'act of self-preservation'.[71]

Likely as that may be, the case of *Stauder*[72] was the first to recognize the possibilities inherent in the EEC Treaty as a means to overcome the difficulty. As an element of its judgment the ECJ determined that in relation to the fundamental right or principle of non-discrimination '[t]he protection guaranteed by fundamental rights is, as regards Community law, assured by various provisions in the Treaty, such as Articles 7 and 40(3); supplemented in its turn by unwritten Community law, derived from the general principles of law in force in Member States'.[73]

It then concluded, almost by way of an aside, that fundamental rights 'were enshrined in the general principles of Community law and protected by the Court'.[74] No in-depth consideration of this crucial statement of principle was provided in the judgment. It was, rather, a bold and pure finding, intensely presumptive, rendered without detailed reasoning, based on a reading of the written text and on an assumption of the unwritten intentions lying behind the Treaty. The opinion of Advocate General Roemer concurred, suggesting that fundamental rights recognized by national law represented 'an unwritten *constituent* part of Community law' (emphasis added).[75]

The reference to 'constituent part' is key. In effect, it meant that *Stauder* had provided a critical form of constitutional remembrance. The ECJ, echoing the sentiments (if not the wording) of the rhetoric of the Commission made at the time, embraced fundamental rights as an-already-present constitutional given. The decision installed a legally authenticated history

---

[70] Lars Bondon Krogsgaard, 'Fundamental Rights in the European Community after Maastricht' *Legal Issues of European Integration* (1993) 101.
[71] M.H. Mendelson, 'The ECJ and Human Rights' *Yearbook of European Law* (1981) 130.
[72] *Stauder*, note 60 above.   [73] Ibid at 422.   [74] Ibid at 425.   [75] Ibid at 428.

of the Community's ethical origins and design. In so doing, the message underpinned the institutional narrative that sought to justify the Community's existence *and* deflect any legal challenge to the assumption of sovereign powers.

The ECJ lost little time in approving its creation of an originating orthodoxy in the subsequent case of *Internationale Handelsgesellschaft*.[76] It suggested that a Community measure could not be rendered invalid on the basis that it contravened fundamental rights contained in a national constitution but went on to conclude 'an examination should be made as to whether or not any analogous guarantee inherent in Community law has been disregarded. In fact, respect for fundamental rights forms an integral part of the general principles of law protected by the Court of Justice'.[77]

The explicit concepts of inherence and integrality again indicate a retrospective representation of the formation of the Community as a system and structure that not only recognized fundamental rights but would have no credibility as an institution of governance in the modern world without their presence.

Advocate General M. Dutheillet de Lamothe substantiated the ECJ's interpretation by drawing attention to the fundamental rights that were already guaranteed expressly in the Treaty. He claimed that these veiled rights were suggestive of an unwritten Community law, 'one of the essential aims of which is precisely to ensure the respect for the fundamental rights of the individual'.[78] Certainly, AG de Lamothe had no difficulty describing Article 40 EEC Treaty in combination with Article 39 in suitable rights language as ensuring 'a more precise guarantee of the rights of individuals than the general principles of Community law'. He therefore echoed the language of rights that had been applied by the ECJ to those non-discrimination provisions of the Treaty in *Stauder*. The ready acceptance of the rhetorical acceptance of rights for the individual was a key precedent for the development of rights as a founding principle. It suggested that human rights issues, although not covered in their entirety, had been embedded throughout the Treaty merely awaiting recognition and suitable application.

So we see another element of the authorized version appear. Professor Bernhardt's study report in 1976 confirmed that it would be 'wrong to infer that the Treaties ascribe no importance to fundamental rights and the

---

[76] *Internationale Handelsgesellschaft*, note 61 above.   [77] Ibid at para 4 at 1134.
[78] Ibid at 1146.

rights of the individual, or even take no cognisance of them'.[79] That the rights might be chiefly 'in relation to economic endeavour' did not negate such a view. Rather, Professor Bernhardt utilized the economic inspired rights as vital precedents for his central contention.

In any event, it became common ground that, setting aside the economic based rights, the Treaty still incorporated provisions that may be interpreted in the language of rights. Twomey, for instance, specifically acknowledges, '[t]hough not formulated in "rights language" many of the provisions in the Treaty are concerned with the rights of the individual'.[80] They included the original Articles 7 (non-discrimination on the basis of nationality), 48 (free movement of workers), and 119 (equal pay) EEC Treaty. The fact that Twomey then points out that many so-called rights do not 'inhere in the individual by his or her humanity, but flow from one's status as a Community national' and that 'non-natural persons do not automatically benefit from the protection afforded'[81] does not negate the starting assumption.

Nevertheless, that this interpretation might be open to doubt was recognized by the Commission in its 1976 *Report on the Protection of Fundamental Rights as Community Law*. It felt compelled to confirm that '[t]here are provisions in the Treaties themselves *whose aim, or at least effect*, is to guarantee and improve the position of the individual in the Community ... It is on the basis of some of these articles that the Court of Justice has been able to give important judgments as regards the protection of fundamental rights' (emphasis added).[82]

The equivocal suggestion as to the 'aim' or 'at least effect' of the listed provisions set up a possible distinction in original design that was quickly rendered less ambivalent within two paragraphs. 'Turning to fundamental rights, strictly speaking, the Community institutions have, since the beginning of the Community, been faced with the question of their existence and with a precise definition of their scope under the Community legal order. Today fundamental rights—however they may be defined—undeniably constitute an essential part of the Community legal order'.[83]

The failure to address the question of definition suggested that definition was unimportant. It confirmed the symbolic attachment to 'human rights' rather than their specific interpretation. The message was that rights, whether called 'fundamental' or 'human' were respected through law and

---

[79] Bernhardt, note 31 above.   [80] Twomey, note 33 above, at 122.   [81] Ibid.
[82] EC Bull Supp 5-1976, para 7 at 8.   [83] Ibid para 8 at 8.

through the Community's political practice. That was all that was deemed necessary for the Community to appropriate authenticity through the language of rights. Further delineation was portrayed as an ancillary concern, which would be addressed by means yet to be determined.

(c) The ECJ and human rights: stage three

Having founded the principle of fundamental rights that underpinned the formative structure of the Community through *Stauder* and *Internationale Handelsgesellschaft* the ECJ then provided a degree of guidance as to how this might be interpreted in practice. In particular the case of *Nold*[84] affirmed that the ECJ would be entitled to 'draw inspiration from the constitutional traditions common to the Member States' and that 'international treaties for the protection of human rights on which the Member States have collaborated or of which they are signatories, can supply guidelines which should be followed within the framework of Community law'.[85]

The ECHR was the 'international treaty' of note in this respect, a fact confirmed by the ECJ through subsequent judgments.[86] Human rights, rather than simply fundamental rights, were therefore drawn into the narrative.

The acknowledgement of the importance of rights in the Community was, however, tempered by practical considerations. Human rights were not unconditionally accepted. They could still be subject to interference through Community law if that were required in the public interest in pursuance of the Community's objectives and the interference was proportionate and the substance of the rights concerned remained guaranteed.[87]

Notwithstanding these limitations, the effect of *Nold* was to encompass within the foundational narrative the authenticity supplied through the international and regional (as well as national) discourses considered earlier in this chapter. It looked not only to the universal precepts of rights but also those that might have developed specifically within Member States. It therefore provided the formal means by which the genealogy of rights within the Community was given substance. Equally, it echoed the institutional promotion of a common tradition focused on human rights. Without in any way specifying what those traditions might amount to, the ECJ succeeded in embracing the rhetoric at work elsewhere in the institution, contributing in

---

[84] *Nold v. Commission*, note 62 above.   [85] Ibid para 13 at 507.
[86] It soon became common practice to relate human rights issues to articles of the ECHR. *Rutili* instituted this tendency, see *Rutili v. Minister for Interior* Case 36/75 [1975] ECR 1219.
[87] See *Nold*, note 62 above.

the process to a substantiation of the myth already under construction. The mythic nature of the enterprise was re-emphasized in Bernhardt's 1976 Report. There he concluded that although there were 'many common features of principle' with regard to the constitutional traditions of rights in the Member States, there were also 'deep-rooted differences in the manner in which these fundamental rights have been elaborated'.[88]

The ECJ's three stage scheme of emplacement of the concept of fundamental and human rights in the Community's formative ideology provided the legal cement for the myth that had already begun to be developed politically. The Court had styled the language of rights into a constitutional and constituting performance, one that was readily adopted and followed by the other organs of the Community.

6.2.4 *The consolidation of the myth of founding principle*

The adoption of the language of rights through the conduit of law filled a gap that might have otherwise threatened to undermine the Community's attempt at structuring its own authenticity. Whether the opponents were the constitutional courts of the Member States or political actors concerned with the transfer of powers to the Community, the Community relied on its story of a pedigree of rights adherence and initiating principle to substantiate its position politically *and* legally. Implicitly, this was recognized by the Parliament, Commission, and Council through the Joint Declaration on Human Rights issued in 1977.[89] Indeed, the Declaration represented the first major rhetorical movement to fuse the forces of law and rights into the very core of the Community. The line of reasoning is clear from the Declaration's text. It is worth quoting in full.

> Whereas the Treaties establishing the European Communities are based on the principle of respect for the law;
>
> Whereas, as the Court of Justice has recognised, that law comprises, over and above the rules embodied in the treaties and secondary Community legislation, the general principles of law and in particular the fundamental rights, principles and rights on which the constitutional law of the Member States is based;
>
> Whereas, in particular, all the Member States are Contracting Parties to the European Convention for the Protection of Human Rights and Fundamental Freedoms signed in Rome on 4 November 1950,

---

[88] Bernhardt, note 31 above, at 45.
[89] Joint Declaration by the European Parliament, the Council, and the Commission on Human Rights [1977] OJ C-103/1.

Have adopted the following declaration:

1. The European Parliament, the Council and the Commission stress the prime importance they attach to the protection of fundamental rights, as derived in particular from the constitutions of the Member States and the European Convention for the Protection of Human Rights and Fundamental Freedoms.

2. In the exercise of their powers and in the pursuance of the aims of the European Communities *they respect* and *will continue to respect* these rights. (emphasis added)

On close reading, the Declaration plays two intersecting themes. First, it substantiates that the Community is imbued with the force of law; it was created in law and operates through law. The project was invested with an authority almost ethereal (certainly mythic) in character. The implication is that 'law' exists outside the institution, independent and therefore wise and trustworthy, an essential guiding power transcending time and political manipulation. In James Bergeron's understanding, Community law looks to the 'mythical structure of national law and the representation of that structure as an external and autonomous, yet transcendent and supreme entity'.[90] Whether or not national law provides the external authority, 'fundamental rights' appear as a vital element of the 'law' in the Declaration's terms. The ECJ's contribution to the scheme is its 'recognition' of this fact. Its decisions merely confirm the Declaration's substance. So much is implied by the preambulatory narrative.

Secondly, the body of the text of the Declaration then proceeds to establish the truth of the story of founding principle by confirming the existing and continuing respect that the institutions have (and by implication, always have had) for human rights. There is no acknowledgement of a change in approach. Rather it is an affirmation of an institutional 'truth'. In order to substantiate the narrative the particular sources of human rights law that would have regional authenticity, namely the ECHR and the constitutional traditions of the Member States, are relied upon. Interestingly rights instruments from a wider background are not explicitly acknowledged. Even the Universal Declaration of Human Rights fails to find a mention.

The Joint Declaration thus channelled the force of law with the force of rights to produce a powerful constituting statement. Although possessing no legal authority, it added to the authentication of the Community (including of course the ECJ) as a site of decision-making and political power through its rhetorical performance. It was given added political

---

[90] For a consideration of the mythology of European law, see Bergeron, note 54 above.

weight by the fact that it would deflect the challenge of national courts to the supremacy of Community law. The Report that gave rise to the Declaration concluded as much. It suggested that an alternative strategy to a catalogue of rights would be to allow the ECJ to develop a rights jurisprudence of its own. It would rely upon 'general legal principles' under the umbrella of a statement that 'the protection of fundamental rights is, in the view of all Community organs, secured under Community law'.[91] The Community 'organs' adopted the approach partly in the hope that the Declaration would 'deal with existing legal uncertainties and dispel misgivings'[92] but also, it is submitted, with a view to entrenching the authenticating foundational narrative of rights.

The Declaration was, however, insufficient to establish the entrenchment on its own. The very nature of narrative and its efficacy depends upon the repetition of the key narrative elements in order to ensure its survival. A constructed myth may require constant re-affirmation to ensure its institutional position as an unquestioned principle. Only then can atrophy of the authenticating process and the forgetting of foundational principles be prevented.

The textual productions that have emanated from the Community since the Declaration have served to cement the story within the constitutional framework. It is possible to trace the lineage through the textual output of the institutions.[93] Taking the form of non-legally binding but official statements and declarations and, in time, Treaty amendments, which have assumed positions of legal doctrine,[94] the first significant constitutional development after 1977 occurred with the determination to hold elections by direct universal suffrage to the European Parliament. The European Council declared in 1978:

The creation of the Communities, which is the foundation of ever closer union among the peoples of Europe called for in the Treaty of Rome, marked the determination of their founders to strengthen the protection of peace and freedom.

---

[91] Bernhardt, note 31 above, at 69.   [92] Ibid.
[93] This same lineage has been identified as 'soft approval' of the ECJ's developed jurisprudence (see Paul Craig and Gráinne de Búrca (eds), *EU Law, Text, Cases and Materials*, 2nd edn (Oxford: Oxford University Press, 1998) 331). However, my interpretation is that the ECJ was a contributor to the narrative of rights constructed, not its sole progenitor. It did not create the response to a need for authenticity. It added a jurisprudential component that the remainder of the institutions was able to enfold into the story that had already begun to be developed. Thus, it was not a situation of 'approval' as such but incorporation.
[94] Culminating in the constitutional assertion of 'founding' principle expressed in Article 6(1) TEU.

The Heads of State and of Government confirm their will ... to ensure that the cherished values of their legal, political and moral order are respected and to safeguard the principles of representative democracy, of the rule of law, of social justice and of respect for human rights.[95]

Human rights were inextricably linked with the 'creation of the Communities'. One flowed from the other, peace and freedom giving rise to, amongst other things, respect for rights. And as a part of the connection, the notion of the rule of law was implicated in the project by appearing as an element of the Member States' 'cherished values', one that must be safeguarded by the Communities. Law and rights in the Community remained interlocked, coupling with democracy to underpin the authenticity sought by the institution and to emphasize its historical and future commitment.

The Parliament also contributed to the developed narrative. Its Committee on Institutional Affairs, through Rapporteur K. De Gucht, reported in 1983 that '[r]espect for fundamental rights and their development are the prerequisite for and the essential foundation of the Union' and would provide, 'the construction of Europe with the necessary legitimacy'.[96] A subsequent Parliamentary Resolution in 1989 stated that 'respect for human rights is indispensable for the legitimacy of the Community'.[97] Whilst it then made clear its determination to 'achieve a basic Community instrument with a binding legal character guaranteeing fundamental rights'[98] it would, in the meantime, restate, 'the legal principles already accepted by the Community'.[99] The attendant Declaration did just that, maintaining that 'it is essential that Europe *reaffirm* the existence of a common legal *tradition* based on respect for human dignity and fundamental rights'[100] (emphasis added).

So we see the formation of the respect for rights played out as a 'legal tradition' re-affirmed rather than created, a tradition echoing the expressions of 'common heritage'. The phrases confirm the mythic nature of the narrative, its inventedness. With little in the way of hard textual support, a myth of origin became fixed through its re-iteration. By repeating the connection between law and rights in the context of a supposed long

---

[95] European Council Copenhagen Declaration on Democracy, EC Bull 3–1978 5–6.

[96] European Parliament, *Working Document on the Law of the Union* (1983) PE 83.326/fin/C (European Parliament Working Documents, 8 February 1983) 5.

[97] European Parliament, *Resolution Adopting the Declaration of Fundamental Rights and Freedoms* [1989] OJ C-120/51-52 at 51, Preamble para B.

[98] Ibid at 52 Preamble para G.   [99] Ibid at 52 Preamble para H.

[100] European Parliament, *Declaration of Fundamental Rights and Freedoms*, para 1 [1989] OJ C-120/52.

history, the statements operated so as to authenticate the Community as a source of decision-making both in the present and in the future.[101] The actual decisions made still required legitimating but this was a matter of programme administration rather than constitution. Thus the Parliament's expressed design to promote the cause of a catalogue of rights did not undermine the current statement of principles. Such a move would clarify operational dilemmas of rights application rather than substantially affect the role of rights in the Community's institutional story.[102]

The Parliament continued to operate on this basis. It would 'contribute to the development of a model of society which is based on respect for fundamental rights and freedoms and tolerance'.[103] It worked with the other Community organs to re-emphasize the Community's rights' traditions and heritage. A noteworthy example was the Preamble to the Joint Declaration by the Parliament, Council, and Commission Against Racism and Xenophobia, which stated 'Whereas the Community institutions attach prime importance to respect for fundamental rights ... Whereas respect for human dignity and the elimination of forms of racial discrimination are part of the common cultural and legal heritage of all the Member States'.[104]

The second part of this Preamble, in particular, indicates the application of myth. Any history of the Member States individually or collectively would find it almost impossible to establish a persuasive case for an effective heritage (legal, cultural, or otherwise) that indicated a resolve to eliminate racial discrimination. Philosophical argument and social programmes designed to counter racism may have existed but to suggest any deeper historical commitment is hardly credible. Yet the Declaration seeks to fix within its historical structure, its institutional story, a *post*-ordained truth that attempts to place the Community on the moral high-ground. Thus an important element of rights, and indeed of general principles of the Community in the form of non-discrimination is set amongst the ethical

---

[101] It might also be said that in attaching the Community to this history, the Community makes clear its resolve to act as a successor to the states of Western Europe *not* their companion but that will take us into a territory that is outside the scope of this book.

[102] This interpretation was given force by the Council at the Cologne IGC in 1999 when in advocating a Charter of Fundamental Rights of the European Union it stated that 'Protection of fundamental rights is a founding principle of the Union and an indispensable prerequisite for her legitimacy'. By implication, therefore, the Charter would merely be a step towards the improvement in the clarity of rights.

[103] See note 97, at 51 Preamble para C.

[104] European Parliament, Council, Commission, *Declaration Against Racism and Xenophobia* [1986] OJ C-158/1.

and, it must be stressed, the *mythical* traditions that make up the foundational principle.

The theme of tradition and heritage of rights, substantiating the founding principle, has also assumed a prominent position in the Parliament's annual resolutions on human rights in the Community. In 1993 it made plain the link between rights and the project of integration by determining that 'respect for human rights is the foundation of democracy and constitutes a basic principle of Community integration'.[105] In 1995 it recommended and declared that, 'the fiftieth anniversary of the end of the Second World War should be celebrated solemnly by the European Institution which, by its democratic nature and purpose, is attached to respect for and the promotion of human rights'.[106]

Equally, the Parliament and the other European organs have seen fit to introduce the notion of values into the rhetoric. The values expressed, including human rights, have been claimed to 'constitute the very essence of European integration'.[107] In 1996 the Commission brought open market economics into the net of an ethical heritage by contending that 'Europe is built upon a set of values shared by all its societies, and combines the characteristics of democracy human rights and institutions based on the rule of law and with those of an open economy underpinned by market forces, internal solidarity and cohesion'.[108]

The principle of respect for human rights has thus become inextricably interwoven into the framework of all aspects of the Community. Stretching from the social and political to the economic, the genealogy of rights as founding principle has become fixed both as an idea, a tradition, as a determinant of future action, and as an element of consistent values that

---

[105] Resolution A3-0025/93 and A3-0025/93/suppl: *Resolution on Respect for Human Rights in the European Community (Annual Report of the European Parliament)* [1993] OJ C-115/178 at 179.

[106] Resolution A4-0078/95: *Resolution on Human Rights in the World in 1993 to 1994 and the Union's Human Rights Policy* [1995] OJ C-126/15 Preamble para A.

[107] Resolution A4-0083/95: *Resolution on Progress in Implementing the Common Foreign and Security Policy* (November 1993–December 1994) [1995] OJ C-151/223 Preamble para D.

[108] Commission Opinion Re-inforcing Political Union and Preparing for Enlargement, 28 February 1996, para 8. See also the Vienna European Council Presidency Conclusions, 11 and 12 December 1998, para 4, which brings the Universal Declaration of Human Rights within the authenticating net by stating '[t]he European Union, which is founded on the principles of liberty, democracy, respect for human rights and fundamental freedoms and the rule of law, shares the values in which the Declaration (UDHR) is rooted and bases its actions on those values'. This returns us to the authentication sought from international instruments that was promoted by the ECJ.

'now inform on everything the Union does'.[109] The Treaty of Amsterdam, the EU Charter of Fundamental Rights, and the Draft Constitutional Treaty of 2003 in particular merely repeat the message. The latter explicitly refers to the 'Union's values' in Article I-2, which includes respect for human rights. In this sense, these texts should not be viewed as a final constitutional word. Rather, they are yet further contributions to the genealogy described.

Nevertheless, such is the power of the narrative described that to challenge its authenticity can be problematic. Even severe critics of the Community's human rights policies have given the story of founding principle credence. In the *Comité des Sages*' Report issued in 1998, *Leading by Example: A Human Rights Agenda for the European Union for the Year 2000*, it was stated that '[a]s the century and the millennium draw to a close, we call upon the European Council to restore human rights to the central role they enjoyed at the dawn of the European construction: that of the cornerstone upon which the fabric of a united Europe must rest'.[110]

Without the founding myth it is difficult to consider how the Community's human rights activities, however limp or effective one considers them to be, could have been enacted. For this reason alone, the story has assumed a position of textual impregnability, a base upon which human rights policies and I suggest their bifurcation, have been instituted.

6.3 Conclusion

We have seen in this chapter that, paradoxically, the narrative of human rights began with a silence on the subject. However, as the Community evolved, as it practised its acquired sovereignty, as it developed its text, the political structure created became capable of 'defining its own past and writing its own history'.[111] Consequently, the Community, in both trying to address the debilitating omission of a human rights dimension in its founding Treaties and seeking an authenticity it otherwise lacked, deployed the discourse of human rights retrospectively. It engaged in the

---

[109] Jacques Santer, 'Foreword' to the *Commission's Report on the External Dimension of the EU's Human Rights policy* (1995) COM(95) 567 final.

[110] Reprinted in Philip Alston *et al* (eds), *The EU and Human Rights* (Oxford: Oxford University Press, 1999) 921–7 at 926.

[111] See J.G.A. Pocock's essay, 'Deconstructing Europe' in Gowan and Anderson (eds), note 16 above, 297–317 at 309, in which he argues that for the Community to possess authority in the present it must capture its past.

formation of an interpretation of text and latent intent that sought to overcome the effects of the original condition. In so doing, it structured a framework for a history of the formation of the Community that is largely mythic in nature.

But why mythic? First, the rhetoric, law, and language employed relate to an assumed fact, that there is a heritage of human rights that belongs to and has been passed down by the peoples and states of Europe. Secondly, they maintain that the Community was and remains a natural successor, or co-owner of the purported common heritage. Together, the two elements combine to provide the Community with an ethical pre-history, a story of its generative ethos, *and* a history in the making, a self-constructed narrative that may authenticate the Community as a continuing and future site of governance. The narrative then serves as an authenticating link between memories of positive and inspiring humanitarian aspects of the European past and the aims of the Community in its moves towards union.

Here we begin to touch upon some of the myths that lie beneath the narrative. Human rights and fundamental freedoms may undoubtedly have a history within Western Europe, a history that can be traced back to the Greek and Roman civilizations, but to suggest that they are uncontested subjects, common throughout the nations of even the Member States of the Community, would be problematic, particularly if considered in terms of states' practice. Since the Declaration of the Rights of Man, history confirms the abuse of all human rights throughout Europe, sometimes on an unimaginable scale. Paul Ricoeur sums it up well. 'The history of Europe is cruel: wars of religion, wars of conquest, wars of extermination, subjugation of ethnic minorities, expulsion or reduction to slavery of religious minorities; the litany is without end'.[112]

Even focusing on civil and political rights, one would be hard pressed to identify any consistent and uniform respect in any state prior to 1945. Admittedly the liberal elite in Europe may have espoused a rhetoric of rights, demonstrated on occasion in practice, but this was invariably expressed in contingent terms. Human rights found little application, for instance, outside national borders in the European colonies.

The mythic elements of the narrative, therefore, came into play not simply in what was said but what was omitted. The abuse, the violence inflicted, the regimes that institutionally incorporated discrimination and

---

[112] Paul Ricoeur, 'Reflections on a New Ethos for Europe' in Richard Kearney (ed), *The Hermeneutics of Action* (London: Sage, 1996) 9.

repression whether at home or abroad were left to one side, forgotten in favour of what was 'good' about 'Europe'—all in the interests of compiling a narrative of constructive commonality. In making that choice the Community composed an essentially mythic story, part history, part 'symbolic discourse', the rhetoric of common heritage providing a foundational institutional narrative for the Project.

The analysis above also refers to Paul Ricoeur's reading of myth as a form of narrative (institutional in my terms) that connected a community's traditions with its projected utopia. That is precisely the interpretation that one might employ in the case of the narrative formed with regard to human rights. In other words, it is through myth that the Community mediates a genealogy of basic values and norms that underpin Western European society and ties it wholesale to the European Project. The former authenticates the latter.

Which brings us to the relevance of this analysis for the condition of incoherence that has been the major concern of this book. The creation of the myth of founding principle *and* the nature of its composition, which has been discussed in this chapter, suggest that 'incoherence' is an inaccurate or rather a simplistic description of the Community's human rights policies. The story of this chapter suggests that far from being beset by a condition of incoherence the Community has been singularly *coherent* in its formation of the narrative of founding principle. Thus when we come to examine the distinction that has arisen between the internal and external human rights policies, evidenced in Chapter 4, we have to apply an analysis that looks for a better description of the condition. Indeed, it is far more apt to describe the progress of the Community's policies as one of 'bifurcation'. In other words, two streams have emerged from a common stem, that stem being the established narrative of founding principle that has been described above.

But how does the narrative suggest that such a bifurcation has taken place? And why does it suggest that we *are* dealing with more than simply an incoherence of policy application and one that demands deeper critique? Two points that emanate from the mythic nature of the narrative of founding principle can be made tentatively to answer these questions.

First, as the concern of the Community's institutions was to stave off criticism on the one hand and gain authenticity on the other, the phrase 'human rights' was employed without regard to its full meaning or possibilities. Using the language of rights as a mythic construct was considered sufficient to satisfy the potential detractors of the Community and its Project. The resulting indeterminacy of human rights, the repeated failure to constitutionalize any definition of the term, ensured that the field was open to interpretation. Thus, the possibility of different human rights discourses, practices and definitions emerging in different arenas inspired by different sources of law and philosophy became apparent. The most significant demonstration of the potential for variance was at the external/internal divide. In both realms, the failure to define what the Community meant by human rights or how they should be applied and promoted in any coherent fashion determined that other forces could influence their evolution. As we have seen in relation to development policy and enlargement, these other influences, perhaps based on prejudices against the 'South' at one level and on supposed political exigencies at another, resulted in quite distinct patterns of human rights discourses and practices between the internal and external arising. The founding principle myth ensured that there was no constitutional, practical (and thus no narrative) base that could guide human rights policies along consistent and parallel lines. Equally, the two connected human rights traditions of the international arena on the one hand and the European on the other that were necessary for the Community's search for authenticity, have also contributed to the sense of bifurcation. The United Nations inspired discourse is not identical to the European. Although highly inter-related the possibility arises for a distinction in interpretation to develop and for different sources of law and meaning to be relied upon in the dichotomous spheres.

Secondly, the mythic nature of the narrative has presented a debilitating factor in any attempt to *rectify* a perceived bifurcation. Due to its lack of substance, its lack of certainty, the narrative of founding principle has become a vapid construction, a wistful statement repeated as law without any certain content or appreciation of practice. It ignores the 'considerable differences' between the attitudes of Member States to rights.[113] It has been incapable of providing a framework for any kind of consistent human rights activity. Instead, the myth has lost its vitality *and* relevance and has left human rights to the vagaries of context and inherent discrimination. As Chapter 4 demonstrated, the resulting distinctions between the internal and external approaches are significant. In this respect the myth's putative role in the authentication of the Community ironically represents the very means for doubting the Community's authenticity in human rights terms. For how can the Community hope to present itself as a polity informed by human rights principles when it has failed to provide any coherent

---

[113] Bernhardt, note 31 above, at 45.

understanding of what those human rights may comprise and how they might be applied?

Ricoeur warned of the political utilization of myths forged around an interpretation of history. He suggested that the past 'can be perverted, usually by monopolistic elites, into a mystificatory discourse that serves to uncritically vindicate the established political powers'.[114] There is a sense that this has occurred in relation to the Community and its discourse of human rights. The reliance upon a mythical tradition to validate the continuation of the European Project is an attempt at authentication that may adhere to the rhetoric but not necessarily the underlying principles of human rights. Significantly, it has enabled a basic discriminatory fault line in the Community's human rights policies to be created.

In essence, therefore, the myth of founding principle provided the *environment* for the distinct approach to internal and external human rights matters, the bifurcation, to develop. But what prompted the distinct policy directions to take the directions they have? The next chapter promotes the view that the adoption of a discourse of European Identity was, and remains, an underestimated factor in this respect, one that possesses severe implications for the future of human rights in the Community.

---

[114] Paul Ricoeur, 'The Creativity of Language: an Interview' in Richard Kearney, *Dialogues with Contemporary Continental Thinkers* (Manchester: Manchester University Press, 1984) 29–30, as quoted in Richard Kearney, 'Between Tradition and Utopia' in David Wood (ed), *On Paul Ricoeur: Narrative and Interpretation* (London: Routledge, 1991) 65.

7

European Identity and Human Rights

The stories that have been told about human rights and the Community rarely touch upon the notion of a European identity as an important influence. But when we look more closely at the development of a bifurcation in human rights policies, as introduced in the previous chapter, we can see that the two discourses of rights on the one hand and identity on the other, are bound tightly together. One could go so far as to suggest that the adoption and subsequent development by the Community of a narrative of European identity was a formative and crucial factor. In an effort to contribute to the construction of an overarching authenticity, one that would have both internal and external application, and promote the credibility of the whole European Project, the Community specifically deployed identity as a unifying and distinguishing concept. The resulting narrative incorporated human rights as an essential element in its definition. It was this that provided the impetus for the central internal/external bifurcation to develop.

Three specific arguments support this proposition. First, by adopting the term 'human rights' as one of the rhetorical components of the Community's initiating discourse of identity the institutional narrative that had already established the base conditions for rights language in the Community was given an added dimension. In other words, the representation that the Community was founded on respect for human rights (as discussed in the previous chapter) was paralleled by the assertion that rights were inherent in the concept of a European identity. Together these components formed the narrative environment for the development of bifurcation.

Secondly, the conscious legal and political construction of '*the* European Identity' as it was to become known, ensured in both practice and in concept that human rights were left to develop along two generally distinct lines. Internally, rights were associated with the desire to create an identity *with* the Community for its constituents. Externally, rights became party to the construction of an identity *of* the Community. The two realms operated with different policy objectives in mind. Thus distinct and bifurcated narratives evolved, applying different forces and conditions on the nature and scope of human rights that emerged in each sphere.[1]

The third argument turns to the theoretical aspects of identity. The bifurcation, encouraged by the adoption of a concept of identity, was rendered inevitable for two inter-related reasons. On the one hand, the nature of the process of collective identity foundation is one of distinction or discrimination. It creates dichotomous dimensions; the internal through a search for definitions of commonality amongst constituents, and the external by delineating differences with others. On the other hand, by making human rights a central component of a concept of identity, and by naming that identity 'European', the Community's institutional narrative of human rights was implicated in the internal/external differentiation. As no explanation or exposition was provided of rights in that narrative foundation, human rights became fluid subjects, open to distinct definition and application through their development in the two separate spheres.

This chapter explores these propositions in an effort to understand further how and why incoherence or rather bifurcation has manifested itself.

7.1 The myth of European identity

The possibility of a 'European identity' in the construction of a continental polity was not a phenomenon introduced by the Community. Its possibility, if not its existence, had been posited for centuries. Since at least Abbé de St. Pierre and Rousseau, it had formed the basic assumption from which strategies for peace within the continent, for co-operation and mutual advancement, for some kind of unity of purpose, had evolved.[2] In particular, as Carlo Gamberale outlined, it was the resistance movement during the Second World War that relied on a notion of a European identity of

---

[1] This is not to say that different dimensions of rights were not constructed within the internal or external spheres. However, the fundamental variance between the interior and the exterior approach is what concerns me.

[2] For a review of this history of a European identity see, for example, Denis de Rougemont, *The Idea of Europe* (New York: Macmillan, 1966), Gerard Delanty, *Inventing Europe: Idea, Identity, Reality* (London: Macmillan Press, 1995) and Derek Heater, *The Idea of European Unity* (Leicester: Leicester University Press, 1992).

values to give strength to its opposition to fascism.[3] Western European attempts to organize international co-operation on the continent immediately after the war took a similar stance. It would have been surprising, therefore, if the Community had not at some stage also drawn on the same discourse. This it did, at first obliquely and then openly. Throughout, as demonstrated below, the narratives that were constructed both established and reflected an external/internal divide.

7.1.1 *Early rhetorical moves*

Although no direct reference was made to the concept of identity in its initiating texts, the Community as a projected idea relied strongly upon notions of commonality for its inspiration. The dominant recurrent theme in the early stages may have been one of a mutuality of economic benefit possible through collective action but the Schuman Declaration, the ECSC Treaty, and the EEC Treaty, were all linked to a greater or lesser extent with the *re*-construction of an identifiable 'European' community.

The Preamble to the ECSC Treaty, for instance, resolved 'to substitute for age old rivalries the merging of their essential interests; to create, by establishing an economic community, the basis for a broader and deeper community among peoples *long divided by bloody conflicts*' (emphasis added).[4]

The emphasis of the text, and that of the Schuman Declaration, from which the rhetoric was borrowed, was not only on the transformation of violent relations but also the return to a community that had purportedly been subjected to an historical division. The natural bonds that somehow defined Europe as a single entity were to be re-established.

The EEC Treaty adopted the inference by looking towards the future of 'an ever closer union' not amongst states but 'the peoples of Europe'.[5] The eradication of division and the improvement in the 'living and working conditions' of the peoples of the Member States provided the dual focus of the programmes. The emphasis was placed on the economic structures to be instituted, an explicit intention of those who advocated a functionalist approach to European integration. Inherent in the scheme was a promise of regeneration and future material benefit. Alan Milward even suggests that European integration was 'the predictable response to the development of a

---

[3] Carlo Gamberale, 'European Citizenship and Political Identity' *Space and Polity* 1/1 (1997) 37–59.
[4] Preamble, ECSC Treaty.
[5] EEC Treaty, Preamble para 1.

universal international capitalist economy'.[6] The originating Treaties readily demonstrate the preference. But to see the enterprise as purely economic would run counter to the significant presence of an authenticating rhetoric that looked far beyond such materialist objectives. Importantly, the Project was supported throughout by association with the mythic entity named 'Europe'. The fact that the initial enterprise could call itself *the* European Community when so many on the continent remained outside was indicative of the central pretension and presumption put to work. In employing the epithet, a definition of the Project had therefore already cast its vision far beyond the politico-economic structures that were actually produced in the founding Treaties.

Even with the lack of direct reference to a European identity within the originating constitutional texts, it did not take long before the rhetoric emanating from the institutions began to play on notions of identification. Gradually during the early to mid-1960s the institutions' self-commentaries transcended the largely technical nature of their work. Increasingly they encompassed the underlying political ambitions of the whole European Project.

Initiatives enacted by the European Parliament in its formative period provide an example. During its plenary session in October 1960, it passed a resolution calling for a 'Right of Legation' and suggested that 'the creation of a flag common to the three Communities' was 'a political exigency'.[7] The blatant regard for the symbolic trappings associated with the nation-state (trappings that have since included an anthem, a passport, an assigned day for Europe) imitated nation-building strategies that might instil, or echo, feelings of popular identification. Indeed, the question of the reception of ambassadors sparked one of the first crises to interrupt the course of the Community. William Wallace described the resulting friction as an 'embittered quarrel between Hallstein [President of the Commission] and de Gaulle' which 'reflected de Gaulle's determination to prevent the EEC developing the symbols of statehood—and Hallstein's intentions that it should acquire them'.[8] So the rhetorical fault lines between the desire for a super-state on the one hand and an intergovernmental agreement on the other were set in place.

---

[6] Alan Milward, 'The Springs of Integration' in Peter Gowan and Perry Anderson (eds), *The Question of Europe* (London: Verso, 1997) 11.
[7] EC Bull 10-1960 at 76.
[8] William Wallace, *The Transformation of Western Europe* (London: Pinter Publishers, 1990) 30.

Even though de Gaulle's opposition to the ambitions of Community actors such as Walter Hallstein largely succeeded in the early part of the 1960s, the rhetoric of identity continued to find expression within the Community. Hallstein in particular drew on the concept of a commonality, stating in 1961 that 'amid all the differences there is a basic substance of identical elements, conditions, capacities, values, and psychological as well as intellectual concepts held in common, a sense of independence in happiness or misfortune, in jointly shaping or suffering our fate, in common weaknesses, but also in brilliant common achievements—cultural, economic and political'.[9]

Hallstein's vision reflected the general tenor of rhetoric as primarily concerned with the internal manifestation of the Community, what it meant, what it could do, for the people *of* the Member States. Ultimately, the expressed wish was for the people 'to be co-citizens in our common Europe', a natural consequence perhaps of their affiliation to the Community Project.[10]

The European institutions adopted similar language. In its introduction to the *Fourth General Report on the Activities of the Community* in May 1961 the Commission described itself as 'contributing to the establishment of a European idea which is penetrating more and more deeply into the consciousness of the public'.[11] It also advocated an awareness of a 'Community spirit' in all aspects of the Member States' activities.[12]

The assimilation of cultural concerns into the deliberations of the Community institutions held an equal significance in this regard. At the Bonn Conference in 1961, the Heads of State and Government produced a Communiqué that was a key document in the textual inception of a myth of identity within Europe.[13] It affirmed the *'valeurs spirituelles'* and the *'traditions politiques'* that formed a *'patrimoine commun'* or common inheritance between the Member States. It drew inspiration from the intent to act in concert to safeguard freedom and peace and expressed the determination to reinforce the *'liens politiques, economiques, sociaux et culturels'* that existed between their peoples. Resonating throughout was the assumption of both a common spirit and a common 'sense', of place, of origin, and of purpose. The myth of identity between peoples (rather than states) provided the rhetorical connection that bound these elements inextricably to one

---

[9] Speech by President Hallstein on receipt of the Charlemagne Prize, see EC Bull 5-1961 at 20.
[10] Ibid at 21. [11] EC Bull 5-1961 at 12.
[12] Ibid at 14. [13] EC Bull 7/8-1961 37–9.

project, that of the union of Europe. It also set a determined agenda designed to attract other European states ready to assume in '*tous les domaines*' the same responsibilities and obligations now accepted by the then current Members. The prospect of embracing an affinity with a past, which was only made coherent by a mythic and undefined notion of what it was to be 'of Europe', and a utopian future, was therefore held out to states who could qualify under those terms. The Project (linked rhetorically to all aspects of society and in particular culture) thus set its own definitional limits.

Other institutional actors in the Community acknowledged the possibilities of the discourse unleashed at Bonn. The European Parliament described the Communiqué as 'a recognition of the fact that education and culture have a considerable effect on the development of a European spirit'.[14] Hallstein commented that progress towards the 'political unity of Europe' would occur not just through 'economic and social policy, the specific subjects of the Treaty establishing the EEC' but also foreign policy and cultural policy.[15]

The Communiqué therefore provided an early impetus *within* the Community for repeated renditions of the notion of an *internally* appreciated European collective identity that extended far beyond the otherwise dominant economic structures. Even at this stage the conditions for bifurcation were beginning to emerge.

In embarking upon the effort to give credence to an internal identity, there was not only a self-conscious recognition that the process was one of 'revelation' (in other words, the 'truth' of the Community's rightful inheritance of the 'European' mantel was being 'revealed' to the people) but also an appreciation, ironically, that it required some degree of 'creative' interference. The Commission's publications on the 'flow of information on Europe', for instance, pointed out that there appeared to be 'little awareness that the *long-heralded concept of Europe* was in the process of becoming a political reality' (emphasis added).[16] It advocated the use of the media 'to foster the sense of being a citizen of Europe through increased knowledge and improved understanding of events'.[17]

Consequently, a keen appreciation of the value of establishing an internal narrative of identity was displayed even at this early stage in the life of the Community. Although not expressed in such stark terms the language

---

[14] EC Bull 8-1963 at 58. [15] Speech, 9 March 1961, EC Bull 3-1961 at 14.
[16] EC Bull 6-1963 42–4. [17] Ibid at 44.

indicated the institutional will to draw on the concept. Equally relevant was the concurrent development of Community law and the language used by the European Court of Justice (ECJ).

7.1.2 Internal identity and the foundations of Community law

Three judgments can be interpreted as giving legal substance to the burgeoning discourse of a European identity. All are of constitutional importance and readily familiar. All provide contributions towards an identity formed with an internal/external divide in mind.

First, the case of *Van Gend en Loos*[18] introduced the doctrine of direct effect into Community law. In deciding that Treaty provisions that give rise to rights or obligations could be relied upon by individuals under national law the ECJ drew on and contributed to the discourse already expressed through the other institutions. In particular, the judgment of the ECJ adopted a method of interpretation in reaching its decision that Paul Craig and Gráinne de Búrca describe as involving 'reading the text—and the gaps in the text—of the Treaty in such a way as to further what it determines to be the underlying and evolving aims of the Community enterprise as a whole'.[19]

The judgment clearly demonstrates an appreciation of the nascent identity rhetoric already considered. It referred to the 'spirit' of the Treaty as an important aspect for its interpretation. It observed that the 'Treaty is more than an agreement which merely creates mutual obligations between the contracting states' confirmed by the Preamble 'which refers not only to governments but to peoples'. It noted that institutions had been 'endowed with sovereign rights, the exercise of which affects Member States and also their citizens'. It confirmed that these citizens were intended to take part in the enterprise through the European Parliament. It concluded that:

The Community constitutes a new legal order of international law for the benefit of which states have limited their sovereign rights, albeit within limited fields, and the subjects of which comprise not only Member States but also their nationals ... Community law therefore not only imposes obligations on individuals but is also intended to confer upon them rights which become part of their legal heritage.[20]

---

[18] *Van Gend en Loos v. Nederlandse Administratie der Belastingen* Case 26/62 [1963] ECR 1.

[19] Paul Craig and Gráinne de Búrca, *EU Law: Text, Cases and Materials*, 3rd edn (Oxford: Oxford University Press, 2003) 184.

[20] *Van Gend en Loos*, note 18 above, at 12.

Although there was no attempt to rely on a *revelation* of identity, by which I mean that the ECJ did not suggest that Europe possessed an identity that awaited re-discovery, there was an implicit acknowledgement that an identity of interests and purpose in a constituency of the people had been created through law. The reference to a 'legal heritage' also inferred a shared history that could now be enhanced by the application of Community law.

The second significant judgment, the case of *Costa v. ENEL*,[21] established the principle that Community law should rule supreme over national law where any conflict arose. There was no constitutional provision to this effect and therefore the ECJ 'once again turned to the "spirit" of the treaty'.[22] It evoked the image of a 'Community of unlimited duration, having its own institutions, its own personality, its own legal capacity ... and real powers stemming from a limitation of sovereignty or a transfer of powers from the States to the Community'.[23] Specifically 'the terms and the spirit of the Treaty, make it impossible for the states ... to accord preference to a unilateral and subsequent measure over a legal system accepted by them on the basis of reciprocity'.[24]

The judgment confirmed the creation of a new legal order, one originating in the idea of the European Project rather than its technical presentation in the Treaties. Again, therefore, the ECJ gave legal credibility to the notion that the Community represented an institution of Europe, an institution that in turn represented Europe and its peoples.

The third judgment, I suggest, provides an example of the ECJ's wide ranging involvement in the shaping of a legal environment for the construction of a European *internal* identity. It involved the determination of the extent of the free movement of workers provisions laid down by Article 39 (ex Article 48) EC Treaty. The Article provided that 'such freedom of movement shall entail the abolition of any discrimination based on nationality between workers of the Member States'.[25] The implication was that internal distinctions would be rendered invalid in law. The case of *Hoekstra*[26] held that the definition of 'worker' was not to be left to national

---

[21] *Flaminio Costa v. ENEL* Case 6/64 [1964] ECR 585.
[22] Renaud Dehousse, *The European Court of Justice* (London: Macmillan, 1993) 42.
[23] *Van Gend en Loos*, note 18 above, at 594.
[24] Ibid.
[25] Article 39(2) (ex Article 48(2)) EC Treaty.
[26] *Hoekstra v. Bestuur der Bedrijfsvereniging voor Detailhandel en Ambachten* Case 75/63 [1964] ECR 177.

legislation. The Court decided that 'the Treaty attributes a Community meaning to that concept'. Consequently, the ECJ would be able to ensure that the free movement of workers as one of the 'foundations' of the Community would be established so as to give it full effect. It could not be undermined by errant national legislatures.

Naturally, the free movement of workers was but one of the principles required to form the internal market. However, the fact that it was the ECJ that was to determine the extent and application of the provisions ensured that fundamental social terms were to receive identification through the Community. Such was the basis for the development of a notion of citizenship. The Commission recognized as much as early as 1968 when M. Levi-Sandri, Vice-President of the Commission, made the connection explicit. He stated, 'Free movement of persons represents something more important and more exacting than the free movement of a factor of production. It represents rather an incipient form—still embryonic and imperfect—of European citizenship'.[27]

The introduction of the concept of citizenship, which was encouraged by *Hoekstra*, implied a clear internal/external divide in the matter of rights. The free movement of workers provisions were only to benefit the citizens of the Community thus excluding those not of Europe.

These judgments helped contribute to the political and legal climate for talking more substantively about a European identity focused on the Community. One could even suggest that a Community legal culture was being created through the ECJ's practices, a culture that would also inspire identity with the Project.[28] The audience was nevertheless primarily the Community's constituents and thus an internal affair.

7.1.3 *The construction of an external expression of identity*

At the same time as the Commission began to talk about the possibility of fostering a sense of citizenship it also considered the implications of the Community acting as an identifiable actor on the world stage. It commented that 'in our thinking as well as in the facts of social and national life the word Europe is imbued with a vitality that assures this Europe of the position due to it in the free world'.[29]

---

[27] EC Bull 11-1968 at 6.
[28] For a discussion on the possibility of a European legal culture see Volkmar Gessner, Armin Hoeland, and Csaba Varga, *European Legal Cultures* (Aldershot: Dartmouth, 1996).
[29] EC Bull 11-1968 at 44.

Here we find the creation of a vision of Europe through an external lens. Hallstein recognized the development of a distinct focus when trying to define 'the European order', as he termed it, suggesting 'The symbol of this order, its concept, remains unchanged. Seen from within, it is democratically constituted Europe built on a federal pattern. To the world around us it is outward looking and is inviting others to join it'.[30]

The presence of a similar double-vision in the thinking of the Community actors at this stage was also evident. At the 1961 Paris Conference the Heads of State expressed the hope that 'Amidst the crises and upheavals which beset the world, Western Europe, so recently ravaged by national rivalries and conflicts, is to become an area of understanding, liberty and progress. In this way, what Europe does will carry more weight in the world'.[31]

Credibility and influence as an international actor were to be achieved, in part, through the display of an 'appropriate' ethos, partially constructed through notions of liberty and freedom and the demonstration of that ethos in practice. The Community could then justify its position as successor to some of the sovereign powers of the Member States in the international arena.

But herein lay a central political tension. On the one hand the Community desired to promote itself as an internally authenticated polity. To achieve that authenticity external recognition would be required. On the other hand, certain Member States, although willing to give up some sovereign powers for the economic benefits that would accrue, still jealously guarded their foreign affairs. France in particular was loath to let slip its position of independent power operating with an individual role in the world. Its seat on the UN Security Council and its continuing colonial presence strengthened that desire.[32] Nevertheless, a functioning internal market *necessitated* an external face for the Community. The founding Treaties had already established the principle. Article 6(2) ECSC confirmed that 'in international relations, the Community shall enjoy the legal capacity it requires to perform its functions and attain its objectives'. The EC Treaty also conferred external powers on the Community,

---

[30] Statement on the Negotiations Concerning the UK's Accession to the EEC and the Causes of their Interruption, EC Bull 2-1963 at 17.
[31] Final Communiqué of the Meeting of Six Heads of State and Government, Paris, 10–11 February 1961, EC Bull 3-1961 at 13.
[32] See Panayiotis Ifestos, *European Political Co-operation: Towards a Framework of Supranational Diplomacy?* (Aldershot: Avebury, 1987) 122 and generally.

enabling the conclusion of agreements in relation to common commercial policy and trade and economic co-operation agreements with non-Member States.[33] Article 310 (ex Article 238) provided for the completion of 'association agreements' with preferred third party states.[34] Article 281 (ex Article 210) conferred legal personality on the Community and the case of *Costa v. ENEL* concluded that the Community possessed 'capacity of representation on the international plane'.[35]

The powers laid down enabled the Community to increase its presence in the world. The Yaoundé Convention, establishing trade relations with the overseas territories and countries in 1963 (considered in Chapter 2), and the GATT discussions seeking to cut tariffs in 1967, were both significant demonstrations of the possibilities.[36]

The affirmations of external competence ensured that the basis for establishing the Community as an entity capable of acting internationally, albeit in the economic realm only, was laid. The economic foundation was then used to enable progressive movement in the political field. Hallstein expressed the view that the Community now had a 'political responsibility in the world'.[37] This accorded with earlier rhetoric. Since, indeed, the erection of the Berlin Wall in 1961, a discourse of an external face founded upon a contrast with other regimes was firmly established. It would be wrong to assume this was all directed towards the East, however. The distinction with Soviet controlled states was based on a notion of 'freedom' but the USA was also singled out for contrast. The relationship with the USA provided the test for the Community's position in global affairs. Again, as Hallstein commented, 'the United States is starting to share—to share willingly—its position as a world power, which it is the only nation in the free world to possess, with a Europe which is increasingly assuming economic and political proportions comparable to its own'.[38]

---

[33] See Articles 133 (ex Article 113) and 300 (ex Article 228) EC Treaty respectively.

[34] Later, the ECJ in *Commission v. Council* [1971] ECR 263 concluded that the Community had the capacity to form contracts with third countries in relation to *any* of the objectives of the Treaty. For a discussion on this subject see I. Macleod. I.D. Hendry, and Stephen Hyett, *The External Relations of the European Communities* (Oxford: Oxford University Press, 1996).

[35] *Costa v. ENEL*, note 21 above.

[36] See Derek W. Urwin, *The Community of Europe: A History of European Integration Since 1945* (London: Longman, 1991) 131.

[37] See Hallstein's address to the Joint Meeting of the European Parliament and Consultative Assembly of the Council of Europe, EC Bull 11-1966.

[38] Address to the European Parliament, 26 June 1963, EC Bull 7-1963 at 10.

The USA was thus represented as a competitor for world influence. Europe had no particular interest in being subsumed as an American satellite. Indeed, it needed to establish its new identity by differentiating itself from the USA as well as the Soviet Union. Failure to do so would imply that Europe had lost its independence. William Wallace even suggests the desire to distinguish the Community from the USA at this time 'represented a claim to greater political autonomy, based on the assertion of "European values" and interests distinct from those which American leadership fostered'.[39] Wallace demonstrates that the Atlantic alliance, although providing essential security against the Soviet Union, also created a feeling of dependence on the USA which France in particular was unhappy in continuing. The possibility of an American dominated continent was perhaps almost as unpalatable for some as a Soviet dominated one. Consequently, the projection of a Europe founded upon distinguishable values indicated the formation of a particular type of identity that was as much 'anti-American' as 'anti-Communism'.[40] How true this was is difficult to gauge, and there have certainly been other interpretations that suggested an attitude of ambivalence towards the USA, an ambivalence that could not determine whether the USA represented a federal form to mimic or resist.[41] Nevertheless, the external condition was beginning to be deployed more frequently to define the European Project in tandem with the internal.

The interior and exterior rhetorical moves described above provided the textual basis upon which was to be constructed a politically promoted narrative of European identity. Internally, the early discourse captured asserted commonalities established in a mythical past and projected the Community as a utopian prospect fulfilling the needs of peace and prosperity. It was aimed at an unspecified constituency but relied on an anticipated ability to create *and* reveal an identity *with* the Community and its Project. Externally, the rhetoric and practice focused upon security and establishing the Community as an independent and distinguishable power on the world stage. It was here concerned with the identity *of* the Community. The basis was thus laid for a more concerted attempt by the Community to capture the two aspects of European identity. It was in

---

[39] Wallace, note 8 above, at 31.
[40] Ibid.
[41] See Stanley Hoffman, 'Europe's Identity Crisis: Between the Past and America' in Stanley Hoffman, *The European Sisyphus: Essays on Europe 1964–1994* (Oxford: Westview Press, 1995) 9–50.

the deliberate construction of *the* European identity, as it became termed, that human rights issues were then explicitly incorporated.

7.2 Human rights and the construction of *the* 'European Identity'

The internal and external projections of a sense of identity grew in intensity towards the end of the 1960s. The success of the customs union venture, realized in July 1968, was the primary reason for this change. The prospect of the Community moving beyond its economic roots now received significant attention. M. Armengaud (French representative of the Liberal and Allied Group) summed up the mood when he suggested in the European Parliament that Europe needed to 'show by results that we can create an economic, political and moral force that will have sufficient power of attraction for our fellow citizens and the Third World'.[42]

The Commission declared, 'Europe is not only customs tariffs ... [i]t must also be the Europe of the peoples, of the workers, of youth, of man himself'.[43] It emphasized the need to break through old structures of national governance inherited from the past whilst still retaining 'the old cultures, traditions, languages, originality, everything which gives the States their personalities and which constitutes the beauty, the diversity, the charm, and the *immanent value of Europe*' (emphasis added).[44]

The direct appropriation of an 'immanent value of Europe' to the Community, of a certain heritage and tradition, a civilization no less, mirrored the projection into the past already encountered when discussing human rights as founding principle in the previous chapter. On one level, it was inherently, and of necessity, an internal matter designed for consumption by constituents actual or potential. It was intended to create perhaps, as Epaminondas Marias suggests, 'a psychological community' or 'feeling of "belonging to" a *Gemeinschaft* with a common destiny, common beliefs and common values'.[45]

---

[42] General Debate in the European Parliament on Problems Connected with the Admission of New Members, EC Bull 3-1968 at 12.

[43] Commission, Declaration on the Occasion of the Achievement of the Customs Union on 1 July 1968, EC Bull 7-1968 5–8.

[44] Ibid.

[45] Epaminondas A. Marias, 'Mechanisms of Protection of Union Citizens' Rights' in Alan Rosas and Esko Antola (eds), *A Citizens' Europe: In Search of a New Order* (London: Sage, 1995) 208.

The narrative constructed in the Community's early phase now began to embrace a concept of 'citizenship' to fulfil this aim. It provided a shorthand for appreciating that the need for authenticity stretched beyond convincing governments and powerful economic interests to the wider constituency of the Community; the people. Already the subject of the mythic bases of community, the people's involvement in the Project continued to occupy the institutions. Public support was necessary if integration was to have any meaning. Mario Scelba, the President of the European Parliament in 1969, drew attention to a lack of 'enthusiastic support of the coming generations' and suggested that it was for the Parliament to take responsibility for the 'diffusion of the European idea and the ideals of European unity'.[46] The desirability of the people participating in the election of the European Parliament was now recalled.[47]

Similarly, greater effort was required if the Community was to confirm its burgeoning external acceptance. The end of de Gaulle's presidency of France in 1969 and the earnest re-opening of negotiations for the enlargement of the membership of the Community provided the opportunity for the external aspects of European union to be re-assessed. It has even been suggested that the then six Member States recognized the need to set in train the future development of European union *before* enlargement took place to ensure the new members, particularly the United Kingdom, did not curtail ambitions.[48]

Consequently, at the end of the 1960s both the internal and external nature of the Community became the subject of keen discussion.[49] The two elements were lodged together during the period 1970 to 1973 and gradually drawn into a common project theme. Human rights were directly implicated in the conjoined discourse. First, they were infused into the internal through their relation to citizenship and public participation. Secondly, they were embroiled in the external through the need to establish a moral identity for Europe on the world stage, one based on the values of human rights and democracy. The development of the process appears in a series of vital texts.

---

[46] Speech to the European Parliament in March 1969, EC Bull 5-1969 5–7.
[47] Article 190 (ex Article 138) EC Treaty required Parliament to be 'elected by direct universal suffrage'.
[48] See Urwin, note 36 above, at 146.
[49] Ibid at 131–46.

7.2.1 *The initiating texts of the 'European Identity'*

The Communiqué issued at the Hague meeting of the Heads of State in December 1969 set the rhetorical scene. It noted the final stage of the Common Market as 'paving the way for a united Europe capable of assuming its responsibilities in the world of tomorrow and of making a contribution commensurate with its traditions and its mission'.[50]

The subsequent Luxembourg Report issued by the Foreign Ministers of the Member States in October 1970 advocated a speedier move towards political union. In particular, it observed that a 'united Europe must be founded upon the common heritage of respect for the liberty and the rights of men'.[51] The integration and co-ordination of Member States' foreign policies was also essential to enable Europe 'to speak with one voice'. This was the base upon which the Community could be formed and developed, politically as well as economically. Europe could then 'show the whole world that [it] has a political mission'.[52]

The Paris Conference that followed in 1972, which saw the Community's enlargement to a membership of nine Member States, pursued the connection between union and external voice. It made the declaration that 'Member States reaffirm their resolve to base their Community's development on democracy, freedom of opinion, free movement of men and ideas and participation by the people through their freely elected representatives'.[53] It went on to state, 'In line with its political aims, the construction of Europe will allow the continent to assert its personality ... and to make its mark in world affairs as a distinct entity'.[54]

The use of the word 'reaffirm' echoes the process of constructing a myth of human rights as a founding principle. It suggests that this set of principles has always been part of the establishment of Europe. Collaboration in the presentation of myths underpinning the Community was underway.

Nonetheless, the new affirmations did much to mark the emphasis that was now placed on the formation of an identity. Commission President Ortoli summed up the intention when he declared, 'If a European Identity

---

[50] EC Bull 1-1970 11–18.

[51] *First Report of the Foreign Ministers to the Heads of State and Government of the European Community's Member States*, 27 October 1970. See Press and Information Office of the Government of the Federal Republic of Germany, *Texts Relating to the European Political Co-operation* (1974) 18–25.

[52] Ibid.

[53] EC Bull 10-1972 at 15.

[54] Ibid at 16.

is to emerge, Europe's place in the world must first be defined'.[55] The external was ascribed as the arena for establishing an 'Identity'. It was in the process of fleshing out the themes that the distinction became more manifest and the involvement of human rights became more concrete.

The two texts that emerged from meetings between the Foreign Ministers of Nine Member States held in Copenhagen in July and December of 1973 were vital in fixing the ground. The first, known as the Copenhagen Report,[56] set the agenda for the work of the newly labelled European Political Co-operation (EPC) (co-operation by the Member States in foreign affairs). It declared that:

The Political Co-operation machinery, which deals on the intergovernmental level with problems of international politics, is distinct from and additional to the activities of the institutions of the Community which are based on the juridical commitments undertaken by the Member States in the Treaty of Rome. Both sets of machinery have the aim of contributing to the development of European unification.[57]

The demarcation ensured that foreign policy would remain the preserve of the individual states acting outside the confines of the Community's regulative control. Specific Ministerial meetings (four times a year), the institution of a political committee to oversee the work required, a group of foreign ministry 'correspondents' to follow the implementation of political co-operation, working parties, studies, were all adopted as part of a strategy to co-ordinate external relations. But it remained clear that control was *outside* the Community's institutional framework. The Commission, the Parliament, and the ECJ had no legal role in the arrangements. Although the extra-Community activity was presented as a means of boosting the image of the Community in the world, it remained steadfastly within the control of the Member States.

7.2.2 *The Declaration on European Identity*

The second document to emerge from Copenhagen, the Declaration on European Identity, was more explicit still in producing an internal/external divide.[58] The Declaration described its intention to enable the Member States to 'achieve a better definition of their relations with other countries

---

[55] Presentation by François-Xavier Ortoli, 6th General Report on the Activities of the Communities 1972.
[56] Second Report of the Foreign Ministers to the Heads of State and Government of the European Community's Member States of 23 July 1973, EC Bull 9-1973.
[57] Ibid at Part II, para 12.   [58] EC Bull 12-1973 118–22.

and of their responsibilities in world affairs'. It set out the parameters of the definition, suggesting that it involved 'reviewing the common heritage, interests and special obligations of the Nine, as well as the degree of unity so far achieved within the Community'. The elements of *the* 'European Identity' (as it was specifically termed) then emerged in a sophisticated and structured narrative framework.

First, the desire to 'ensure that the cherished values of their legal, political and moral order are respected, and to preserve the rich variety of their national cultures' was expressed. The shared 'attitudes to life, based on a determination to build a society which measures up to the needs of the individual' were noted. The will 'to defend the principles of representative democracy, of the rule of law, of social justice—which is the ultimate goal of economic progress—and of respect for human rights' was affirmed. Notions of a common heritage coursed through the words providing a kind of general ethos for the Community. However, none of the terms was given any definition. They were presented as self-explanatory and axiomatic.

Secondly, the parties noted that the Common Market and the 'common policies and machinery for co-operation' qualified as 'an essential part of the European Identity'. Thus, the Community Project was coupled with the ethos described and re-affirmed as an 'essential' component of the identity being proposed. One was implicit in the other. The deliberate sense of capture was palpable.

Thirdly, the document proposed that the 'diversity of cultures within the framework of common European civilization, the attachment to common values and principles, the increasing convergence of attitudes to life, the awareness of having specific interests in common and the determination to take part in the construction of a united Europe, all give the European Identity its originality and its own dynamism'.

'Unity in diversity' was the catchphrase to be employed. It pleaded internal difference but argued an essentialist discourse of commonality through an intangible, value-based construct. The European Identity was therefore a concept enabling the Community to subsume all those factors, cultural, economic, political, which might define Europe. Portraying the Community in this way was an exercise in filling the ethical and moral void that otherwise remained.

Fourthly, the Declaration considered the European Identity 'in relation to the world'. Member States agreed to co-operate where possible in foreign policy so as to help manufacture a European Identity 'as a function of the dynamic of the construction of a united Europe'. They concluded that in 'their external relations the Nine propose progressively to undertake the definition of their identity in relation to other countries or groups of countries'. The external was to be employed as a method of providing meaning for the European Identity through contrast or conceivably through comparison.

The four-part construction outlined above set the pattern for the Community's discursive practices when acting upon or defining value-based concepts. For human rights no definition was provided. Their meaning, scope, and practical effect were open to future formulation. As internally and externally policy construction operated independently, with different frameworks, different political agendas, and different legal bases, the potential for distinct understandings and applications forming in each sphere was set within the institutional narrative. Human rights were shaped by two separate attitudes towards identity. Internally, human rights developed in conjunction with a narrative that sought to construct an identity *with* the Community. Externally, the narrative was concerned with identity *of* the Community. The distinction is a subtle but important one and is considered below.

7.2.3 *Rights and identity* with *the Community*

Internally, embracing human rights as a general governing principle of a potential union was presented as a necessary strategy to acquire popular support. The Report on European Union in 1975 indicated the Commission's perspective.

> European Union will naturally rest on certain general principles which are held by all the Member States. These principles, which have repeatedly been reaffirmed, whether in existing Treaties or in statements approved by the meetings of the Heads of Government, are democracy, freedom of opinion, the free movement of people and of ideas, participation by the peoples through their freely elected representatives, and the protection of human rights.[59]

The ethical location of human rights within the framework of a union of peoples was thus strongly advocated. In practice, however, reliance was placed on the development of rights through the jurisprudence of the ECJ. The alternatives, namely the creation of a separate catalogue of legally enforceable rights or accession by the Communities to the European Convention on Human Rights (ECHR) could not acquire the necessary

---

[59] Report on European Union, EC Bull Suppl. 5-1975 para 4 at 9.

political and legal support. The Joint Declaration on Human Rights of 1977[60] and the preceding Commission Report[61] acknowledged the compromise. The ECJ was left to operate independently and piecemeal in establishing a rights discourse in Community law. This it did, relying heavily on the ECHR for inspiration. Subsequent moves by the Commission to acquire a concrete definition of rights applicable in the Community failed to find a solid constitutional foundation but the efforts made continued to mark the connection between human rights and identity *with* the Community. A Commission Report in 1979, for instance, noted the potential advantage of acceding to the ECHR as 'improving the image of Europe as an area of freedom and democracy'.[62] Eventually, however, the EU Charter of Fundamental Rights appeared as a compromise measure, initially neither acceding to the ECHR nor creating a justiciable instrument, but at least formulating a 'more visible' presence of rights in the Community,[63] before the Draft Constitutional Treaty of 2003 (DCT) proposed a fundamental realignment. Article I-7 DCT looked to the Community to 'recognise the rights, freedoms and principles set out in the Charter' and to 'seek accession to the [ECHR]'.[64] The underlying desire remained to 'bring citizens ... closer to the European design and the European institutions ... and how to develop the Union into a stablising factor and a model in the new, multipolar world'.[65]

Human rights have also been subject to definition internally through their association with the burgeoning concept of a European citizenship. Although Gamberale has a point in refusing to equate citizenship with identity (the former he asserts is based on the principle of action, the latter on the principle of being)[66] the discourse that made up the identity narrative did not rely upon such a distinction. Rather identity *with* the Community was to be encouraged through, at first, the granting of 'special

---

[60] [1977] OJ C-103/1.

[61] *Report on the Problems of Drawing up a Catalogue of Fundamental Rights for the European Communities* EC Bull Supp 5-1976.

[62] Commission, 'Memorandum on the Accession of the European Communities to the Convention for the Protection of Human Rights and Fundamental Freedoms', EC Bull Supp 2-1979 at 11.

[63] EU Charter of Fundamental Rights [2000] OJ C-364/08 Preamble.

[64] See Draft Constitutional Treaty 2003 (available at http://european-convention.eu.int/docs/Treaty/cv00850.en03.pdf).

[65] See Declaration of the Laeken Council (available at http://european-convention.eu.int/pdf/LKNEN.pdf).

[66] Gamberale, note 3 above.

rights', the development of economic and social rights emanating from the Treaties, and the right to participate in the election of the European Parliament. Leo Tindemans suggested the purpose of such developments in his famous report on European Union in 1975:

> The construction of Europe is not just a form of collaboration between States. It is a *rapprochement* of peoples who wish to go forward together, adapting their activity to the changing conditions in the world while preserving those values which are their common heritage. In democratic countries the will of governments alone is not sufficient for such an undertaking. The need for it, its advantages and its gradual achievements must be perceived by everyone so that effort and sacrifices are freely accepted. Europe must be close to its citizens.[67]

The link between values, Europe, and a citizenry of the Community therefore seemed uppermost in Tindemans' rhetorical presentiment of the Community's future. Questions of identity *with* the Community by the people were key to the political construction in view.

The European Parliament also expressed the connection between citizenship rights and identity in 1975 by suggesting, 'practical measures capable of contributing to the development of a European Community consciousness will be adopted'.[68] These measures related to rights that could be given to citizens under the existing Treaty provisions. They were what Antje Wiener has called the 'legal ties of belonging'.[69] As the internal narrative of human rights developed from the 1970s onwards, the ties became more defined and set into the constitutional framework of the Community, culminating in the establishment of citizenship in the Treaty on European Union. Citizens' rights have since been outlined in the EU Charter of Fundamental Rights.[70]

However, this is not the place to enter into detailed discussion concerning the nature and scope of the narrative of citizenship. That project has been the subject of intensive studies in recent times.[71] The point for

---

[67] EC Bull Supp 1-1976 at 26.
[68] European Parliament Resolution, 6 August 1975 [1975] OJ C-179 at 28.
[69] Antje Wiener, 'Assessing the Constructive Potential of Union Citizenship: A Socio-Political Perspective' (European Integration Online Papers, 1997) vol 1 no 17 (available at http://eiop.or.at/eiop/texte/1997-017a.htm) at 16.
[70] See note 63 above, Articles 39–46.
[71] Carole Lyons lists many of the relevant works in 'A Voyage around Article 8: An Historical and Comparative Evaluation of the Fate of European Union Citizenship' *Yearbook of European Law* 17 (1997) 135–63 at note 2. See, in particular, Siofra O'Leary, 'The Relationship between Community Citizenship and the Protection of Fundamental Rights in Community Law' *CML Rev* (1995) 519–54 in which the potential for linking citizenship with fundamental rights is explored.

my purposes is that the definition of rights internally was subject to a dual process, first through the jurisprudence of the ECJ and second through the initiatives of the Community with regard to citizenship. In both cases, identity with the Community was sought through human rights. As Griánne de Búrca has suggested they 'may be seen as capable of providing a moral grounding to a legal order which on its face was established principally to support the pursuit of economic goals, and also to forge an identity which could simultaneously (i) have a cross-national appeal to individuals and to groups within the Community and (ii) emphasize shared or common values already existing within the member states'.[72]

Human rights were thus a 'tool of integration'. They were not defined in relation to a predetermined set of ethical precepts but were rather the subject of political and legal negotiation and argument. The consistent theme, however, was that they had internal application. Both human rights discourse, as developed in the ECJ, and citizenship and other Treaty-based rights provided the means by which the Community could acquire acceptance from its constituents and encourage a sense of identification with its institutional existence. In this sense, rights and citizenship are inseparable from the institutional construction of an identity with the Community. Both affect the scope and character of the other. Whether that process necessarily reflected an exclusionary project is something that cannot be discounted.[73]

7.2.4 *Rights and identity* of *the Community*

Externally, the picture was somewhat different. The terminology of European Identity was here retained and frequently recited. Ortoli, referred to the 1973 Paris Conference, for instance, in the following terms:

Ever present in the minds of those taking part in the Conference was a concern to establish a European identity. In this, they were expressing a heartfelt desire, shared by all our peoples, to differentiate ourselves from the rest of the world, not only to play our own role in the world and thus take Europe's destiny into our own hands,

---

[72] Griánne de Búrca, 'The Language of Rights and European Integration' in Jo Shaw and Gillian More (eds), *New Legal Dynamics of European Union* (Oxford: Clarendon Press, 1995) 43. The Reflection Group Report at Messina 1995 specifically linked citizenship with the Community as a 'unique design based on common values'.

[73] For a discussion of this possibility see Jo Shaw, 'The Many Pasts and Futures of Citizenship in the European Union' *EL Rev* (1997) 554–72.

but also to formulate and implement the plan for a civilisation which, to quote Leon Blum, would again be human.[74]

The Commission's 1975 Report on European Union stated that 'peace, security, stability and cooperation with the Third World, will be the expression of the European identity defined in the Copenhagen document'.[75] In neither case was mention made of human rights. Indeed, the way the EPC developed in the early 1970s it was clear that respect for human rights was not such a fundamental principle to promote to the world as the Copenhagen rhetoric may have implied. Issues that affected individual Member States were paramount.[76] The concern of external relations was initially acknowledged by the Commission as focusing on 'energy' (understandable given the oil crisis of 1973/4) 'raw materials and general relationship with industrialized and developing countries'.[77] Political concerns of the Member States reigned in the projection of the Community to the outside world. The so-called 'London Report' in 1981, produced by the Foreign Ministers as the third report on EPC, confirmed that a 'flexible and pragmatic approach' would be maintained.[78] The 'political aspects of security' were identified as the key issues.

However, over time human rights began to acquire a greater presence in foreign affairs. In the field of development policy and in accession matters, as we have seen, human rights promotion evolved as an issue that demanded attention. As Chapters 2 and 3 have demonstrated, the Community has made an explicit and implicit correlation between its projection and the human rights it chooses to promote. The link is specific. This was eventually enhanced by the Treaty structure itself with the Single European Act of 1986.[79] The Preamble stated that the Community should 'display the principles of democracy and compliance with the law and with human rights' in speaking with 'one voice' to the world. No mention of human rights was made in the Title on European co-operation in the sphere of foreign policy but the Foreign Ministers of the Member States did confirm in the same year as the SEA that 'respect for human rights is an

---

[74] Address by Mr Francois-Xavier Ortoli, President of the Commission, 13 February 1973, EC Bull 2-1973 6–7.
[75] See note 59 above, para 5 at 9.
[76] For a review of the work of EPC during these formative years, see Ifestos, note 32 above.
[77] See note 59 above, para 146 at 41.
[78] EC Bull Supp 3-1981
[79] EC Bull Supp 2-1986.

important element in relations between third countries and the Europe of the Twelve'.[80]

Nevertheless, the constitutional seal was finally placed on the connection between the European Identity, external affairs, and human rights in the TEU. The Preamble stated that a common foreign and security policy (CFSP) would reinforce 'the European identity'. Article B stated that the European Union would set objectives to include the assertion of 'its identity on the international scene'. And Article J.1 established that a key principle of the CFSP was to 'develop and consolidate democracy and the rule of law, and respect for human rights and fundamental freedoms'. The connection, always present since Copenhagen, now had constitutional form subsequently confirmed, and clarified, by the Draft Constitutional Treaty of 2003.[81]

The two facets of identity related above, identity with the Community and identity of the Community, do not of themselves explain why rights practice should have developed differently in each sphere. However, it is my contention that the very association made between rights and identity ensured that different standards and attitudes would be applied. A bifurcation would evolve *because* of the nature of identity and the effects of its deployment as a political tool. The theoretical appreciations of identity in the context of the Community that justify this conclusion are considered below.

7.3 Identity as unity; identity as distinction

Identity formation and assertion has assumed a critical importance for new social and political movements in recent times. In the fields of ethnicity, feminism, regionalism, and particularly incipient nationalism (to name a few), identity has been used as a focus for gathering people together under the banner of some unifying notion or characteristic in order to critique or challenge existing socio-political structures or form new ones in their stead. The deployment of collective identities in this way has thus always been fundamentally concerned with acts of power. They represent sites of struggle and inevitably attract the attention of groups competing for political influence.

---

[80] EC Bull 7/8-1986 as quoted by Andrew Clapham, 'Where is the EU's Human Rights Common Foreign Policy, and How is it Manifested in Multilateral Fora?' in Philip Alston *et al* (eds), *The EU and Human Rights* (Oxford: Oxford University Press, 1999) 627–83 at 633.

[81] See, in particular, Articles I-3(4) and III-193 DCT, note 64 above.

Stuart Hall has described how two possibilities exist for the shaping of these collective identities, the second in effect opposing the first.[82]

From the first perspective Hall suggests that identities may be constructed through the recognition by people of 'an unchanging "oneness" or cultural belongingness' that overcomes any 'superficial differences'.[83] For A.D. Smith, and his studies of national identities, the unity will occur through a complex intersection of common appreciations; a recognized geographical territory accompanied by 'common memories and myths of origin, a mass, standardized public culture, a common economy and territorial mobility, and common legal rights and duties for all members of the collectivity'.[84]

Through a sense of 'kinship', based on a unity of understanding and common heritage, national identities may appear strong enough to underpin a feeling of nationalism.[85]

Laurence Grossberg describes this model type as one where 'there is some intrinsic and essential content to any identity which is defined by either a common origin or a common structure of experience or both'.[86] Where people see different commonalities at the same location, the struggle then becomes bounded by the search for *the* 'authentic' identity.

Hall argues that the essentialist nature of the above model is unsustainable in itself. In some respects it is self-deluding. It is based on a premise that there can be an unchanging universal truth that binds people together irrespective of their actions. Identities are 'found' or 'revealed', or even created, a process that denies the impact of time and changing social relationships as well as modes of communication.

Hall refuses to accept the notion of an 'absolute' identity, composed of immutabilities, and proposes an alternative reading. His second perspective, or model, is preferred to the essentialist approach. It recognizes that identities are in a constant state of flux, subject to negotiation over time and

---

[82] See Stuart Hall, 'Cultural Identity and Diaspora' in J. Rutherford (ed), *Identity: Community, Culture, Difference* (London: Lawrence and Wishart, 1990) 222–37 and 'Introduction: Who Needs Identity' in Stuart Hall and Paul du Gay (eds), *Questions of Cultural Identity* (London: Sage, 1996) 1–17.

[83] Hall 'Introduction', note 82 above, at 4.

[84] Anthony D. Smith, 'National Identity and the Idea of European Unity' in Peter Gowan and Perry Anderson, *The Question of Europe* (London: Verso, 1997) 318–42 at 323.

[85] See Anthony D. Smith, *National Identity* (London: Penguin, 1991) for a full discussion of Smith's views on identity and nationalism.

[86] Laurence Grossberg, 'Identity and Cultural Studies: Is That All There Is?' in Hall and du Gay (eds), note 82 above, at 89.

space, and can never be truly unified. They are contingent on context or 'position', historical, linguistic, cultural, and are 'multiply constructed across different, often intersecting and antagonistic, discourses, practices and positions'.[87] 'All forms of fixity and essentialism', as Rutherford claims, are eschewed in favour of a 'politics of articulation' that refuses to accept 'social, political and class formations' as existing *a priori*.[88]

Three interconnected appreciations help to understand the significance of Hall's interpretations. First, as Grossberg suggests, 'struggles over identity no longer involve questions of adequacy or distortion, but of the politics of representation itself'.[89] In other words, identities are 'constituted within, not outside, representation' and are crucially concerned with 'using the resources of history, language and culture in the process of becoming rather than being'.[90] Thus 'practices of representation' operate so as to constitute the field of any collective sense of identity. Commonalities, mythic or otherwise, are the subject of 'articulations', which combine to provide a discourse of identity open to continual alteration, definition, and manipulation. 'Identity politics' has been used to describe the struggles that emerge as a result.

The second appreciation takes us to the importance of narrative in the socio-political sphere. Representations or discourses of identity are structured and communicated through narrative. It is 'through narrativity that we come to know, understand, and make sense of the social world' and it is through narrativity and narratives that social identities are constituted.[91] Paul Ricoeur asks, 'do not human lives become more readily intelligible when they are interpreted in the light of the stories that people tell about them?'[92] and proposes that identities are formed through narratives as a result. The narrative process is, therefore, the means by which people structure the representations of their understandings of their identity over time and communicate that understanding to others. Equally, it is the means by which represented identities of others are comprehended.

---

[87] Hall 'Introduction', note 82 above, at 4.

[88] Jonathan Rutherford, 'A Place Called Home: Identity and the Cultural Politics of Difference' in Rutherford (ed), note 82 above, 9–27 at 20.

[89] Grossberg, note 86 above, at 89.

[90] Hall 'Introduction', note 82 above, at 4.

[91] Margaret R. Somers and Gloria D. Gibson, 'Reclaiming the Epistomological "Other": Narrative and the Social Constitution of Identity' in Craig Calhoun (ed), *Social Theory and the Politics of Identity* (Oxford: Blackwell, 1994) 58–9.

[92] Paul Ricoeur, 'Narrative Identity' in David Wood (ed), *On Paul Ricoeur: Narrative and Interpretation* (London: Routledge, 1991) 188–99 at 188.

David Rasmussen interprets the process as, 'A narrative can link the past with the future by giving a sense of continuity to an ever changing story of the self. Because narrative has this potentiality it is uniquely qualified to express the ongoing dialectic of selfhood and sameness'.[93] People are able to conjoin with others in a sense of shared identity by accepting and repeating a particular narrative, or in other words, telling similar stories about themselves. At the site of the collective, an institutional narrative may be constructed that is concerned with substantiating the institution's 'authentic' position to speak for its purported members. From that location a collective identity may therefore be promoted both to reinforce a unity of constituents and provide the institution with justification for its existence.

Thirdly, and most important for an analysis of bifurcation, is the appreciation that the construction of identities through representation (or rather narrative) inherently involves a process of definition, of delineation played out over time. Articulations of identities, 'produced in specific historical and institutional sites within specific discursive formations and practices, by specific enunciative strategies' as Hall maintains, 'emerge within the play of specific modalities of power, and thus are more the product of the marking of difference and exclusion, than they are the sign of an identical, naturally-constituted unity'.[94] In particular, Hall claims that, 'It is only through the relation to the Other, the relation to what it is not, to precisely what it lacks, to what has been called its *constitutive outside* that the "positive" meaning of any term—and thus its identity—can be constituted'.[95]

The process of constitution described consciously evokes the work of Jacques Derrida. Most significantly it echoes Derrida's understanding of difference. Through the tendency of Western systems of knowledge to impose a fixed meaning on words and terms so as to stabilize or universalize them (and impose them on others) different world-views, different conceptions of culture and values are obscured and suppressed. Words are thus employed to maintain power structures through their denial of alternative. The effect is to create a language based on opposition and an opposition that assumes the domination of one term over its opposite.

---

[93] David Rasmussen, 'Rethinking Subjectivity: Narrative Identity and the Self' in Richard Kearney (ed), *Paul Ricoeur: The Hermeneutics of Action* (London: Sage, 1996) 164–5. For the inspiration for the thesis of narrative identity, see Paul Ricoeur, *Time and Narrative Vol III* (Chicago: University of Chicago Press, 1988).
[94] Hall 'Introduction', note 82 above, at 4.
[95] Ibid.

Derrida describes the process as one 'not dealing with the peaceful coexistence of a *vis-à-vis*, but rather with a violent hierarchy. One of the two terms governs the other'.[96] Thus masculine is opposed to feminine, rational to irrational, civilized to uncivilized, advanced to backward, internal to external. If a term is used institutionally it therefore immediately distinguishes and separates its alternative. And in the exercise of power, where words are infused with particular importance and sited as preferential, the effect is to portray the alternative as unworthy and dangerous. Identity construction through articulation can then become a process of definition through distinction, creating 'margins' to a core of projected essential truths.

In Derrida's conception, it is here that the sense of '*differance*' is deployed as a term to describe 'the process of differentiation'.[97] The suggestion is that 'without relations of *differance* no representation could occur'[98] and meaning is deferred or postponed, dependent always upon the 'margin' to give it definition. The margin then operates as a 'supplement, marking what the centre lacks but also what it needs in order to define fully and confirm its identity'.[99] Deconstruction is Derrida's method for uncovering the whole scheme of *differance*.

Hall recognizes the value of Derrida's work in the analysis of identity formation and the dangers it uncovers. Differences that provide a conceived identity with meaning can change across time and space. Such is the play of identity formation. The danger occurs when presenting an identity as possessing a 'natural and permanent' meaning rather than one that is 'arbitrary and contingent'.[100] Then the possibility for discrimination and violence becomes incorporated into the very political structures of an institution.

At the site of the institution, therefore, narratives that draw on a concept of identity may well display a tendency, if not inevitability, to be fundamentally engaged in a practice of distinction. By making a choice of identity construction, an institution defines who is *not* part of its constituency as much as who is. The process of definition may be conscious or unconscious but it is always concerned with power relations, with determining the rights and interests of those who may be heard and authorized

---

[96] Jacques Derrida, *Positions* (London: Athlone Press, 1981) 41.
[97] Ibid at 101 note 13.
[98] Hall 'Cultural Identity', note 82 above, at 229.
[99] Rutherford, note 88 above, at 22.
[100] Hall 'Cultural Identity', note 82 above, at 230.

to take part in the politics of the institution. As such, there is always the question of narratives of identity providing the conditions for violent discrimination and oppression at worst and exclusion at best.

The exclusionary effects of identity narratives proclaimed by political institutions such as the Community (or nations or communities for that matter) might therefore result in an interior/exterior divide. Internally, the discourse will be concerned with defining unity, defining constituents, their original link with the institution, their rights to belong to and take part in the institution. Externally, the tendency will be to present a collective unity already formed, distinct from other collectivities. The *terms* for creating or revealing an internal identity *with* the collective inside, and those utilized for determining an external identity *of* the collective outside, become shaped by the domain in which they find themselves. Even if identical terms are applied initially in each sphere, as I have attempted to show is the case with human rights in the Community's identity discourse, their conceptualization in and through practice may well be subject to differentiation as the internal and external narratives develop and deviate. It is this condition and process that I argue has provided the impetus for bifurcation.

The theoretical position advanced above has not been lost on studies of the idea of Europe and the attendant notion of a European identity. Many works have concerned themselves with the related questions of identity and legitimacy.[101] But then, the European Project has always been infused with the need to bring the people of Europe together and in so doing cause a distinction to be made as to who is not of Europe. Derek Heater argues that:

> No project for voluntary political integration would be at all credible unless the putative member states shared some cultural and political traditions and values. This sense of identity necessary for a successful union of states is Janus-faced. In looking inward it must recognise the characteristics which the members have in common and which thus provide at least a modicum of homogeneity. In looking outward it must recognise the distinctiveness, incompatability, even enmity of those outside the union.[102]

Whether or not Heater is correct in assuming the necessity of the 'Janus-faced' identity, the fact is that observers have noted the interior/exterior consequences of the Community adopting a discourse of European identity

---

[101] For one of the many examples see Thomas Banchoff (ed), *Legitimacy and the European Union: the Contested Polity* (London: Routledge, 1999).

[102] Derek Heater, *The Idea of European Unity* (Leicester: Leicester University Press, 1992) 180.

into its institutional narrative. Philip Schlesinger for instance recognizes that 'the making of identities is an active process that involves inclusion and exclusion' and in the context of the Community the construction of a collective identity will entail engaging with both the 'official identities of existing nation states, and ... the emergent identities of regions' but also with definitions imposed from without.[103]

Similarly, although Zenon Bańkowski and Emilios Christodoulidis do not accept that exclusion is a necessary consequence of identity constructions in the Community (suggesting 'the identification "Europe"' could be considered as a 'contested rather than a natural setting ... one that hosts mutually underwriting and mutually denying identifications') they acknowledge the powerful pull towards exclusion and discrimination.[104] Their solution, however, seems to deal only with the exclusion of the internal 'other'. Those of the external, those not of Europe, are not considered and are potentially excluded by the very terms 'Europe' and 'European', which are not subjected to critique in their analysis.

Here, the importance of attaching the term 'Europe' to identity, as the Community has done, is thrown into sharp focus. 'Europe' as a definitional term involves a discriminatory process, *excluding* the 'other' through geography firstly, but also through the notion of a European society and civilization, frequently presented as superior, developed, advanced, all in opposition to the uncivilized, inferior, undeveloped, backward other. 'Europe' reflects those hierarchical relations of dominance that were employed as a hallmark of colonialism. And the terms 'Europe' and 'Europeans' continue to signify separation and distinction with 'non-Europe' and 'non-Europeans'.

The possible violent effects of subsuming the discourse of superiority into the narrative of identity adopted by the Community (through the almost synonymous treatment of Europe and the Community, Europe appropriated by the Community 'as shorthand for itself')[105] has, of course, worried numerous commentators. Hence, there has been a great search for alternative methods of satisfying the perceived need to possess an identity. However, the concern has usually been with resolving the tensions that

---

[103] Philip Schlesinger, *Media State and Nation: Political Violence and Collective Identities* (London: Sage 1991).

[104] Zenon Bańkowski and Emilios Christodoulidis, 'The European Union as an Essentially Contested Project' *European Law Journal* 4/4 (1998) 341–54 at 354.

[105] Victoria Goddard, Josep Llobera, and Cris Shore, 'Introduction: The Anthropology of Europe' in Goddard *et al* (eds), *The Anthropology of Europe* (Oxford: Berg, 1994) 26.

might exist between a putative European identity and competing national or regional identities *within* the Community. A.D. Smith, for instance, has sought to look to the past for inspiration, addressing potential unifying commonalities in his oft-quoted phrase:

> The heritage of Roman Law, Judeo-Christian ethics, Renaissance humanism and individualism, Enlightenment rationalism and science, artistic classicism and romanticism, and, above all, traditions of civil rights and democracy which have emerged at various times and places in the continent—have created a common European cultural heritage and formed a unique cultural area straddling national boundaries and interrelating their different national cultures through common motifs and traditions.[106]

Overcoming internal conflict is the aim. Equally, Daniela Obradovic may dispute the possibility of Smith's suggested enterprise, and the search for new myths, but her concern is that 'the Union simply lacks the mythical ground for reinforcing its policy legitimacy in a way which would stabilize and institutionalize the community'.[107] The internal play of identities provides the focus of attention. Admittedly this is a very important area for those concerned with internal legitimacy and social cohesion within the Community. However, the possibility of distinction with the external and exclusion on a wider scale, remains a constitutional issue of equal importance even if the internal situation can be decided, which also must be doubtful.[108]

Consequently, rather than focus on the works concerned with promoting 'a stronger "sense of community"' as 'necessary if the Union is to overcome its shallow political roots',[109] my interest lies with the genealogy of exclusion that the discourse of identity implies. Onora O'Neill suggests that the dangers of such a discourse, one 'idealizing community and unity', are that 'we obscure the *distinctness* of others and overlook plurality'.[110] In similar vein, it is the attempt to establish an institutionalized identity through shared commonalities and defining distinctions, I argue, that has provided the pre-scription for bifurcation. Put simply, by adopting a narrative of distinction that incorporated human rights without definition in that distinction, the Community also set in train the conditions for the scope

---

[106] Smith, note 85 above, at 174.

[107] Daniela Obradovic, 'Policy Legitimacy and the European Union' *JCMS* 34/2 (1996) 215.

[108] See, for instance, the question of migrants, refugees, and asylum seekers that continues to pose significant policy and ethical difficulties.

[109] Brigid Laffan, 'The Politics of Identity and Political Order in Europe' *JCMS* 34/1(1996) 81–100 at 100.

[110] Onora O'Neill, 'Justice and Boundaries' in Chris Brown (ed), *Political Restructuring in Europe: Ethical Perspectives* (London: Routledge, 1994) 83.

and application of human rights between the external and the internal condition to develop along separate lines. Human rights became subject to a process of differentiation as they became interpreted and applied in the two separate spheres.

7.4 Conclusion

Carole Lyons has maintained that, 'the constitutional forces in the EU are aware and desirous of the creation of an identity for the Union and this is formulated in the main in terms of an external identity, one which has a manifestation outside rather than inside the entity'.[111] There is some truth in this, although my interpretation of identity politics precludes such a simplistic reading. Equally, there are some commentators who have endeavoured to forge a new understanding for a European identity through the Community that focuses on internal values and 'post-national' notions of citizenship. On the whole these are aspirational rather than reflective of the discourse that has materialized in and from the Community.[112]

Nevertheless, no matter which approach is taken the adoption of a discourse of identity has created two narratives, one adapted for the internal the other for the external. The explicit use of a 'European Identity' may have become the preserve of the Community's exterior projections but the discourse remains a dual-faced enterprise.

It is also clear that human rights have been implicated in each of the internal and external streams through their appearance as an undefined fundamental principle. But it is this lack of definition, coupled with the effects of adopting a discourse of identity, that I suggest has provided the roots of bifurcation. The conditions for distinction, difference, and exclusion were thus set into the Community's narrative structure. The incoherence detailed in Chapter 4 indicates the extent and nature of the bifurcation that emerged as a result. But precisely what is the significance of the phenomenon of bifurcation? This is a matter to which we must now turn.

---

[111] Carole Lyons, 'The Politics of Alterity and Exclusion in the European Union' in Peter Fitzpatrick and James Henry Bergeron (eds), *Europe's Other: European Law Between Modernity and Postmodernity* (Aldershot: Ashgate, 1998) 170.

[112] See, for instance, Jurgen Habermas, 'Citizenship and National Identity: Some Reflections on the Future of Europe' *Praxis International* 12 (1992) 1–19 and David Jary, 'Citizenship and Human Rights—Particular and Universal Worlds and the Prospects for European Citizenship' in Dennis Smith and Sue Wright (eds), *Whose Europe? The Turn Towards Democracy* (Oxford: Blackwell, 1999) 207–31.

8

The Irony of the Community's Human Rights Policies

In this book I have examined a sequence of stories. From an investigation into those narratives concerning human rights externally and internally to those that explain the generation of human rights as a founding principle of the Community and its identity, I have attempted to demonstrate how the Community has constructed a policy that has affected both its constitution and its practice. The result has not been the rendition of a linear history or a chronicle. More accurately, it has been a genealogy, an excavation of the plurality of the Community's institutional narratives on human rights, how they are constructed and how they are read.

My aim throughout has not been simply to uncover these stories but to interpret them, specifically to understand what they tell us about the Community and the role of human rights within it. At a time when human rights have acquired emblematic status, representing the imposition of order for Europe and the world, this is an increasingly necessary undertaking. Without a critical approach to human rights and the Community there is a danger that practices undertaken in the name of human rights and the narratives constructed around them, will be accepted without question. They will be *assumed* to be legitimate and justified accordingly. Any contradictions, inconsistencies, and open hostilities that emanate from those practices will be dismissed as irrelevant, heretical to the established order. The threat then is that the very values and standards that are proclaimed as defining the institution will undermine and destabilize it.

We can see something of this tension in the work of the Convention on the Future of Europe that gave rise to the Draft Constitutional Treaty (DCT) proposals that emerged in 2003. Despite providing the forum within which a re-assessment of the role of human rights in the

Community could have taken place we were presented with a fairly tired discussion. It was as if the subject had exhausted itself so that there was little energy to re-examine the tightly patrolled parameters of human rights and the Community. It was perhaps not surprising, therefore, that both the Convention and the DCT should have ignored any direct reference to a human rights policy, that they should have dealt meaningfully only with the legal status of the EU Charter of Fundamental Rights and possible accession to the European Convention on Human Rights, that they should have avoided any consideration of incoherence in the Community's human rights affairs as described in this book. We cannot then be surprised that the condition of bifurcation was not even acknowledged let alone analysed. It is not much of a risk to suggest, therefore, that any final Constitutional Treaty will do nothing to address the issue.

This does not mean that a book such as this is fruitless. It becomes more important. For without critique the prospect of achieving a human rights policy that is effective and credible becomes more distant. In this spirit, the purpose of this final chapter is to draw together the arguments that have underpinned the book and then to consider the significance of the bifurcation of human rights policies for the Community. In doing so some consideration is given to how the condition might be further explored and perhaps rectified.

8.1 The arguments

A number of propositions have been advanced in this book. Three are of particular importance.

The first proposition is that a fundamental and defining distinction between the Community's narratives of human rights projected externally and those assembled internally has evolved over the last 30 years or more. Both emanate from a rhetoric of respect for human rights and yet both have developed along distinct paths from this base. I have called the phenomenon a 'bifurcation' although it is usually, and incompletely, labelled as incoherence. By analysing the human rights narrative in development co-operation and accession policies and comparing these with the internal condition, three specific aspects of human rights have been identified where the bifurcation can be observed: first, in the definition ascribed to rights; secondly, in the practice of scrutiny of human rights conditions; thirdly, in the enforcement of rights. In each case evident differences between the two spheres have been uncovered.

The analysis has enabled a delineation of the general distinctions in the Community's human rights policies to emerge. Internally, human rights are contingent. They are often referred to as 'fundamental rights' thus signifying an underlying Community conception that owns a restricted definition. Rights are conceived as possessing a distinct European heritage. The European Convention on Human Rights is the primary source. Other international instruments apart from the Universal Declaration of Human Rights are treated with caution. Rather, the 'constitutional traditions' of the Member States provide a more accessible precedent but even these remain vague in terms of their potential application. There is also a basic lack of structure to the Community's scrutiny of rights internally. Both with regard to its own institutions and more particularly the Member States, there is no systematic approach to the monitoring or investigation of human rights conditions in the Community. Due in part to self-imposed legal constraints, the Community possesses neither the capacity nor the resources to monitor human rights effectively. The field is left to other agencies and organizations, in particular the Council of Europe and the European Court of Human Rights. Equally, there are few effective methods of enforcement of human rights beyond those prompted by individual rather than institutional initiative. Restraint in rhetoric and action by the Community in relation to the Member States and their human rights record is a constant feature of policy and practice.

Externally, the story is different. Human rights are broad in concept and considered with a global perspective in mind. In particular, collective notions of rights (such as minority rights and the right to development) are given some credence and considered worthy of promotion and protection. Scrutiny can also be intrusive and effective. Although often subject to political interests (both of individual Member States and the Community) the Community has assumed the necessary capacity to take action and ensured it has the financial resources and legal authority to do so. There may be a lack of consistency in this respect but it has been able to adopt methods and systems of enforcement that have become increasingly severe in scope and strength depending on context. The range of measures the Community lauds as available to it is extensive, and it is all too willing to pronounce and publish the actions it takes as a result.

The second proposition is that the bifurcation described above has emerged from an institutionally constructed narrative, essentially mythic in character. This myth attempts to ascribe to the Community a respect for human rights that purportedly underpins the Community's ethos, its creation, and its continuing evolution. In composing the myth, however, the Community failed to determine the content of its subject or recognize the importance of human rights beyond their symbolic role as providing legitimization (or authentication in my more restricted terms) of the Community and its activities. The nature and scope of the myth have provided an environment for human rights that has made them subject to diverse influences dependent on context. Thus the conditions have been established for a bifurcation of human rights policies or narratives to emerge.

Finally, the third proposition I have advanced is that the search for a European Identity by the Community, whilst initially contributing to the enabling narrative environment described, has been instrumental in constituting the specific characteristics of the bifurcation.[1] By bonding rights to notions of identity that both reflect and generate a narrative of exclusion and differentiation, the bifurcation has developed along an internal/external fault line. One stream of narrative has evolved in the Community's internal human rights policies and one stream in its external. Underlying the demarcation is a discrimination based on a conception of Europe as superior and non-Europe as beneath, inferior, somehow deficient in moral and ethical standards that are expressed in human rights terms.

These three main propositions are of course not the end of the story. A final pressing question remains to be answered: Does the presence of the bifurcation described hold any significance for the Community? In short, should we, or the Community, care about bifurcation?

8.2 The significance of bifurcation

That distinctions exist between the Community's internal and external approaches to human rights has been well documented. However, the state of bifurcation suggests that we are dealing with more than a number of discrete inconsistencies. Rather, the analysis of the whole narrative of

---

[1] In this respect I acknowledge that other forms of bifurcation may be found. In particular, the divergent approaches to human rights with regard to citizens on the one hand and to refugees or asylum seekers on the other have been the subject of increasing concern over the last few decades. However, this subject lies outside the scope of analysis and represents an issue that would require a work of its own.

human rights in the Community suggests that a systematic and systemic division has been created along the internal/external fault line. Indeed, by adopting a more searching reading of the Community's texts a pervading sense of irony is revealed. This takes two related forms: the irony of distance and the irony of concealment.

As far as the former is concerned, in Philip Alston's weighty edited collection of reports on human rights and the Community, Martti Koskenniemi observed pertinently that, 'A political culture that officially insists that rights are foundational ... but in practice constantly finds they are not, becomes a culture of bad faith. A gap is established between political language and normative faith that encourages a strategic attitude as the proper political frame of mind as well as an ironic distance to politics by the general population'.[2]

The distinction between rhetoric and practice is a common concern. Whether the actions of the Community match its fine words and authoritative statements on matters of ethics and values frequently underscores research agendas. And the discovery of such a distinction does indeed draw attention to a dangerous and destructive possibility. It suggests a failure of resolve on an issue of principle that sends messages of hypocrisy to those whom the Community purportedly wishes to influence, if not govern. It encourages an institutional lack of regard for human rights that may in turn lead to abuse or the failure to deal with abuse whenever and wherever it occurs. Ultimately, one can imagine that it might even undermine the whole structure of the European Project. Either the precepts it advocates as essential to its existence are rendered unbelievable, thus cutting the Community adrift from the very public whose support and allegiance it says it requires, or it attracts opposition from legal, political, and social quarters that take away its foundations of authority.

In one respect, the significance of bifurcation does indeed lie in its manifestation as a gap between rhetoric and practice. Through first the promotion of a narrative that attempts to portray the Community as bound by a single concept of human rights, one that purportedly recognizes their universal and indivisible nature, and secondly the contradictory adoption of policies and practices that apply different definitions of rights, different methods of monitoring and scrutiny, and different measures of enforcement, the 'gap' is of an order that goes to the heart of the Community's

---

[2] Martti Koskenniemi, 'The Effect of Rights on Political Culture' in Philip Alston *et al* (eds), *The EU and Human Rights* (Oxford: Oxford University Press, 1999) 100.

credibility with regard to human rights. Internally, the distinctions leave those fighting for, say, the recognition of minority rights or those looking for an effective European political response to human rights violations, doubting the ability *and* the will of the Community to engage seriously in such matters. Externally, the distinctions threaten to leave the Community adrift on the international stage if it becomes apparent that it is promoting a double-standard, attempting to push for policies and actions abroad that it fails to embrace internally.

An 'ironic distance' as a result of bifurcation might therefore arise for two constituencies, the people of the Community on the one hand and the international community on the other. For each, the reading of the Community's human rights policies and activities may be undertaken with an ever-present scepticism, a questioning that focuses on the political rather than ethical nature of human rights initiatives. The fundamental principles of human rights might be by-passed altogether, rendering the interpretation of the Community's policies always contingent upon the perception of its hidden purposes.

Evidence of this possibility has already emerged. The criticisms levelled against the Community for its failure to adopt a human rights policy that is consistent in both external and internal spheres have grown over the last decade. Joseph Weiler and Sybilla Fries provide one example. In their review of the Community's competences in human rights they make the point that the Community 'is extremely apt to preach democracy to others when it, itself, continues to suffer from serious democratic deficiencies and to insist that all newcomers adhere to the ECHR when it, itself, refuses to do the same'.[3]

Andrew Clapham notes also that the Community's participation in 'multilateral fora', such as the United Nations, is rendered incredible because of the lack of consistency between external and internal policies. Thus he points out that the 'schism ... whereby external policy is divorced from internal policy and different considerations apply inside and outside the European Union, currently contributes to the credibility deficit in the context of UN human rights debates'.[4]

To these observations should be added the inconsistencies identified in Chapter 4. All are symptoms or effects of the bifurcation of human rights,

---

[3] Joseph Weiler and Sybilla Fries, 'A Human Rights Policy for the European Community and Union: The Question of Competences' in Alston *et al*, note 2 above, 147–65 at 149.

[4] Andrew Clapham, 'Where is the EU's Human Rights Common Foreign Policy, and How is it Manifested in Multilateral Fora?' in Alston *et al*, note 2 above, 627–83 at 642.

and all highlight the phenomenon's significance both for human rights and the Community's relations with its constituents and the outside world. This alone suggests that bifurcation signifies an approach by the Community that warrants rectification.

The credibility gap that has become evident through the Community's practices does not represent the only significant consequence of bifurcation. There is a further ironic strain that permeates the Community's narratives of human rights. This is irony not in a post-modern sense of interpretation by the Community as author whereby every statement, pronouncement, and decision is subjected to self-critique. Such a sophistication seems beyond the inherently conservative nature of the Community. Rather, it is irony in the sense of dissimulation, of an attempt to present a fixed vision of the world and the Community's values and standards that in practice *conceal* more persistent, differentiated, complex, and contradictory appreciations.

As I have already indicated, the nature and scope of bifurcation, the character of its history, and the narratives that have been woven throughout, are indicative of more than mere 'inconsistency'. Bifurcation has been generated through the unconscious differentiation practised by the Community *and* the conscious adoption of a rhetoric of identity fundamentally concerned with establishing, reinforcing, and maintaining a hegemonic position. Such a position distinguishes between the zenith of values that is represented by the Community, and the nadir of an external that is particularly characterized as 'under-developed' or 'newly democratized'. It is the product of a basic institutional discrimination. The external is excluded through the process of bifurcation and rendered inferior, subject to different rules and more stringent review. Those classified as 'outside' or 'other' may not enter the world of Europe and sully the Community's otherwise taken-for-granted and self-promoted sanctified position on human rights.

The portrayal of the bifurcation of human rights as a story of discrimination relies upon a number of observations. First, the adoption of a myth that Europe possessed a heritage of respect for human rights ensured that the other histories *within* of abuse, violation, and violence were effectively silenced or suppressed institutionally. As I considered at the end of Chapter 6 the myth presupposed a history of Europe that in essence was unproblematic. Thus, a self-critical evaluation of Europe and the values it stands for and promotes has failed to materialize. Human rights within this narrative have been left adrift without precise institutional analysis or definition. The implication has been that the Community does not believe that it needs to address the past of Europe or its own value conceptions. It can present itself as breaking with the violent and conflictual tradition of Euro-centrism, colonialism, and imperialism whilst at the same time as trying to promote an invented counter-tradition of integrity and virtue that is 'European' in character. The presumptive nature of the constructed (and mythic) narrative is coursed through with irony. It creates an institutional 'distance' within the Community that separates it from its own discourse. In contravention of its own mythic precepts it disallows others, who desire to question the Community from within, from participating in its development and in the composition of its narratives. The extent of the democratic deficit so often related is just one such manifestation of this irony.

At the same time, the voices of others, those that might wish to present a different vision of the world, of rights and society, have been institutionally denied. Through the purported espousal of an unproblematized universalist thinking in relation to human rights whilst putting policies into practice that allow distinctions to be made between the internal and external conditions, an inherent discrimination can be read as underlining bifurcation. The past external activities of Europe have been forgotten. The colonial tradition has been suppressed, even denied, in the text, leaving the Community to present itself as virtuous in external affairs, unblemished by its Member States' histories and current actions. In doing so, the Community has maintained the discrimination that lay at the heart of colonialism: the presupposition of superiority that begat a belief in the 'civilizing mission' of Europe. Both Chapters 2 and 3 provide evidence of the presupposition. The very adoption of a discourse of development can be interpreted as promoting the sense of superiority. Equally, the negotiations with applicant states have been suffused with a discourse that holds the Europe of the Community as the pinnacle of progress and values to which others should aspire. Together these narratives reinforce the projection of the Community as heir to a civilization that is European.

In sum, therefore, the bifurcation is indicative of an ironical institutional narrative that at the same time opposes and promotes fundamentally discriminatory thinking. Internally, the Community has adopted an assumption that human rights conditions within its borders do not require attention on the whole. Although open to some degree of institutional review, at no time has it turned its eyes with any force upon its Member States. One of the reasons put forward for this abrogation of responsibility has been that the Council of Europe and other international human rights regimes provide adequate protection and coverage. And yet, when assessing applicants for accession to the Community, such human rights regimes are not deemed sufficient. Another reason proffered is that the human rights standards in the Member States are superior to any external condition. But this is a dangerous assumption, one that is certainly not warranted as a statement of principle.

By contrast, the Community has presented itself externally as a practising guardian of human rights, a beacon of virtue. It has attempted to impose standards and values and interpretations on the tacit understanding that, unlike its own constituents, 'others' require constant scrutiny and the presence of potential sanction to ensure human rights are respected. The Community has, as I have demonstrated, consistently applied a wholly different approach to human rights between the two spheres to the extent that in some respects even the definition of human rights applicable internally and externally can be distinguished. Discrimination thus flows through the story presented of the Community's policies. As a consequence, the authenticity suggested in Chapter 6 which was originally sought through the adoption of a human rights discourse is severely undermined. Bifurcation questions the seriousness, commitment, and integrity of the Community with regard to human rights.

Similar but related analyses support the notion of an underlying institutional discriminatory tendency. Verena Stolke, for instance, applied an anthropological perspective to the rhetoric of exclusion practised by the Community with regard to its advance of an immigration policy. She noted that there had arisen, 'since the seventies a rhetoric of inclusion and exclusion that emphasizes the distinctiveness of cultural identity, traditions, and heritage among groups and assumes the closure of culture by territory'.[5] Her concern was not only with the upsurge in racist action throughout Europe but also initiatives instituted by the Community that gave rise to 'external boundaries' that 'are ever more tightly closed'.[6] The implication of her findings is that the political rhetoric of common heritage lends itself to interpretation as imposing a cultural identity that emphasizes its 'incommensurability' with other traditions and value systems. Thus, one can argue that the adoption of any discourse that attempts to define a

---

[5] Verena Stolke, 'Talking Culture: New Boundaries, New Rhetorics of Exclusion in Europe' *Current Anthropology* 36/1 (1995) 2. See also Peter Fitzpatrick, 'New Europe, Old Story: Racism and the European Community' in Paddy Ireland and Per Laleng (eds), *The Critical Lawyers' Handbook 2* (London: Pluto Press, 1997) 86–95.

[6] Stolke note 5 above.

territory by reference to a particular culture is an act of exclusion. More significantly, perhaps, is Stolke's analysis that at the core of collective exclusion 'predicated on the idea of the "other" as a foreigner, a stranger, to the body politic is the assumption that formal political equality presupposes cultural identity'.[7] Hence 'cultural sameness is the essential prerequisite for access to citizenship rights'.[8] As discussed in Chapter 7, the promotion of an identity by the Community, which relies in part upon a narrative of human rights distinguishing between the internal and external conditions, substantiates the sense of exclusion and discrimination.

My reading of the story of human rights and the Community confirms and expands the occasional critiques of latent discrimination present in the Community's structure. Indeed, the analysis I have provided suggests that the extent of discrimination is deeper set and more influential than has been previously considered. The fact that the identification of bifurcation indicates that discrimination attaches to those very precepts that purport to advance human rights (of which one would be the right not to be discriminated against) takes the issue on to an altogether more serious level. Indeed, one consequential critique is that the discrimination may signify a racist subtext. By uncovering a sense of superiority that is based upon the fact that the Community is European suggests that issues of race may lie beneath the surface. This is a grievous charge and requires further investigation that lies beyond the scope of this work to determine whether it possesses any substance. However, one cannot discount the possibility given the presence of such discrimination as I have described.

In light of the above, one can be forgiven for assuming that the institutional narratives of the Community in relation to human rights are consumed by irony. Perhaps Jean-Francois Lyotard identified the reason for the condition when he suggested that 'unification of Europe means the unification of hatreds'.[9] Perhaps Conor Gearty is closer the mark when he claims that 'at the centre of the plan for a new European landscape there is to be found a hard seed of hate'.[10] Faced with such an environment the question must be asked: Has the Community truly attempted to combat the conditions of discrimination and exclusion that have scarred Europe over generations? Or has it subconsciously and subtextually allowed its human

---

[7] Stolke note 5 above at 8.   [8] Ibid.
[9] Jean-François Lyotard, *Europe, the Jews and the Book* (London: UCL Press, 1993) 159.
[10] Conor A. Gearty, 'The Internal and External "Other" in the Union Legal Order: Racism, Religious Intolerance and Xenophobia in Europe' in Philip Alston *et al* (eds), note 2 above, 325–58 at 327.

rights policies to be constructed by a discriminatory and exclusionary ideology?

It is hard to suggest that such questions are not fundamental to the future of human rights in the Community *and* the future of the European Project itself. The possibility alone that the critique of discrimination evidenced through bifurcation can be substantiated must engender a reaction. To some extent the Community has accepted the critique through its acknowledgement of the symptoms of bifurcation. Chapter 4 discussed those measures that have been introduced to counter the charges of incoherence and inconsistency. But such approaches will not, and cannot, address the core problem, the cause of that incoherence and inconsistency. Bifurcation will not be dismissed by a piecemeal strategy that seeks to introduce a Charter here, a Treaty amendment there. 'Mainstreaming' human rights simply will not alter the condition. Nor will the laudable efforts of the European Parliament, which adopts a diplomatic approach without the resources to engage in diplomacy. Indeed, the Community's attempts to create a space for itself where it can pursue a human rights policy that is not based on the central discrimination I have described will continue to be beset by a sense of irony unless it returns to basic principles.

How this change could be achieved requires the commitment of commentators and institutions alike to acknowledge the problem as a problem. As a prerequisite it would necessitate counteracting directly the entrenched bifurcated institutional narrative that the Community has adopted. At the very least it would require an intellectual revision of the institutional discourse of identity that provokes a differentiation based on origin. Failure to address these narratives will, in my reading, ensure that future human rights activity remains constrained by that bifurcation and plagued by discrimination and a sense of irony. Policy will continue to be crafted along bifurcated lines, following what has preceded it and maintaining the underlying discrimination that is present. If this is to be avoided new narratives will need to be moulded. A consciousness of the bifurcation and not simply its manifestations will be necessary. A deep analysis of the meaning of human rights, and the application of strategies to realize them, must also be undertaken. The disparate narratives will need to be drawn together, challenging and realigning a whole institutional culture. A choice will then have to be made in the process. If the Community is to assume the role of guardian of human rights both in relation to its Member States *and* its dealings with the rest of the world, perhaps to assume a role as a human rights organization, then it must be able to ensure that distinctions in definition, scrutiny, and enforcement of human rights can be erased. If not, it is difficult to see how the bifurcation can be overcome.

The signs are that such a radical alteration is beyond the Community at the moment. It does not have the best record in confronting its own history or that of its Member States. Its approach to a Constitutional Treaty does little to alter that perception. Nevertheless, the change may be forced upon it. The enlargement of the Community to incorporate much of central Europe will affect the whole presentation of the issue of human rights internally. Whether the present and future Member States are willing to accept a policy that challenges the system of scrutiny and enforcement against themselves as well as the newcomers will perhaps be the severest test. If they are not, the bifurcation will continue to undermine those attempts at acquiring legitimacy for the Community. How the Community could function as a true Union in such circumstances, one to provide a model to the world, is difficult to imagine.

BIBLIOGRAPHY

Addo, M., 'Some Issues in European Community Aid Policy and Human Rights' *Legal Issues of European Integration* 1 (1988) 71–7

Alston, Philip *et al* (eds), *The EU and Human Rights* (Oxford: Oxford University Press, 1999)

Alston, Philip, and Weiler, Joseph, 'An Ever Closer Union in Need of a Human Rights Policy: The European Union and Human Rights' in P. Alston *et al* (eds), *The EU and Human Rights* (Oxford: Oxford University Press, 1999) 3–97

Amato, Guiliano, and Batt, Judy, 'Minority Rights and EU Enlargement to the East: Report of the First Reflection Group on the Long-Term Implications of EU Enlargement' (European University Institute, RSC Policy Paper no 98/5, 1998)

Arikan, Harun, 'A Lost Opportunity? A Critique of the European Union's Human Rights Policy Towards Turkey' *Mediterranean Politics* 7/1 (2002) 19–50

Arts, Karin, *Integrating Human Rights into Development Cooperation: the Case of the Lomé Convention* (The Hague: Kluwer International, 2000)

Babarinde, Olufemi, 'The European Union's Relations with the South: A Commitment to Development' in C. Rhodes (ed), *The European Union in the World Community* (London: Lynne Rienner, 1998) 127–46

Banchoff, Thomas (ed), *Legitimacy and the European Union: the Contested Polity* (London: Routledge, 1999)

Bañkowski, Zenon, and Christodoulidis, Emilios, 'The European Union as an Essentially Contested Project' *European Law Journal* 4/4 (1998) 341–54

Barthes, Roland, *Mythologies* (London: Vintage, 1993)

Baxi, Upendra, 'Human Rights: Suffering Between Movements and Markets' in R. Cohen, and S. Rai (eds), *Global Social Movements* (London: Athlone Press, 2000) 33–45

Beetham, David, and Lord, Christopher (eds), *Legitimacy and the European Union* (London: Longman, 1998)

Bergeron, James Henry, 'An Ever Whiter Myth: The Colonization of Modernity in European Community Law' in P. Fitzpatrick, and J. H. Bergeron (eds), *Europe's Other: European Law Between Modernity and Postmodernity* (Aldershot: Ashgate, 1998) 3–26

Besselink, Leonard F.M., 'Entrapped by the Maximum Standard: on Fundamental Rights, Pluralism and Subsidiarity in the European Union' *CML Rev* 35 (1998) 629–80

Boyle, Kevin, 'Stock-Taking on Human Rights' in D. Beetham (ed), *Politics and Human Rights* (Oxford: Blackwell, 1995) 79–95

Brandtner, Barbara, and Rosas, Allan, 'Human Rights and the External Relations of the European Community: An Analysis of Doctrine and Practice' *European Journal of International Law* 9/3 (1998) 468–90

Brandtner, Barbara, and Rosas, Allan, 'Trade Preferences and Human Rights' in P. Alston *et al* (eds), *The EU and Human Rights* (Oxford: Oxford University Press, 1999) 699–722

Cassese, Antonio, *International Law* (Oxford: Oxford University Press, 2001)

Clapham, Andrew, *Human Rights and the European Community: A Critical Overview* vol 1 (Baden-Baden: Nomos, 1991)

Clapham, Andrew, 'Where is the EU's Human Rights Common Foreign Policy, and How is it Manifested in Multilateral Fora?' in P. Alston *et al* (eds), *The EU and Human Rights* (Oxford: Oxford University Press, 1999) 627–83

Coppel, J., and O'Neill, A., 'The ECJ: Taking Rights Seriously' *Legal Studies* 12 (1992) 227–45

Craig, Paul, and de Búrca, Gráinne, *EU Law: Text, Cases and Materials*, 2nd edn (Oxford: Oxford University Press, 1998)

—— *EU Law: Text, Cases and Materials*, 3rd edn (Oxford: Oxford University Press, 2003)

Cremona, Marise, 'Human Rights and Democracy Clauses in the EC's Trade Agreements' in N. Emiliou, and D. O'Keefe (eds), *The European Union and World Trade Law* (Chichester: John Wiley & Sons, 1996) 62–77

—— 'External Relations and External Competence: the Emergence of an Integrated Policy' in P. Craig, and G. de Búrca (eds), *The Evolution of EU Law* (Oxford: Oxford University Press, 1999) 137–75

Damrosch, Lori, 'Politics Across Borders: Non-Intervention and Non-Forcible Influence Over Domestic Affairs' *AJIL* 83 (1989) 1–50

Dauses, Manfred, 'The Protection of Fundamental Rights in the Community Legal Order' *EL Rev* 10 (1985) 398–419

de Búrca, Gráinne, 'The Language of Rights and European Integration' in J. Shaw and G. More (eds), *New Legal Dynamics of European Union* (Oxford: Clarendon Press, 1995) 29–54

—— 'Drafting the EU Charter on Fundamental Rights' *European Law Review* 26/2 (2001) 126–38

de Giustino, David, *A Reader in European Integration* (London: Longman, 1996)

de Rougemont, Denis, *The Idea of Europe* (New York: Macmillan, 1966)

de Sousa Santos, B., *Toward a New Common Sense: Law, Science and Politics in the Paradigmatic Transition* (London: Routledge, 1995)

de Witte, Bruno, 'Politics Versus Law in the EU's Approach to Ethnic Minorities' (EUI Working Paper, RSC no 2000/4, 2000)

Dehousse, Renaud, *The European Court of Justice* (London: Macmillan, 1993)

Delanty, Gerard, *Inventing Europe: Idea, Identity, Reality* (London: Macmillan Press, 1995)

Derrida, Jacques, *Positions* (London: Athlone Press, 1981)

di Fabio, Udo, 'Some Reflections on the Allocation of Competences Between the European Union and its Member States' *CML Rev* 39 (2002) 1289–1301

Donnelly, Jack, *Universal Human Rights in Theory and Practice* (New York: Cornell University Press, 1989)

Douglas-Scott, Sionaidh, *Constitutional Law of the European Union* (Harlow: Longman, 2002)

Duparc, Christiane, *The European Community and Human Rights* (Brussels: European Commission, 1993)

Ellerman, C., 'Command of Sovereignty Gives Way to Concern for Humanity' *Vanderbilt Journal of Transnational Law* 26/2 (1993) 341

Escobar, Arturo, *Encountering Development: The Making and Unmaking of the Third World* (Princeton: Princeton University Press, 1995)

Estébanez, M.A.M., 'The Protection of National, or Ethnic, Religious and Linguistic Minorities' in N. Neuwahl, and A. Rosas (eds), *The European Union and Human Rights* (The Hague: Kluwer Law International, 1995) 133–63

Esteva, Gustavo, and Prakash, Madhu Suri, *Grassroots Post-Modernism* (London: Zed Books, 1998)

Falk, Richard, *Human Rights Horizons: the Pursuit of Justice in a Globalizing World* (London: Routledge, 2000)

Fitzpatrick, Peter, 'New Europe, Old Story: Racism and the European Community' in P. Ireland and P. Laleng (eds), *The Critical Lawyers' Handbook 2* (London: Pluto Press, 1997) 86–95

Flynn, Leo, 'The Implications of Article 13 EC' *CML Rev* 36 (1999) 1127–52

Føllesdal, Andreas, 'Democracy, Legitimacy and Majority Rule in the European Union' in A. Weale and M. Nentwich (eds), *Political Theory and the European Union: Legitimacy, Constitutional Choice and Citizenship* (London: Routledge, 1998)

Franklin, M., Marsh, M., and McLaren, L., 'Uncorking the Bottle: Popular Opposition to European Unification in the Wake of Maastricht' *JCMS* 32 (1994) 455–72

Freeman, Heather Berit, 'Austria: the 1999 Parliamentary Elections and the European Union Members' Sanctions' *Boston College International and Comparative Law Review* (2002) 109–24

Friis, Lykke, and Murphy, Anna, 'The EU and Central and Eastern Europe: Governance and Boundaries' *JCMS* 37 (1999) 211–32

Gamberale, Carlo, 'European Citizenship and Political Identity' *Space and Polity* 1/1 (1997) 37–59

Gearty, Conor A., 'The Internal and External "Other" in the Union Legal Order: Racism, Religious Intolerance and Xenophobia in Europe' in P. Alston *et al* (eds), *The EU and Human Rights* (Oxford: Oxford University Press, 1999) 325–58

Gessner, Volkmar, Hoeland, Armin, and Varga, Csaba, *European Legal Cultures* (Aldershot: Dartmouth, 1996)

Ghai, Yash, 'Universalism and Relativism: Human Rights as a Framework for Negotiating Interethnic Claims' *Cardozo Law Review* 21 (2000) 1095–140

Giddens, Anthony, *The Nation-State and Violence: Volume Two of a Contemporary Critique of Historical Materialism* (Cambridge: Polity Press, 1985)

Goddard, Victoria, Llobera, Josep, and Shore, Cris, 'Introduction: The Anthropology of Europe' in Goddard *et al* (eds), *The Anthropology of Europe* (Oxford: Berg, 1994)

Gow, James, and Freedman, Lawrence, 'Intervention in a Fragmenting State: the Case of Yugoslavia' in N. Rodley (ed), *To Loose the Bands of Wickedness: International Intervention in Defence of Human Rights* (London: Brassey's, 1992) 93–132

Grossberg, Laurence, 'Identity and Cultural Studies: Is That All There Is?' in S. Hall and P. du Gay (eds), *Questions of Cultural Identity* (London: Sage, 1996)

Habermas, Jurgen, 'Citizenship and National Identity: Some Reflections on the Future of Europe' *Praxis International* 12 (1992) 1–19

Hall, Stuart, 'Cultural Identity and Diaspora' in J. Rutherford (ed), *Identity: Community, Culture, Difference* (London: Lawrence and Wishart, 1990) 222–37

—— 'Introduction: Who Needs Identity' in S. Hall and P. du Gay (eds), *Questions of Cultural Identity* (London: Sage, 1996) 1–17

Heater, Derek, *The Idea of European Unity* (Leicester: Leicester University Press, 1992)

Hobsbawm, Eric, and Ranger, Terence (eds), *The Invention of Tradition* (Cambridge: Canto, 1992)

Hoffman, Stanley, *The European Sisyphus: Essays on Europe 1964–1994* (Oxford: Westview Press, 1995)

Holland, Martin, *The European Union and the Third World* (Basingstoke: Palgrave, 2002)

Ifestos, Panayiotis, *European Political Co-operation: Towards a Framework of Supranational Diplomacy?* (Aldershot: Avebury, 1987)

Jacobs, Francis, *The European Convention on Human Rights*, 2nd edn (Oxford: Clarendon Press, 1996)

Jacobsen, Hanns-D., 'The European Union's Eastward Enlargement' *EIoP* 1/14 (1997) (available at http://eiop.or.at/eiop/texte/1997-014a.htm)

Jary, David, 'Citizenship and Human Rights: Particular and Universal Worlds and the Prospects for European Citizenship' in D. Smith and S. Wright (eds), *Whose Europe? The Turn Towards Democracy* (Oxford: Blackwell, 1999) 207–31

Kearney, Richard, 'Between Tradition and Utopia' in D. Wood (ed), *On Paul Ricoeur: Narrative and Interpretation* (London: Routledge, 1991)

King, Toby, 'The European Community and Human Rights in Eastern Europe' *Legal Issues of European Integration* 2 (1996) 93–125

Koskenniemi, Martti, 'The Effect of Rights on Political Culture' in P. Alston *et al* (eds), *The EU and Human Rights* (Oxford: Oxford University Press, 1999) 99–116

Krogsgaard, Lars Bondon, 'Fundamental Rights in the European Community after Maastricht' *Legal Issues of European Integration* (1993) 99–113

Laffan, Brigid, 'The Politics of Identity and Political Order in Europe' *JCMS* 34/1 (1996) 81–100

Lenaerts, Koen, 'Fundamental Rights in the European Union' *EL Rev* 25/6 (2000) 575–600

Lister, Marjorie, *The European Community and the Developing World* (Aldershot: Avebury, 1988)

Lyons, Carole, 'A Voyage around Article 8: An Historical and Comparative Evaluation of the Fate of European Union Citizenship' *Yearbook of European Law* 17 (1997) 135–63

—— 'The Politics of Alterity and Exclusion in the European Union' in P. Fitzpatrick and J. H. Bergeron (eds), *Europe's Other: European Law Between Modernity and Postmodernity* (Aldershot: Ashgate, 1998) 157–76

Lyotard, Jean-François, *Europe, the Jews and the Book* (London: UCL Press, 1993)

Macleod, I., Hendry, I.D., and Hyett, Stephen, *The External Relations of the European Communities* (Oxford: Oxford University Press, 1996)

Mancini, G. Federico, 'The Making of a Constitution for Europe' *CML Rev* 26 (1989) 595–614

Marantis, Demetrios James, 'Human Rights, Democracy, and Development: the European Community Model' *Harv HRJ* 7 (1994) 1–32

Marias, Epaminondas A., 'Mechanisms of Protection of Union Citizens' Rights' in A. Rosas and E. Antola (eds), *A Citizens' Europe: In Search of a New Order* (London: Sage, 1995) 207–33

Mayhew, Alan, 'EU Policy Toward Central Europe' in C. Rhodes (ed), *The European Union in the World Community* (London: Lynne Reiner, 1998) 105–25

McInerney, Siobhan, 'Bases for Action Against Race Discrimination in EU Law' *EL Rev* 27 (2002) 72–9

Mendelson, M.H., 'The ECJ and Human Rights' *Yearbook of European Law* 1 (1981) 125–65

Milward, Alan, *The European Rescue of the Nation-State* (London: Routledge, 1992)

Milward, Alan, 'The Springs of Integration' in P. Gowan and P. Anderson (eds), *The Question of Europe* (London: Verso, 1997) 5–20

Murdoch, Jim, 'The European Convention for the Prevention of Torture and Inhuman or Degrading Treatment or Punishment: Activities in 2000' *EL Rev Human Rights Survey* 26 (2001) 398–412

Neusse, Peter, 'European Citizenship and Human Rights: An Interactive European Concept' *Legal Issues of European Integration* 24 (1997) 47–66

Nogueras, Diego, and Martinez, Luis, 'Human Rights Conditionality in the External Trade of the European Union: Legal and Legitimacy Problems' *Columbia Journal of European Law* (2001) 307–36

Nowak, Manfred, 'Human Rights Conditionality in the EU' in P. Alston *et al* (eds), *The EU and Human Rights* (Oxford: Oxford University Press, 1999) 687–98

Nugent, Neill, *The Government and Politics of the European Union* (London: Macmillan, 1994)

O'Leary, Siofra, 'The Relationship between Community Citizenship and the Protection of Fundamental Rights in Community Law' *CML Rev* 32 (1995) 519–54

O'Neill, Onora, 'Justice and Boundaries' in C. Brown (ed), *Political Restructuring in Europe: Ethical Perspectives* (London: Routledge, 1994) 69–88

Obradovic, Daniela, 'Policy Legitimacy and the European Union' *JCMS* 34/2 (1996) 191–221

Pocock, J.G.A., 'Deconstructing Europe' in P. Gowan and P. Anderson (eds), *The Question of Europe* (London: Verso, 1997) 297–317

—— 'The Politics of History: The Subaltern and the Subversive' *Journal of Political Philosophy* 6/3 (1998) 219–34

Rack, Reinhard and Lausegger, Stefan, 'The Role of the European Parliament: Past and Future' in P. Alston *et al* (eds), *The EU and Human Rights* (Oxford: Oxford University Press, 1999) 801–37

Rasmussen, David, 'Rethinking Subjectivity: Narrative Identity and the Self' in R. Kearney (ed), *Paul Ricoeur: The Hermeneutics of Action* (London: Sage, 1996)

Rich, Roland, 'Right to Development: A Right of Peoples?' in J. Crawford (ed), *The Rights of Peoples* (Oxford: Clarendon Press, 1988) 39–67

Ricoeur, Paul, *Time and Narrative Vol III* (Chicago: University of Chicago Press, 1988)

—— 'Narrative Identity' in D. Wood (ed), *On Paul Ricoeur: Narrative and Interpretation* (London: Routledge, 1991) 188–99

—— 'Reflections on a New Ethos for Europe' in R. Kearney (ed), *The Hermeneutics of Action* (London: Sage, 1996) 3–13

Riedel, Eibe and Will, Martin, 'Human Rights Clauses in External Agreements of the EC' in P. Alston *et al* (eds), *The EU and Human Rights* (Oxford: Oxford University Press, 1999) 723–54

Rist, Gilbert, *The History of Development* (London: Zed Books, 1997)

Rodley, Nigel, 'Collective Intervention to Protect Human Rights and Civilian Populations: the Legal Framework' in N. Rodley (ed), *To Loose the Bands of Wickedness: International Intervention in Defence of Human Rights* (London: Brassey's, 1992) 14–42

Rutherford, Jonathan, 'A Place Called Home: Identity and the Cultural Politics of Difference' in J. Rutherford (ed), *Identity: Community, Culture, Difference* (London: Lawrence and Wishart, 1990) 9–27

Sacerdoti, Giorgio, 'The European Charter of Fundamental Rights: From a Nation-State Europe to a Citizens' Europe' *Columbia Journal of European Law* (2002) 37–52

Schermers, H.G., 'The New European Court of Human Rights' *CML Rev* 35 (1998) 3–8

Schlesinger, Philip, *Media State and Nation: Political Violence and Collective Identities* (London: Sage, 1991)

Scott, Joanne, *Development Dilemmas in the European Community; Rethinking Regional Development Policy* (Buckingham: Open University Press, 1995)

—— 'Regional Policy: An Evolutionary Perspective' in P. Craig and G. de Búrca (eds), *The Evolution of EU Law* (Oxford: Oxford University Press, 1999) 625–52

Shaw, Jo, 'The Many Pasts and Futures of Citizenship in the European Union' *EL Rev* 22 (1997) 554–72

Shuibhne, Niamh Nic, 'The European Union and Minority Language Rights' *MOST Journal on Multicultural Societies* 3/2 (2001) (available at www.unesco.org/most/v13n2shui.htm)

Sidentop, Larry, *Democracy in Europe* (London: Allen Lane, 2000)

Simma, B., Aschenbrenner, J. Beatrix, and Schulte, C., 'Human Rights and Development Co-operation' in P. Alston *et al* (eds), *The EU and Human Rights* (Oxford: Oxford University Press, 1999) 571–626

Smith, Anthony D., *National Identity* (London: Penguin, 1991)

—— 'National Identity and the Idea of European Unity' in P. Gowan and P. Anderson, *The Question of Europe* (London: Verso, 1997) 318–42

Somers, Margaret R., and Gibson, Gloria D., 'Reclaiming the Epistemological "Other": Narrative and the Social Constitution of Identity' in C. Calhoun (ed), *Social Theory and the Politics of Identity* (Oxford: Blackwell, 1994)

Spencer, Michael, *States of Injustice: A Guide to Human Rights and Civil Liberties in the European Union* (London: Pluto Press, 1995)

Steiner, Henry, and Alston, Philip, *International Human Rights in Context: Law, Politics, Morals* (Oxford: Clarendon Press, 1996)

Stolke, Verena, 'Talking Culture: New Boundaries, New Rhetorics of Exclusion in Europe' *Current Anthropology* 36/1 (1995) 1–24

Tomaševski, Katarina, *Development Aid and Human Rights Revisited* (London: Pinter, 1993)

Toth, A.G., 'The European Union and Human Rights: the Way Forward' *CML Rev* 34 (1997) 491–529

Twomey, Patrick, 'The European Union: Three Pillars Without a Human Rights Foundation' in D. O'Keefe and P. Twomey (eds), *Legal Issues of the Maastricht Treaty* (London: Wiley Chancery Law, 1994) 121–32

Urwin, Derek W., *The Community of Europe: A History of European Integration Since 1945* (London: Longman, 1991)

von Bogdandy, Armin, 'The European Union as a Human Rights Organisation? Human Rights and the Core of the European Union' *CML Rev* 37 (2000) 1307–38

Wallace, William, *The Transformation of Western Europe* (London: Pinter Publishers, 1990)
Ward, Ian, *The Margins of European Law* (London: Macmillan Press, 1996)
Weiler, Joseph, 'The Transformation of Europe' *Yale Law Journal* 100 (1991) 2403–83
—— 'Does the EU Need a Human Rights Charter?' *European Law Journal* 6 (2000) 95–7
Weiler, Joseph and Fries, Sybilla, 'A Human Rights Policy for the European Community and Union: the Question of Competences' in P. Alston *et al* (eds), *The EU and Human Rights* (Oxford: Oxford University Press, 1999) 147–65
Weiler, J.H.H., 'Does Europe Need a Constitution? Reflections on Demos, Telos and Ethos in the German Maastricht Decision' in P. Gowan and P. Anderson (eds), *The Question of Europe* (London: Verso, 1997) 265–94
—— *The Constitution of Europe* (Cambridge: Cambridge University Press, 1999)
Wiener, Antje, 'Assessing the Constructive Potential of Union Citizenship: A Socio-Political Perspective' (European Integration Online Papers, vol 1 no 17, 1997) (available at http://eiop.or.at/eiop/texte/1997-017a.htm)
Williams, Andrew, 'EU Human Rights Policy and the Convention on the Future of Europe: A Failure of Design?' *European Law Review* 28 (2003) 794–813
—— 'Mapping Human Rights, Reading the European Union' *European Law Journal* 9/5 December (2003)

INDEX

Accession Partnerships, *see* Community Accession Policy
Accession Policy, *see* Community Accession Policy
ACP states, *see* Community Development Policy
Acquis communautaire 64, 72
Action Plan Against Racism 67, 86
African Charter of Human and Peoples' Rights 41
Agenda 2000, *see* Community Accession Policy
Aid, *see* Community development policy
Amnesty International ix, 86, 123
Annual Reports on Human Rights 6, 9, 13, 80, 98–102, 116
Apartheid 29, 30
Asian-African Bandung Conference 22
Athens Declaration 116
Austria:
  Freedom Party 5
  Roma, and 88–9
  TEU, and 5, 108
Authenticity:
  Community, of 129–37

Banda, Hastings ix–x
Belgium 69
  racism, and 86, 122
Bifurcation xi, 14, 129
  discrimination, as 199–203
  European identity and origins of 162–3, 167, 184, 189, 191–2
  irony and 194–204
  myth of founding principle 157–60
  significance 196–204

Bonn Conference 143, 166–7
Bulgaria 70–1, 71, 73

Central and Eastern European states, *see* Community Accession Policy
Citizenship:
  European citizenship, origins of 170, 175
  European identity and human rights 180–2
  post-national concept of 192
Civil rights, *see* Human rights
Civil society 2, 47, 48, 93, 120–1
Collective rights 67, 69, 84, 88, 92–4, 123
Colonialism, *see* Community development policy
Comité des Sages:
  human rights report, 157
Commission, *see* European Commission
Common Foreign and Security Policy 44, 49, 100, 113
  European identity, and 184
Community Accession Policy:
  Accession Partnerships 75–6
  Agenda 2000 59, 69, 73–5, 106
  Central and Eastern European states, and 59–78
  Cold War, end of 59
  conditionality 75
    implicit 53–9
    explicit 59–65
  Copenhagen Criteria 64–5, 73
  Europe Agreements 61–3
  European Commission, and 61–3, 69–70, 73–6
  Greece 58

Community Accession Policy (*contd*)
  human rights:
    civil and political 71–2
    collective notions 67, 69
    definition 66–73, 79
    economic, social, and cultural 72–3
    enforcement 73–8
    history 53–65
    minorities 66–71, 87–9
    scrutiny 73–7
  New Europe, and 59–61
  Portugal 56
  'selective entry' 55–7
  Spain 56
  Turkey, and 76–7
Community Development Policy 4, 12, 16–52
  ACP states 26–32
  aid 22, 23, 25, 27, 30, 33, 36, 38, 44, 49–51, 81, 91, 92, 95
  colonialism 17–23, 51
  conditionality 36, 49–51, 93
  Cotonou Agreement 39–40, 45, 50
  Council Regulation 975/1999 41, 46–7
  Diplomatic Pressure (*démarches*) 33, 44–5
  European Commission 37–8, 47
  European Court of Justice 35–6
  European identity 25–34, 40
  formative period 17–25
  France 18, 19
  General System of Preferences 49
  good governance 43
  human rights:
    definition 40–4
    history 17–40
    scrutiny and enforcement 44–51
  Joint Resolution of 28 November 1991 33–4, 46
  Lomé I 25–7
  Lomé II 27–8
  Lomé III 28–31
  Lomé IV 31–3
  military spending 34
  positive measures 46–9
  post-Cold War period 34–40
  right to development 30
  sanctions 49–51
  Treaty of Rome 16, 18–19, 24
  UN Charter 29
  Yaoundé Convention 23, 26
Competence:
  Annual Reports on Human Rights, and 116
  authentication, and 129, 131
  Draft Constitutional Treaty, effect on 114–16
  EU Charter of Fundamental Rights 114
  external 113, 172
  human rights, in 112–18, 198
  internal 114–17
  subsidiarity, and 117
  Treaty of Rome, and 113
Conditionality:
  accession policy, and 59–65
  development policy, and 36, 49–51, 93
Convention on the Prevention and Punishment of the Crime of Genocide 41
Copenhagen Criteria, *see* Community Accession Policy
Cote d'Ivoire 50
Cotonou Partnership Agreement, *see* Community development policy
Council, *see* European Council
Council of Europe 69, 74, 111, 118–19, 138
  Statute of 143
Customs Union 141
Czech Republic 63, 71, 73

De Gaulle, Charles 165, 175
Declaration on European Identity 25, 40, 55
Démarches, *see* Community development policy
Democracy, *see* European values
Democratic deficit:
  Community, and 130
Derrida, Jacques 187–8
Development, *see also* Community development policy concept, of 16–17
Development policy, *see* Community development policy
Dignity 29, 32
Direct effect 132, 168
Discrimination 88
  EC Treaty, and 100, 103
Doctrine of non-interference 23, 37, 57–8, 106, 124, 138
Double standards, *see* Incoherence
Draft Constitutional Treaty 3–4, 95, 114–16, 120, 193–4
  European identity 180
  founding principle, myth of 140

Economic and Social Committee 8
Economic rights, *see* Human Rights
Enlargement 3–4, 127
  accession 59–65
Estonia 69, 73
Ethnic cleansing 68
EU Charter of Fundamental Rights 13
  citizenship 180
  collective rights 83
  Community competence, and 114
  creation 2, 180
  enforcement, restriction of 107
  European values 80
  founding principle, myth of 139
  incoherence, and 9–10, 13
  minority rights, absence of 91
  monitoring the Community, and 97
  sources of law, and 81
  universality, and 80
EU Human Rights Policy:
  accession, and 53–78
  bifurcation 159–61, 162–3, 167, 184, 187, 191–2, 194–204
  Community actions, scrutiny of 95–7
  Community's legal competence 112–18
  Council Annual Reports on Human Rights 99–102
  development, and 16–52
  enforcement 44–51, 73–7, 105–10
  European Convention on Human Rights, and 118–21
  European Parliament reports 98–9
  founding principle, myth of 137–57
  human rights, conceptions of 84–94, 129–61
  European identity, relationship to 162–92
  incoherence 6–11, 79–110
    orthodox explanations for 111–27
  institutional authenticity, and 129–37
  irony of 193–204
  Member States, scrutiny of 97–105
  original silence of 137–40
  reform 1–6
  scrutiny 44–51, 73–7, 94–105
  sources of law 80–4
Europe Agreements 61–3
European Commission
  accession policy, and 63–5, 69–71, 73–6
  citizenship 176–7
  development policy, and 36–8, 47
  EU Charter of Fundamental Rights 9, 80, 84

European Commission (*contd*)
  EU Monitoring Centre for Racism and Xenophobia, and 104
  European identity, origins of 166, 167
  external identity 179–80
  founding principle, contribution to myth of 138, 141, 145, 151–2
  incoherence of human rights policy, response to 9
  Member States, and 86–7
  Race Directive, and 123
  Roma, and 89
  TEU, and 109
European Commission Against Racism and Intolerance 86, 87, 104, 122
European Convention on Human Rights 3, 13, 71
  Accession Policy, in 81, 115
  Accession, by Community 95, 115, 179–80
  Authenticity of Community, and 136
  reverence for 118–21
  source of law 81, 82
European Council:
  Annual Reports on Human Rights 80, 99–102, 116
  founding principle, contribution to myth of 151–4
  incoherence of human rights policy, response to 9
European Court of Human Rights 118
European Court of Justice:
  Community accession to European Convention on Human Rights 95
  Community acts, review of 96
  European identity, and 168–70
  founding principle, contribution to myth of 144–51
  human rights, and 54, 97, 118
  Member States 107

minority rights 90–1
sources of human rights law 67, 81–2
European common heritage 56, 142
  enlargement, and 60, 62–3
  EU Charter of Fundamental Rights 83, 142
  European identity 174, 178, 181–2, 185, 191
  respect for human rights, and 87, 94, 117, 154–6
European Human Rights Forum 99
European Identity 54–5
  bifurcation 162–3, 167, 184, 189, 191–2
  Community law 168–70
  concept of identity 184–92
  EU human rights policy, and 162–92
  external dimension 170–4
  internal dimension 167–70
  key texts 176–7
  myth 163–74
  origins in the Community 164–8
European Initiative for Democracy and the Protection of Human Rights 46
European Monitoring Centre for Racism and Xenophobia 13, 102–5
  establishment 82
  limitations 96–9
European Ombudsman 96
European Parliament:
  approach to association agreements 57
  Community, scrutiny of 96–7
  discrimination, approach to 85–6
  European identity 165, 167, 174, 181
  European Monitoring Centre for Racism and Xenophobia 103–4

founding principle, contribution to
  myth of 153–6
human rights, and 8–9
Member States, scrutiny of 98–9
principle of non-interference,
  and 58
TEU reform, and 109–10
European Parliament Committee on
  Civil Liberties and Internal
  Affairs 85, 88
European Political Co-operation 44,
  56, 177, 183
European Project 63, 69, 124
  enlargement, and 54
  irony, and 197, 203
  myth, and 159
European Roma Rights Centre 88
European values, *see also* European
  common heritage
  development policy, and 37
  Draft Constitutional Treaty,
    and 116, 140
  enlargement, and 54, 56–7, 63
  European identity 163–4, 173,
    174–5, 178–82, 189, 192
  human rights, and 80, 83, 136, 154,
    156
  legitimacy 130
  myth of common heritage 129, 136,
    144, 157, 159

Fiji 45
Florence European Council 65
Framework Convention for the
  Protection of National
  Minorities 69, 81, 82–3, 91
France:
  Community development policy,
    and 18, 19
  Framework Convention for the
    Protection of National Minorities,
    and 81

racism, and 122
stability pact for Europe 67
Freedom Party, *see* Austria

General System of Preferences 49
Geneva Convention relating to the
  Status of Refugees 41
Geneva Conventions 41
Good governance 33
  definition 43, 92–3
  enlargement, and 64
Gorbachev, Mikhail 61
Greece 58

Haiti 45, 49
Hall, Stuart 185–7
Hallstein, Walter 142, 165–6, 167, 172
Haughey, Charles 61
Heritage, *see* European common
  heritage
Human Rights, *see also* Community
  development policy, EU human
  rights policy
  civil and political 71–2
  collective rights 42, 43, 51, 67, 71
  definition 40–4, 66–73, 79–94
  development 92–4
  discourse 133–7
  distinct conditions 121–4
  economic, social, and cultural 72–3
  enforcement 44–51, 73–7, 105–10
  European identity, and 162–92
  generations, of 84
  invention of, in the
    Community 128–61
  minorities, and 42, 66–71
  right to development 30
  scrutiny 44–51, 73–7, 94–105
Human Rights Watch 85

Identity, *see* European Identity
Incoherence:

218 *Index*

Incoherence (*contd*)
    bifurcation, and 159–61, 194–204
    enforcement, in 105–10
    EU human rights policy, and 6–11, 79–110
    human rights definitions, in 79–94
    lack of analysis 9–11
    orthodox explanations for:
        legal competence 112–18
        legal reverence 118–21
        distinct conditions 121–4
        Realpolitik 124–6
    scrutiny, in 94–105
Indivisibility:
    rights, of 7, 31, 32, 42
Institutional Narratives 11, 141, 144, 150, 154–7
    bifurcation, and 182–92
Interdependence
    human rights 42–3
International Covenant on Civil and Political Rights 31, 41
International Covenant on Economic, Social and Cultural Rights 31, 41
International Labour Organisation 112
Invented tradition:
    EU human rights policy 143–4
Irony:
    EU human rights policy, of 14–15, 193–204

Joint Declaration on Human Rights 151–3

Laeken Declaration 119
Legitimacy 128–30
    Community, of 128–37
Lomé Conventions, *see* Community development policy
Luxembourg European Council 32

Madagascar 21, 48

Madrid European Council 65
Mainstreaming 101, 203
Malawi ix-x
Margin of Appreciation 123
Membership of the EU, *see* Community Accession Policy
Minority Language rights, *see* Minority rights
Minority Rights:
    Community Accession Policy, in 66–71
    Community development policy, in 42
    EU human rights policy, incoherence in 85 92
    linguistic minorities 91
Mitterand, François 60
Monitoring, *see* Human Rights, Scrutiny
Myth:
    EU human rights policy, and 14, 137–57
    European identity, and 14, 163–74
    human rights as Community founding principle, of 137–57
    meaning of 140–1

Neo-colonialism 51, 135
New Europe, *see* Community Accession Policy
Nigeria 46

Overseas Territories, *see* Community development policy

Paris Conference 25
PHARE 59, 62
Political rights, *see* human rights

Racism:
    Annual Reports on Human Rights, and 5, 101

Community, within 85–92, 122–3, 155
European Monitoring Centre for Racism and Xenophobia 102–5
Ricoeur, Paul 159, 161, 186
Right to Development 30, 92–4
Roma 70–1, 88–90
Romania 70, 72, 73
Rule of law 25, 34, 38, 39–40, 47, 47, 48, 60, 62, 63, 92, 128–9, 133, 152

Sanctions, *see* Human rights
Santer, Jacques xi,
Schuman Declaration 164
Selective entry 55–7
Single European Act 183
Slovakia 69–70, 72, 74
Smith, A.D. 185, 191
Social rights, *see* Human rights
South Africa 30–1
Strasbourg European Council 59–60
Supremacy:
   story of 132

TACIS 59, 62
Third generation rights, *see* Human rights
Trade and Co-operation Agreements 56, 57, 61–3, 100
Treaty of Amsterdam 2, 8, 86, 107–8
Treaty of Maastricht 1, 8, 34
Treaty of Nice:
   human rights, and 2, 9, 96–7, 109
Treaty of Rome:
   Community development policy, and 16, 19–20

European identity, and 164–5
founding principle, myth of 137–9
Treaty on European Union 1, 5, 113, 181
Turkey:
   application for EU membership 3, 76–7

Uganda 27
UN Charter 29, 41, 57
UN Committee on the Elimination of Racial Discrimination 88
UN Conference on Trade and Development 23
UN Convention on the Rights of the Child 72
UN Declaration on Social Progress and Development 30
UN Declaration on the Right to Development 30, 43
United Kingdom 25, 110
Universal Declaration of Human Rights 31, 41, 42, 134, 152
Universality:
   Community development policy 42–3
   discourse, of 7, 79–80, 123, 134–5
USA 172–3

World Bank, *see* Good governance

Yaoundé Convention, *see* Community Development Policy
Yugoslavia 68

Zimbabwe 50